# THE SARBANES-OXLEY SECTION 404 IMPLEMENTATION TOOLKIT, Second Edition

## Practice Aids for Managers and Auditors

**MICHAEL RAMOS**

**WILEY**

John Wiley & Sons, Inc.

Published by John Wiley & Sons, Inc., Hoboken, New Jersey.
Published simultaneously in Canada.

For general information on our other products and services, or technical support, please contact our Customer Care Department within the United States at 800-762-2974, outside the United States at 317-572-3993 or fax 317-572-4002.

Wiley also publishes its books in a variety of electronic formats. Some content that appears in print may not be available in electronic books.

*Library of Congress Cataloging-in-Publication Data:*

ISBN: 978-0-470-16931-5

Printed in the United States of America

10  9  8  7  6  5  4  3  2  1

# Contents

| Part III | Internal Control Testing Programs | 113 |
|---|---|---|

# About the Author

Michael Ramos was an auditor with KPMG and now works as an author and consultant. He is the author of *How to Comply with Sarbanes-Oxley Section 404: Assessing the Effectiveness of Internal Control, Third Edition.* This is his book.

# Preface

This book started out as a collection of forms and checklists. It turned out to be something much different and, hopefully, more valuable. What I discovered was that creating this book was not about the forms; it's about the underlying process for SOX 404 compliance that the forms describe. Writing this book turned out to be an exercise in process engineering, not in form design. The critical questions asked during writing were always "what should people do to comply?" "What's the best way for them to do that? "How do the results of this work tie-in to other parts of the process?" Once I figured out those questions, designing the checklist was fairly easy. All the practice aids in this book are just parts of a roadmap to lead you through a process that I've mapped out.

Since Sarbanes-Oxley became the law of the land, common approaches and methodologies have emerged, and these practice aids have evolved to take these best practices into account. A good starting point for understanding this process I've laid out is the first practice aid, the General Work Program (Form ADM-1). All the other practice aids are just footnotes to this General Work Program, providing more structure and detail to the overall process. The practice are integrated to provide a consistency of approach for all the main phases in the internal control assessment: planning, documentation, testing and reporting.

As I have refined my thoughts about how to create an effective and efficient SOX 404 compliance, process I came to realize that a project team basically does two things:

- It gathers information, and then
- It assesses that information and "pulls it together," to form a reasoned, supportable conclusion.

Most of these practice aids are designed to help in information gathering, and what I've tried to do is find ways to structure that information so it helps you understand what it means.

In the area of testing, most successful SOX projects have been the ones where project teams have been actively engaged with operating personnel to discover "what really goes on" at the company. I've spoken with project team leaders and seen work programs that describe a testing approach that seems too hands off to me. I'm concerned about the quality of the conclusions reached by a project team that relies primarily on a discussion with a single individual, or the reading of a document, or the observation that a code of conduct has been posted to the Intranet to draw conclusions about control design or operation. You'll see that the testing process I've laid out is much more involved and requires the project team to be more active—asking multiple questions, making observations, corroborating single instances of control compliance until a clear pattern emerges.

To use these practice aids as they were intended, I think it might also be helpful if I shared my basic principles for design. Over the years I've worked with a number of CPAs who perform the same types of tasks required of a SOX 404 engagement. I've observed many, many instances where auditors have equated their *work* with the *documentation of the work*. If the subject matter of their tests is quantitative, this relationship holds true. For example, if an auditor is asked to test the accuracy of recorded interest expense, he or she would make a calculation of the expected expense (using average loan balance, the interest rate, etc.) and compare that expectation to the recorded amount. The auditor would then prepare a worksheet to show the calculation and the comparison. The process of doing the work—pushing around numbers to make a calculation—is the same as the documentation of the work.

Equating the work with the work product becomes less valid when dealing with subjective subject matters—like internal control—where the primary tests are inquiry, observation, and analysis. Under these circumstances, if we put a checklist in front of someone, they too often believe that their task is to complete the checklist. They focus their energy on filling out the checklist. This approach is misguided. The task is to gather and assess information and draw a supportable conclusion. The checklist is there to aid in their information gathering and assessment and to document conclusions. The checklist is only a means to an end, not an end in itself.

These practice aids are designed to be work product, a culmination of the work performed. To reinforce that idea, you'll see that the forms and checklists are addressed from the project team member to an audience of reviewers such as project team leaders, senior management, or the external auditors. They are designed to have the project team members "fill in the blank" about—

- The work they performed
- What they observed, or the results of their tests
- What they concluded based on their observations or the results of the tests

By writing the forms in this fashion, I hoped to remind the project team member completing the checklist is not the primary objective.

Preceding each form is a brief set of instructions on how to complete the form. These instructions are addressed from me to the project team. These instructions are not intended to be included in your final work product. These instructions provide reference to SEC rules, PCAOB standards and other guidance, but they do not summarize or explain these requirements. These practice aids are intended to supplement the guidance you already have on SOX 404, and to the extent that questions arise about the information required to complete a form (for example, 'what is a material weakness?') you should turn to those other sources of guidance.

Working on this book has forced me to clarify my own thoughts on what project teams should do to comply with SOX 404. By refining the 404 compliance process and creating this integrated tool set, I hope I have helped to make the process repeatable and therefore more efficient and effective.

Enjoy!

Michael Ramos
*January 2008*

# Acknowledgments

## TECHNICAL ADVISORY BOARD

This book was written with the assistance of several individuals and their firms, who provided financial support, input, and feedback during the lengthy development of these materials. I am very grateful to the following individuals and their firms for their generous support and encouragement.

The members of the Technical Advisory Board are:

**John Compton**
Partner
Cherry Bekaert & Holland, LLP

**Michelle Thompson**
Partner
Cherry Bekaert & Holland, LLP

**Krista M. Kaland**
Partner, Director of Assurance Services
Clifton Gunderson LLP

**Ronald P. Pachura**
Business Risk Services Practice Director
Clifton Gunderson LLP

**Michael C. Knowles**
Partner
Frank, Rimerman & Co.

**Randy von Feldt**
Senior Manager
Frank, Rimerman & Co.

I would like to thank Ginny Carroll for her fine attention to detail and the significant improvements she made to the overall readability of the book. A sincere thanks also to the staff at North Market Street Graphics for all their hard work during the production process.

Finally, I would like to thank John DeRemigis and Judy Howarth for their encouragement and patience in the development of these materials.

# PART I
# Tools for Management

# General Work Program

## PURPOSE

This form has been designed to

- Facilitate the organization of an efficient process for evaluating the effectiveness of the company's internal control
- Help ensure that the company's assessment of internal control effectiveness complies with all applicable requirements
- Facilitate an external auditor's understanding and evaluation of the company management's process for assessing the effectiveness of the company's internal control over financial reporting

## INSTRUCTIONS

Use this form to guide the design and performance of the company's project to assess internal control effectiveness. As each step in the program is completed, the person responsible for performing that step should put his or her initials and the date in the indicated column on the worksheet. If the step is not applicable, indicate that by noting "N/A." Use the "Notes" column to cross-reference to where the performance of the procedure is documented or to make other notations.

*Notations in italics are additional instructions to the preparer of the form and should be removed before the form is considered final.*

### ASSESSMENT OF INTERNAL CONTROL EFFECTIVENESS
### GENERAL WORK PROGRAM

Company: _____     Reporting Date: _____

Prepared by: _____     Date Prepared: _____

This form summarizes the procedures we performed to document, test, and report on the effectiveness of the company's internal control over financial reporting.

| Procedure Performed | N/A Performed by | Date | Notes |
|---|---|---|---|
| **Project Planning** | | | |
| 1. Form the project team. Consider both internal and external resources and the expertise needed to successfully complete the project, including IT expertise.<br>a. Determine the extent to which management intends to have the external auditors rely on the work of the project team in their audit of the company's internal control. For each project team involved with those areas<br>  i. Assess its competency.<br>  ii. Assess its objectivity. | | | |
| *[Consider using form ADM-2, Project Planning Summary, to document the performance of this step.]* | | | |
| 2. Determine the nature of the internal control services, if any, that the company's external auditors will provide or have provided to the company during the current audit period.<br>a. If the external auditors have provided internal control services to the company, obtain approval of the board and determine that this approval has been documented in the minutes. | | | |
| 3. Gather current information relevant to the internal control assessment and make this available to the project team members to allow them to better plan the project. | | | |

| Procedure<br>Performed | N/A<br>Performed<br>by | Date | Notes |
|---|---|---|---|
| *Determine Project Scope* | | | |
| *[For all steps listed in this subsection, related to project scope, consider using form ADM-2, Project Planning Summary, to document the performance of the step.]* | | | |
| 4. *Entity-level controls*<br>   a. Identify entity-level controls required to be documented, evaluated, and tested.<br>   b. Identify other entity-level controls designed to meet significant control objectives. | | | |
| 5. *Centralized processing and controls*<br>   a. Identify all centralized processes and controls, including shared service environments, that affect the relevant assertions of significant accounts and disclosures. | | | |
| 6. *Activity-level controls*<br>   a. Identify the significant accounts and disclosures within the financial statements.<br>   b. For all significant accounts identified in step 6a, identify the relevant assertions.<br>   c. For all significant accounts identified in step 6a, identify the major transactions affecting these accounts. Separately identify<br>      i. Routine transactions<br>      ii. Nonroutine transactions<br>      iii. Estimates | | | |

| Procedure Performed | N/A Performed by | Date | Notes |
|---|---|---|---|
| d. *Routine transactions.* For each routine transaction, identify the significant processing procedures.<br>e. *Nonroutine transactions and estimates.* Determine that nonroutine transactions identified in step 6c are included in the consideration of entity-level controls in step 4. | | | |
| 7. Determine the locations or business units to be included in the scope of the project. | | | |
| 8. Identify the significant processing procedures that are performed by third-party organizations.<br>a. Determine which of the services performed by a third party are part of the company's information system.<br>b. Determine how the project team will obtain the information necessary to understand and evaluate the design and operating effectiveness of controls at the third party (for example, by obtaining a Type 2 SAS No. 70 report). | | | |
| 9. Consider how unusual circumstances will affect the scope of the project, including<br>• Business acquisitions made since the last internal control evaluation<br>• Variable-interest entities (VIEs) included in the company's consolidated financial statements<br>• Installation of a new accounting system | | | |

| Procedure Performed | N/A Performed by | Date | Notes |
|---|---|---|---|
| 10. Determine which business process owners will be required to provide subcertifications. | | | |
| *Project Administration* | | | |
| 11. Prepare a timeline of the scheduled performance and completion of major project phases. | | | |
| 12. Document significant planning decisions, for example by completing form ADM-2, Project Planning Summary. | | | |
| *Coordination with External Auditors—Project Planning* | | | |
| 13. Communicate with the auditors, preferably in writing, to provide them with information that will help them plan their audit of internal control over financial reporting, including<br>a. The extent of recent changes, if any, in the company, its operations, or its internal control<br>b. Preliminary judgments about factors relating to the determination of material weaknesses<br>c. Control deficiencies previously communicated to the audit committee or management<br>d. Legal or regulatory matters of which the company is aware | | | |
| 14. In order to help the external auditors understand management's process for evaluating internal control effectiveness, consider providing the auditors with a copy of the documentation of significant planning matters prepared in step 12. | | | |

| Procedure Performed | N/A Performed by | Date | Notes |
|---|---|---|---|
| a. If you provide a copy of the documentation of significant planning matters, consider preparing a written request for consideration and feedback to clarify why management is providing the documentation to the auditors. | | | |
| *Documentation of Internal Control* | | | |
| 15. *Documentation completeness.* For all locations, business segments, service organizations, or other units included within the project scope (see steps 7, 8, and 9), determine that the company has documented all significant controls relating to<br>a. Entity-level controls identified in step 4<br>b. Centralized processes and controls identified in step 5<br>c. Activity-level controls identified in step 6 | | | |
| 16. *Documentation currency.* Determine that the content of the internal control documentation is up to date and reflects current practices at the company.<br>a. Identify all changes to internal control procedures since the documentation was last prepared.<br>b. Determine that all changes to internal control procedures have been reflected in the documentation.<br>c. Identify all changes to the internal control documentation since the last internal control audit and determine that the changes | | | |

| Procedure<br>Performed | N/A<br>Performed<br>by | Date | Notes |
|---|---|---|---|
|     i.  Were authorized<br>   ii.  Are reflective of actual<br>      changes to control proce-<br>      dures | | | |
| 17.  *Documentation content.* Review the content elements of the documentation identified in step 15 to determine that it contains all necessary elements.<br>    a.  Entity-level and centralized controls should be described in sufficient detail to understand the nature of the control procedure and<br>       • Its relationship to control objectives<br>       • Who performs the procedure<br>       • How often it is performed<br>       • Whether and how performance of the procedure is documented<br>       • Other information necessary to assess the design effectiveness of the control<br>    b.  Activity-level controls should include all items listed in step 17a plus<br>       • Information about how significant transactions are initiated, authorized, recorded, processed, and reported<br>       • Sufficient information about the flow of transactions to identify the points at which material misstatements due to error or fraud could occur | | | |
| 18.  Assess the efficiency and effectiveness of the company's processes for maintaining adequate documentation of internal control and recommend improvements, if applicable. | | | |

| Procedure<br>Performed | N/A<br>Performed<br>by | Date | Notes |
|---|---|---|---|
| *[If the company is considering the use of an integrated computerized software documentation solution, consider form DOC-4, Checklist for Evaluating SOX 404 Software.]* | | | |
| 19. Confirm the design of internal control by performing procedures to understand how and how consistently the documented control procedures are performed by company personnel. For example, consider performing walkthrough procedures for the significant processes of major transactions. | | | |
| *[For suggestions on how to perform walkthrough procedures, see form TST-ACT-1.]* | | | |
| *Coordination with External Auditors—Documentation* | | | |
| 20. If this is the first year the current external auditors will be performing an audit of the company's internal control, consider providing them with an example of the company's documentation of internal control.<br>   a. If you provide a copy of example documentation, consider preparing a written request for consideration and feedback to clarify why management is providing the documentation to the auditors. | | | |

| Procedure Performed | N/A Performed by | Date | Notes |
|---|---|---|---|
| 21. If the company uncovers inadequacies in its documentation of internal control, these inadequacies are considered control deficiencies that are required to be reported to the external auditors, even if corrected prior to year-end. Communicate these deficiencies to the auditors, preferably in writing, including a separate disclosure of all deficiencies believed to be significant deficiencies or material weaknesses.<br>a. If material weaknesses in the documentation of the company's internal control are discovered, consider the need for disclosure in the company's interim SEC filings. | | | |
| 22. In order to provide support for the company's assessment of internal control effectiveness in the future should such support be requested, prepare and archive a copy of the documentation of the company's internal control as it exists as of the end of the current fiscal year. | | | |
| *Design Tests of Operating Effectiveness* | | | |
| *[The following steps should be performed for all entity-level, centralized, and activity-level controls. Generally, entity-level and centralized control tests are performed before performing tests of activity-level controls.]* | | | |
| 23. Describe the parameters of the test, including<br>a. The test objective<br>b. Definition of deviations | | | |

| Procedure Performed | N/A Performed by | Date | Notes |
|---|---|---|---|
| 24. For each control identified in steps 4, 5, and 6, select the control procedures to be tested. | | | |
| 25. Determine the nature of the tests to be performed, for example<br>• Inquiries or written surveys of company personnel<br>• Inspection of documentation of control performance<br>• Observations of control performance<br>• Reperformance of controls | | | |
| 26. Determine the point in time at which the controls will be tested. | | | |
| 27. Determine the period of time to be covered by the tests. | | | |
| 28. Determine the extent of the tests to be performed. For example<br>• If inquiries or surveys are to be made of company personnel, how many and which individuals will be chosen to participate?<br>• If the control procedure is to be observed or reperformed, how many times?<br>• If documentation is to be inspected, which ones? | | | |
| 29. If the company receives a Type 2 SAS No. 70 report from one or more third-party organizations that are part of the company's information system, review these report(s) and evaluate their findings. | | | |
| *Consider using forms TST-ACT-3 and TST-ACT-3a to help you review a Type 2 SAS No. 70 report.* | | | |

| Procedure Performed | N/A Performed by | Date | Notes |
|---|---|---|---|
| 30. If sampling techniques are to be used to select items to be tested, develop a sampling plan that addresses<br>  a. The population from which the sample will be drawn<br>  b. The sample size<br>  c. Sample selection methodology | | | |
| 31. Schedule the timing of the tests, for example,<br>  • Determine which controls will be tested first and the sequencing of the tests to follow. | | | |
| *[Note: Generally, entity-level and common controls are tested prior to testing activity-level controls.]* | | | |
|   • Make any necessary arrangements to coordinate with company personnel or project team members included in the testing. | | | |
| *Coordination with External Auditors— Test Design* | | | |
| 32. Consider providing the external auditors with a summary of the nature, timing, and extent of planned tests of control operating effectiveness.<br>  a. If you provide a summary of the planned tests of controls, consider preparing a written request for consideration and feedback to clarify why management is providing the summary to the auditors. | | | |
| *Perform and Document Tests* | | | |
| 33. Perform the tests designed in steps 23–32. | | | |

| Procedure Performed | N/A Performed by | Date | Notes |
|---|---|---|---|
| 34. Prepare documentation of the tests performed and their results. | | | |
| 35. Identify testing exceptions and determine whether they indicate the existence of one or more control deficiencies.<br>a. If a determination is reached that a testing exception did *not* indicate a control deficiency<br>   i. Perform and document additional procedures.<br>   ii. Document the reasons for concluding that the testing exception was *not* considered to be a sign of a control deficiency. | | | |
| 36. Obtain and review subcertifications from selected business process owners. | | | |
| 37. For identified control deficiencies, develop a plan and take remedial action to correct the deficiencies. | | | |
| 38. Disclose to the external auditors all deficiencies in internal control, including separately disclosing all deficiencies determined to be significant deficiencies or material weaknesses.<br>a. If material weaknesses in the company's internal control are discovered, consider the need for disclosure in the company's interim SEC filings. | | | |
| *Evaluate and Report* | | | |
| 39. Assess the need to update tests of controls performed in advance of year-end. If necessary, update tests. | | | |

| Procedure Performed | N/A Performed by | Date | Notes |
|---|---|---|---|
| 40. For controls implemented since the testing date, including newly designed controls to remediate control deficiencies, <br> a. Review the documentation of the control and assess its adequacy. <br> b. Test the operating effectiveness of the control as of year-end (see steps 23–38). | | | |
| 41. Summarize and evaluate results of the tests. | | | |
| 42. Prepare management's report on internal control effectiveness. | | | |
| 43. Consider the need for other internal control–related disclosures in SEC filings. | | | |
| 44. Determine whether there was any material fraud or any other fraud that, although not material, involved senior management or management or other employees who have a significant role in the company's internal control. | | | |
| 45. Summarize all significant deficiencies and material weaknesses reported by the external auditors to company management as part of previous audits of internal control. Identify how each of these deficiencies was, or was not, corrected. | | | |

| Procedure<br>Performed | N/A<br>Performed<br>by | Date | Notes |
|---|---|---|---|
| 46. Determine whether, subsequent to the date being reported on, there were any changes in internal control or other factors that might significantly affect internal control, including any corrective action taken with regard to significant deficiencies and material weaknesses. Consider<br>• Relevant internal audit reports issued during the subsequent period<br>• External auditor reports of significant deficiencies or material weaknesses<br>• Regulatory agency reports on the company's internal control<br>• Information about the effectiveness of the company's internal control obtained from other sources | | | |
| 47. Prepare a written representation letter for the external auditors that conforms to the requirements of PCAOB Auditing Standard No. 5. | | | |
| *[See COM-2, Example Management Representation Letter.]* | | | |

# Project Planning Summary

## PURPOSE

This form has been designed to

- Help make important decisions in planning management's project for testing the effectiveness of the company's internal control
- Document key planning decisions and the basis for those decisions

## INSTRUCTIONS

Use this form to guide the planning of the company's project to assess internal control effectiveness. The completed form can be circulated to project team members, business process owners, external auditors, and others involved in the project. The form is divided into the following six sections.

- Project Team Members and Responsibilities
- Project Team Members' Competence and Objectivity
- Internal Control Information Sources
- Project Scope
- Internal Control Documentation Sources
- Project Schedule

Each section of the form includes an introduction that describes its purpose and content. These introductions have been written from the *project manager's* point of view, so they should be read carefully and modified by the project manager, as appropriate.

Included as appendixes to the form are the decision aids to help you make and document key planning decisions. Attach the completed aids (to the extent that you use them) to the final planning document.

*Footnoted comments in italics are additional instructions to the preparer of the form and should be removed before the form is considered final.*

## ASSESSMENT OF INTERNAL CONTROL EFFECTIVENESS PROJECT PLANNING

Company: _____    Reporting Date: _____

Prepared by: _____    Date Prepared: _____

This form summarizes the most significant decisions made about our planning of the company's process for evaluating the effectiveness of its internal control and our support for making these decisions. This form has been prepared to

- Assist the company's independent auditors in their understanding and evaluation of our process
- Communicate the project plan to project team members
- Establish a concise, permanent record of the significant facts and circumstances that influenced the design of our project and the company's compliance with the requirements to review the effectiveness of internal control

## PROJECT TEAM MEMBERS AND RESPONSIBILITIES

Company management is responsible for evaluating the effectiveness of internal control and presenting a written assessment of that assessment as of the end of the fiscal year. Our chief executive officer and chief financial officer bear the ultimate responsibility for the planning and performance of our project to assess internal control effectiveness.

To carry out the day-to-day performance and administration of the project, we formed a project team, which reports directly to those individuals responsible for management's report on internal control effectiveness. To form our project team, we considered the need for individuals both internal and external to the company that possessed the following:

- Knowledge of company business processes and operations
- Knowledge of company control policies and procedures
- Expertise in information technology systems and controls
- Knowledge of financial accounting and reporting matters, including SEC reporting requirements
- Expertise in the design, documentation, testing, and evaluation of internal control

The following table summarizes key project team members.

| Project Team | Name(s) | Internal/ External | Summary of Responsibilities |
|---|---|---|---|
| **Management** | | | |
| Chief executive officer (CEO) | | Internal | With CFO, shares ultimate responsibility for the assessment of internal control effectiveness |
| Chief financial officer (CFO) | | Internal | With CEO, shares ultimate responsibility for the assessment of internal control effectiveness |

| Project Team | Name(s) | Internal/ External | Summary of Responsibilities |
|---|---|---|---|
| Overall project manager | | Internal | Day-to-day planning and project performance |
| **Individual Project Teams[1]** | | | |
| | | | |
| | | | |
| **Technical Specialists[2]** | | | |
| | | | |
| | | | |

[1] For example, "documentation," "testing," etc. The individual teams described in this section will vary according to how your project is organized. The three rows indicated here are for example purposes only and should not be construed to limit the number of your individual project teams.

[2] For example, "information technology." Your project may include more than the two specialists suggested by this example form.

## PROJECT TEAM MEMBERS' COMPETENCE AND OBJECTIVITY

As part of their audit of the company's internal control, the company's external auditors may rely on certain tests of controls performed by project team members. The following summarizes the project team members and the control areas that may meet the applicable auditing standards, thus allowing the external auditors to rely on their work. The third column indicates where information on the project team's competence and objectivity can be located.

| Project Team Member | Control Area(s) Tested | Ref. to Information on Competence and Objectivity[1] |
|---|---|---|
|  |  |  |
|  |  |  |
|  |  |  |

[1] Consider attaching form ADM-2a, Checklist for Summarizing Project Team Competence and Objectivity, for each project team listed.

## INTERNAL CONTROL INFORMATION SOURCES

The project gathered and reviewed the following relevant, current information about the company's operations, financial reporting, and internal controls for the purpose of helping plan the project.

| Description | Reviewed | Reference |
|---|---|---|
| Recent SEC filings, including the most recent 10-K and all 10-Qs subsequently filed | Y    N |  |
| Documentation of tests performed in previous assessments of internal control effectiveness | Y    N |  |
| Previously identified testing exceptions or control deficiencies | Y    N |  |
| Current efforts to remediate previously identified control deficiencies | Y    N |  |
| Internal control reports of the company's internal auditors | Y    N |  |
| Communications from the company's external auditors on internal control matters | Y    N |  |
| Guidance on internal control assessment or reporting from the PCAOB or SEC that has been issued since the previous assessment project | Y    N |  |
| Relevant findings or recommendations of the disclosure committee | Y    N |  |

# PROJECT SCOPE

This section summarizes the factors considered and decisions made regarding the controls that were included in the scope of our project. These decisions were made for the areas indicated below.

|  | Yes | N/A |
|---|:---:|:---:|
| Entity-level controls | ❏ | ❏ |
| Activity-level controls | ❏ | ❏ |
| Multiple business units or locations | ❏ | ❏ |
| Controls at service organizations | ❏ | ❏ |
| Other considerations | | |
| Describe _____ | ❏ | ❏ |

## *Entity-Level Controls*

PCAOB Auditing Standard No. 5 provides definitive guidance on the entity-level controls required to be included in the scope of our internal control assessment. Our project was designed to comply with these requirements and accordingly, the scope of the project included the following.

|  | Yes | N/A |
|---|:---:|:---:|
| Control environment | ❏ | ❏ |
| Controls related to management override | ❏ | ❏ |
| Management's risk assessment process | ❏ | ❏ |
| Controls to monitor other controls | ❏ | ❏ |
| Controls to monitor results of operations | ❏ | ❏ |
| Period-end financial reporting process | ❏ | ❏ |
| Policies that address significant business controls and risk management practices | ❏ | ❏ |
| Selection and application of accounting policies | ❏ | ❏ |
| Information technology general controls | ❏ | ❏ |

In addition to the preceding entity-level controls, our project included the documentation, testing, and evaluation of the following entity-level controls:

_____

_____

_____

## Centralized Processes and Activity-Level Controls

To determine the common processes and activity-level controls included within the scope of the project, we performed the following three steps:

1. Identified the significant financial statement accounts or account groups

2. Identified significant financial statement disclosures

3. Identified the major transactions/business processes for each significant financial statement account and disclosure

### SIGNIFICANT ACCOUNTS AND DISCLOSURES

A listing of the significant financial statement accounts and disclosures is included as attachment ■■ to this form. *[Attach a list of significant financial statement accounts and disclosures. Alternatively, you may wish to complete and attach form ADM-2b.1, Worksheet for Determining and Documenting Significant Accounts and Disclosures.]*

### MAJOR TRANSACTIONS/BUSINESS PROCESSES

The scope of our project includes the major "transactions" for each significant account and disclosure. We use the term "transactions" interchangeably with "business processes." We consider "major" business processes to be those that are significant to the company's financial statements.

The documentation, testing, and evaluation of company activity-level controls are organized according to the significant processes relating to major business processes. Included as attachment ■ to this form is a list of major business processes. *[Alternatively, you may wish to complete and attach form ADM-2b.2, Mapping of Business Processes to Significant Accounts and Disclosures.]*

## Consideration of Multiple Business Units or Locations

The table on the following page is a summary of all the business units or locations of the company and an indication of which were included within the scope of our project.

| Business Unit | Financial Summary (in Thousands of Dollars) | | | Financially Significant? | Specific Risks | Nature of Risk | Significant in Aggregate | Excluded from Project |
|---|---|---|---|---|---|---|---|---|
| | Revenues | Net Income | Assets | | | | | |
| Consolidated Financial Statements | $ | $ | $ | | | | | |
| Business Unit #1 | $ | $ | $ | | | | | |
| Business Unit #2 | $ | $ | $ | | | | | |
| Business Unit #3 | $ | $ | $ | | | | | |
| Business Unit #4 | $ | $ | $ | | | | | |
| Business Unit #5 | $ | $ | $ | | | | | |

**INSTRUCTIONS FOR COMPLETING THE SUMMARY**

- List each business unit or location in the first column of the worksheet.
- Financial summary. Provide a summary (in dollars) of the operations and financial position of the company at the consolidated level and for each business unit. This information will be helpful in supporting conclusions about which business units have been included within the scope of the project.
- Assess the overall risk of material misstatement associated with the business unit or location.
- At some business units or locations, the risk may be isolated to one or more "specific risks." The scope of the project will include only the controls related to these specific risks, rather than all controls of the business unit or location.
- Some locations or business units may not present a reasonable possibility of a material misstatement. Those locations of business units are excluded from the scope of the project.
- Review the completed summary and determine that the scope of the project includes testing a "large portion" of the company's operations and financial condition. Consider the guidance provided in paragraph A17 of the PCAOB Staff Questions and Answers (June 23, 2004) to make this determination.

**OTHER CONSIDERATIONS**

In choosing which business units and locations to include within the scope of our project, we encountered certain conditions not summarized in the preceding section. Those conditions and how they affected our decisions relating to project scope are summarized as follows.

_____

_____

_____

_____

_____

_____

CONCLUSION

We believe that our selection of the business units indicated in the preceding summary results in our testing a large portion of the company's operations and financial position.

## *Consideration of Controls at Service Organizations*

The company uses one or more service organizations to process certain of its transactions. For those service organizations that we determined were part of the company's information system we

- Obtained an understanding of the controls at the service organization that are relevant to our company's internal control
- Obtained an understanding of the controls maintained by the company over the activities of the service organization
- Obtained evidence that the controls (both at the service organization and at the company) that are relevant to our assessment of internal control effectiveness are operating effectively

The following table summarizes the service organizations whose services are considered part of the company's information system, together with our overall approach to how we included them within the scope of our engagement.

## SUMMARY OF APPROACH TO SERVICE ORGANIZATIONS

| Service Organization | Testing Approach | | | SAS 70 Type II Report | Reference |
|---|---|---|---|---|---|
| | Services Provided | Company Controls | Service Organization Controls | | |
| | | | | | |
| | | | | | |
| | | | | | |
| | | | | | |
| | | | | | |
| | | | | | |
| | | | | | |
| | | | | | |
| | | | | | |
| | | | | | |
| | | | | | |
| | | | | | |
| | | | | | |
| | | | | | |
| | | | | | |

## INSTRUCTIONS FOR COMPLETING THE TABLE

- Determine which of the service organizations used by the company provide services (i.e., process major transactions) that are part of the company's information system.

Summarize the organization and the service(s) they provide in the first two columns of the table.

- Determine which of the testing approaches the company will use to obtain information about the design and operating effectiveness of the controls related to major transactions that are processed by a service organization. Place an X in each column that applies.
  - "Company Controls" indicates that you will document, test, and evaluate the company's controls over the activities of the service organization.
  - "Service Organization Controls" indicates that you will test the controls at the service organization.
  - "SAS 70 Type II Report" indicates that you will obtain and review a service auditor's report on controls placed in operation and tests of operating effectiveness.
- Provide a reference to where the relevant documentation and the results of tests of operating effectiveness can be found.

# INTERNAL CONTROL DOCUMENTATION SOURCES

*[This section of the Planning Summary may be helpful to project team members and the external auditors by allowing them to understand the scope and relative magnitude of the documentation of internal control and how that documentation can be accessed.]*

## Entity-Level Controls

The following table summarizes the entity-level controls included within the project scope and where the documentation related to the design of these controls can be found.

### INSTRUCTIONS FOR COMPLETING

- Identify the documents the company maintains relating to entity-level controls. Examples might include the following:
  - Code of conduct
  - Board of directors or audit committee charter
  - Human resources policies relating to the recruiting, hiring, training, compensation, promotion, or termination of employees
  - Organizational chart
- List the title of these documents across the horizontal axis.
- For each document, determine which entity-level control(s) the document addresses. Put an X in the appropriate cell.

## Where to Find Documentation of Control Design

| Entity-Level Controls | Corporate Governance Documents | Human Resources Policies | Information Technology Documents | Type 2 SAS 70 | Other |
|---|---|---|---|---|---|
| Control environment | | | | | |
| Management's risk assessment process | | | | | |
| Controls to monitor other controls | | | | | |
| Period-end financial reporting process | | | | | |
| Board-approved policies that address significant business control and risk management practices | | | | | |
| Audit committee effectiveness | | | | | |
| Antifraud programs and controls | | | | | |
| Information technology general controls | | | | | |
| Controls on which other controls are dependent | | | | | |
| Controls over significant nonroutine and nonsystematic transactions | | | | | |
| Other entity-level controls | | | | | |

## *Documentation of Internal Control Policies and Procedures*

The company's documentation of its major business processes and related activity-level controls is maintained and can be accessed as follows.

_____

_____

_____

_____

_____

_____

_____

### INSTRUCTIONS FOR COMPLETING THIS SECTION

Summarize the methods and the technology used to prepare, maintain, and store the company's documentation of internal control. For example, if the company uses an automated software solution for the documentation of internal control, provide pertinent information related to that solution in this section of the form.

# PROJECT SCHEDULE

*[It will be helpful to all those involved in the project if you include a proposed project schedule in your Planning Summary. The following is just one example of how such a summary might be prepared. Note that the first column should contain all the entity- and activity-level controls previously identified as being included within the scope of the project. The schedule should indicate the timing of the major phases of the project, such as review of documentation, testing, and evaluation.]*

| Legend | | |
|---|---|---|
| Review documentation | | |
| | | |
| Test effectiveness | | |
| | | |
| Evaluate and/or report | | |

| Weeks | Month #1 | | | | Month #2 | | | | Month #3 | | | | Month #4 | | | |
|---|---|---|---|---|---|---|---|---|---|---|---|---|---|---|---|---|
| | 1 | 2 | 3 | 4 | 1 | 2 | 3 | 4 | 1 | 2 | 3 | 4 | 1 | 2 | 3 | 4 |
| Entity-level | | | | | | | | | | | | | | | | |
| Entity-level #1 | ▧ | | | | | | | | | | | | | ▨ | | █ |
| Entity-level #2 | | | ▨ | ▨ | ▨ | ▨ | | | | | | | | ▨ | | █ |
| Entity-level #3 | | ▧ | | | | | | | | | | | | ▨ | | █ |
| Entity-level #4 | | | | | | ▨ | ▨ | | | | | | | ▨ | | █ |
| Activity-level | | | | | | | | | | | | | | | | |
| Activity-level #1 | | | | | | ▧ | ▧ | | ▨ | ▨ | ▨ | ▨ | ▨ | ▨ | | █ |
| Activity-level #2 | | | | | | ▧ | ▧ | | ▨ | ▨ | ▨ | ▨ | ▨ | ▨ | | █ |
| Activity-level #3 | | | | | | ▧ | ▧ | | ▨ | ▨ | ▨ | ▨ | ▨ | ▨ | | █ |
| Activity-level #4 | | | | | | ▧ | ▧ | | ▨ | ▨ | ▨ | ▨ | ▨ | ▨ | | █ |

# Checklist for Summarizing Project Team Competence and Objectivity

## PURPOSE

This form has been designed to

- Summarize your evaluation of the competence and objectivity of the individuals performing tests of controls, for the primary purpose of supporting the external auditor's decisions about using these tests in their audit of internal control

## INSTRUCTIONS

In the spaces provided along the horizontal axis, insert the names of the individuals who will be testing controls, together with the areas to which they have been assigned. This information should correspond to the information entered into "Project Team Members' Competence and Objectivity" in form ADM-2, Project Planning Summary.

For each testing team member, answer the questions listed in the first column. For additional guidance on these questions, please refer to paragraphs 117–120 of PCAOB Auditing Standard No. 2.

To support your answers to questions relating to educational level, professional experience, and continuing education, consider attaching relevant documentation, such as resumes of the project team members.

Provide an explanation of any "No" responses.

*Footnoted comments in italics are additional instructions to the preparer of the form and should be removed before the form is considered final.*

## ASSESSMENT OF INTERNAL CONTROL EFFECTIVENESS
## PROJECT TEAM COMPETENCE AND OBJECTIVITY

Company: _____     Reporting Date: _____

Prepared by: _____     Date Prepared: _____

This form summarizes our pertinent information related to the competence and objectivity of individuals who performed tests of controls.

## Individuals Performing Tests of Controls

| | Individual #1 | Individual #2 | Individual #3 | Individual #4 | Individual #5 |
|---|---|---|---|---|---|
| Work area(s) assigned | | | | | |
| Professional designation (e.g., CIA, CPA) | | | | | |
| If the individual is an internal auditor, does he or she follow the International Standards for the Professional Practice of Internal Auditing? | | | | | |

## Competence

| | Individual #1 | | Individual #2 | | Individual #3 | | Individual #4 | | Individual #5 | |
|---|---|---|---|---|---|---|---|---|---|---|
| | Yes | No | Yes | No | Yes | No | Yes | No | Yes | No |
| Are the educational level and professional experience of the individual appropriate for the work area(s) assigned? [Consider attaching resume or equivalent.] | ❑ | ❑ | ❑ | ❑ | ❑ | ❑ | ❑ | ❑ | ❑ | ❑ |
| Has the individual received adequate continuing education on matters relevant to testing internal control in the work areas assigned? [Consider attaching resume or equivalent.] | ❑ | ❑ | ❑ | ❑ | ❑ | ❑ | ❑ | ❑ | ❑ | ❑ |
| Is the person's work adequately supervised? | ❑ | ❑ | ❑ | ❑ | ❑ | ❑ | ❑ | ❑ | ❑ | ❑ |
| Is the documentation of the tests performed and their results adequate? | ❑ | ❑ | ❑ | ❑ | ❑ | ❑ | ❑ | ❑ | ❑ | ❑ |

## Objectivity

| | Individual #1 | | Individual #2 | | Individual #3 | | Individual #4 | | Individual #5 | |
|---|---|---|---|---|---|---|---|---|---|---|
| | Yes | No | Yes | No | Yes | No | Yes | No | Yes | No |
| Is the individual prohibited from testing controls in the following areas? | | | | | | | | | | |
| • Areas in which relatives are employed in important or internal control–sensitive positions | ☐ | ☐ | ☐ | ☐ | ☐ | ☐ | ☐ | ☐ | ☐ | ☐ |
| • Areas to which the individual was recently assigned | ☐ | ☐ | ☐ | ☐ | ☐ | ☐ | ☐ | ☐ | ☐ | ☐ |
| • Areas to which the individual is scheduled to be assigned upon completion of control testing responsibilities | ☐ | ☐ | ☐ | ☐ | ☐ | ☐ | ☐ | ☐ | ☐ | ☐ |
| If the individual is responsible for the work of others who test controls | | | | | | | | | | |
| • Does the individual report to an officer of sufficient status within the company? | ☐ | ☐ | ☐ | ☐ | ☐ | ☐ | ☐ | ☐ | ☐ | ☐ |
| • Does the individual have direct access and report regularly to the board of directors or audit committee? | ☐ | ☐ | ☐ | ☐ | ☐ | ☐ | ☐ | ☐ | ☐ | ☐ |
| • Does the board of directors or audit committee oversee decisions related to the individual's employment? | ☐ | ☐ | ☐ | ☐ | ☐ | ☐ | ☐ | ☐ | ☐ | ☐ |

# Worksheet for Determining and Documenting Significant Accounts and Disclosures

## PURPOSE

This form has been designed to

- Aid in the determination of which financial statement accounts and disclosures are considered significant
- Provide documentation related to project scope considerations for common processing and activity-level controls

## INSTRUCTIONS

First, determine whether this form is necessary. Based on your knowledge of the company and your previous experience, you may determine that all or almost all of the company's financial statement accounts are considered significant. If so, then you should consider documenting that fact, together with a list of those accounts *not* included in the project scope, along with an explanation for why these accounts are not considered significant.

The following discussion describes how the form should be completed, in the event that you determine it would be helpful for your project.

The horizontal axis of this matrix lists several factors that you may consider when determining whether an account is significant. These factors are presented in the first column of the following table, together with an interpretation of how the factors might be considered.

| Guidance Included in the Auditing Standard | How the Factor Might Be Considered | |
|---|---|---|
| | Indicates *More* Significant | Indicates *Less* Significant |
| Size and composition of the account | Large balance | Small balance |
| Susceptibility of loss due to errors or fraud | Highly susceptible | Less susceptible |

| | How the Factor Might Be Considered | |
|---|---|---|
| **Guidance Included in the Auditing Standard** | **Indicates *More* Significant** | **Indicates *Less* Significant** |
| Volume of activity, complexity, and homogeneity of the individual transactions processed through the account | Large volume, complex transactions, great variety of transactions included in the account | Small volume, simple, homogeneous transactions |
| Nature of the account (for example, suspense accounts generally warrant greater attention) | To be determined based on your judgment | To be determined based on your judgment |
| Accounting and reporting complexities associated with the account | Complex accounting and reporting | Relatively simple accounting and reporting |
| Exposure to losses represented by the account (for example, loss accruals related to a consolidated construction contracting subsidiary) | Significant exposure to loss | Minimal exposure to loss |
| Likelihood (or possibility) of significant contingent liabilities arising from the activities represented by the account | Greater than remote possibility of significant contingent loss | Remote possibility of significant contingent loss |
| Existence of related-party transactions in the account | Related-party transactions included in account | No related-party transactions included in account |
| Changes from the prior period in account characteristics (for example, new complexities or subjectivity or new types of transactions) | Substantial changes from prior period | Minimal changes from prior period |

The vertical axis lists the account groups and selected individual accounts reported in the company's financial statements. *The listing in the attached example is for illustrative purposes only and should be modified for your company's unique circumstances.*

For each account group or account, assess the factor listed in the column heading and determine whether it poses a high, medium, or low risk of material misstatement. Once all factors have been considered, determine whether the account is considered significant, based on the assessed risks of material misstatement.

*Footnoted comments in italics are additional instructions to the preparer of the form and should be removed before the form is considered final.*

# ASSESSMENT OF INTERNAL CONTROL EFFECTIVENESS
# SIGNIFICANT ACCOUNTS AND DISCLOSURES

Company: _____          Reporting Date: _____

Prepared by: _____        Date Prepared: _____

This matrix documents the accounts we identified as significant and therefore included within the scope of its assessment of internal control effectiveness.

- *Size and composition.* Size and composition of the account.
- *Exposure to loss.* Susceptibility of loss due to errors or fraud; exposure to losses represented by the account (e.g., loss accruals related to a consolidated construction contracting subsidiary).
- *Transactions.* Volume of activity, complexity, and homogeneity of the individual transactions processed through the account.
- *Complexity.* Accounting and reporting complexities associated with the account.
- *Contingent liability.* Likelihood (or possibility) of significant contingent liabilities arising from the activities represented by the account.
- *Related party.* Existence of related-party transactions in the account.
- *Changes from prior period.* Changes from the prior period in account characteristics (e.g., new complexities or subjectivity or new types of transactions).
- *Other.* Any other factor, including the nature of the account (e.g., suspense accounts generally warrant greater attention).

    Risks were assessed as

- *High.* The risk of material misstatement caused by the factor is probable.
- *Moderate.* The risk of material misstatement caused by the factor is reasonably possible.
- *Low.* The risk of material misstatement caused by the factor is remote.

    Overall, we considered an account to be significant if there is more than a remote likelihood that the account could contain misstatements that individually, or when aggregated with others, could have a material effect on the financial statements, considering the risks of both overstatement and understatement.

## Risk Assessment Criteria

| Account Group/ Subgroups | Size and Composition | Exposure to Loss or Liability | Transactions | Complexity | Contingent Liabilities | Related Party | Change from Prior Period | Other | Significant Account? |
|---|---|---|---|---|---|---|---|---|---|
| Cash | | | | | | | | | |
| Accounts receivable | | | | | | | | | |
| Investments Trading Available for sale Held-to-maturity | | | | | | | | | |
| Inventory Raw materials Work in process Finished goods | | | | | | | | | |
| Property, plant, and equipment | | | | | | | | | |
| Goodwill and intangible assets | | | | | | | | | |
| Prepaid expenses and other assets | | | | | | | | | |

**Risk Assessment Criteria**

| Account Group/ Subgroups | Size and Composition | Exposure to Loss or Liability | Transactions | Complexity | Contingent Liabilities | Related Party | Change from Prior Period | Other | Significant Account? |
|---|---|---|---|---|---|---|---|---|---|
| Accounts payable | | | | | | | | | |
| Accrued liabilities | | | | | | | | | |
| Minority interest | | | | | | | | | |
| Other current liabilities | | | | | | | | | |
| Long-term debt Current Noncurrent | | | | | | | | | |
| Deferred taxes Current Noncurrent | | | | | | | | | |
| Subordinated debt | | | | | | | | | |
| Stockholders' equity Common stock Preferred stock Paid-in-capital Retained earnings Other comprehensive income | | | | | | | | | |

**Risk Assessment Criteria**

| Account Group/ Subgroups | Size and Composition | Exposure to Loss or Liability | Transactions | Complexity | Contingent Liabilities | Related Party | Change from Prior Period | Other | Significant Account? |
|---|---|---|---|---|---|---|---|---|---|
| Revenues | | | | | | | | | |
| Cost of sales | | | | | | | | | |
| Personnel costs | | | | | | | | | |
| Occupancy costs | | | | | | | | | |
| Selling costs | | | | | | | | | |
| Administrative expenses | | | | | | | | | |
| Income taxes | | | | | | | | | |

# Mapping of Business Processes to Significant Accounts and Disclosures

## PURPOSE

This form has been designed to help you

- Identify the major transactions associated with each significant account and disclosure
- Organize the overall approach to the project

## INSTRUCTIONS

Paragraph 72 of PCAOB Auditing Standard No. 2 identifies the following three types of transaction:

- *Routine transactions* are recurring financial activities reflected in the accounting records in the normal course of business (e.g., sales, purchases, cash receipts, cash disbursements, payroll).
- *Nonroutine transactions* are activities that occur only periodically (e.g., taking physical inventory, calculating depreciation expense, adjusting for foreign currencies). A distinguishing feature of nonroutine transactions is that data involved generally are not part of the daily flow of transactions.
- *Estimation transactions* are activities that involve management judgments or assumptions in formulating account balances in the absence of a precise means of measurement (e.g., determining the allowance for doubtful accounts, establishing warranty reserves, assessing assets for impairment).

When completing the attached matrix, *you should consider only routine transactions.* Controls related to nonroutine transactions and estimates are considered as part of the documentation, testing, and evaluation of entity-level controls. Similarly, the period-end financial reporting process also is considered as part of the evaluation of entity-level controls.

The horizontal axis of the matrix lists all significant accounts and disclosures you previously identified as being significant to the financial statements and, therefore, included within the scope of the project. *The listing in the example is for illustrative purposes only and should be modified for your company's unique circumstances.*

The vertical axis lists the company's major transactions. Included as an appendix to this form is a list of example routine business processes/major transactions that provides more detail on the nature of the transactions listed in the matrix. *The listing in the example is for illustrative purposes only and should be modified for your company's unique circumstances.*

The company's internal control and your project teams are most likely to be organized according to major transactions and the related processes, rather than by financial statement account title. For example, one project team would be responsible for assessing controls related to cash disbursements for *all* accounts.

Completing the matrix is a two-step process.

1. Review each major transaction. Determine which financial statement account(s) the transaction affects. Place an X in the corresponding cell(s).

2. Each financial statement account may be affected by more than one transaction. For example, cash accounts are affected by both cash receipts and cash disbursements. Once you have completed the matrix, review each significant account (column). Determine that all *routine* debits and credits to the account have been encompassed in the identified business processes. If some routine debits and credits have not been included, you will need to add a new business process to the vertical axis. Once you have determined that all routine debits and credits to the account have been included in the scope of the project, indicate this conclusion by signing off in the first row of the matrix.

*Footnoted comments in italics are additional instructions to the preparer of the form and should be removed before the form is considered final.*

---

## ASSESSMENT OF INTERNAL CONTROL EFFECTIVENESS
## MAPPING OF BUSINESS PROCESSES TO SIGNIFICANT
## ACCOUNTS AND DISCLOSURES

Company: _____          Reporting Date: _____

Prepared by: _____          Date Prepared: _____

**ASSETS**

| Business Process | Cash | Accounts Receivable | Investments | Inventory | Property, Plant, and Equipment | Goodwill and Intangibles | Prepaids and Other |
|---|---|---|---|---|---|---|---|
| Manage logistics and receive inventory | | | | | | | |
| Process product costs | | | | | | | |
| Process and ship customer orders | | | | | | | |
| Process accounts receivable | | | | | | | |
| Authorize purchases | | | | | | | |
| Process accounts payable | | | | | | | |
| Cash receipts | | | | | | | |
| Cash disbursements | | | | | | | |
| Safeguard assets | | | | | | | |
| Process investment transactions | | | | | | | |
| Process finance transactions | | | | | | | |
| Record fixed assets activity | | | | | | | |
| Safeguard assets | | | | | | | |
| Process payroll | | | | | | | |

## LIABILITIES AND EQUITY

| Business Processes | Accounts Payable | Accrued Liabilities | Minority Interest | Other Current Liabilities | Long-term Debt | Deferred Taxes | Equity |
|---|---|---|---|---|---|---|---|
| Manage logistics and receive inventory | | | | | | | |
| Process product costs | | | | | | | |
| Process and ship customer orders | | | | | | | |
| Process accounts receivable | | | | | | | |
| Authorize purchases | | | | | | | |
| Process accounts payable | | | | | | | |
| Cash receipts | | | | | | | |
| Cash disbursements | | | | | | | |
| Safeguard assets | | | | | | | |
| Process investment transactions | | | | | | | |
| Process finance transactions | | | | | | | |
| Record fixed assets activity | | | | | | | |
| Safeguard assets | | | | | | | |
| Process payroll | | | | | | | |

# REVENUES AND EXPENSES

| Business Processes | Revenues | Cost of Sales | Personnel Costs | Occupancy Costs | Selling Costs | Administrative Expenses | Income Taxes |
|---|---|---|---|---|---|---|---|
| Manage logistics and receive inventory | | | | | | | |
| Process product costs | | | | | | | |
| Process and ship customer orders | | | | | | | |
| Process accounts receivable | | | | | | | |
| Authorize purchases | | | | | | | |
| Process accounts payable | | | | | | | |
| Cash receipts | | | | | | | |
| Cash disbursements | | | | | | | |
| Safeguard assets | | | | | | | |
| Process investment transactions | | | | | | | |
| Process finance transactions | | | | | | | |
| Record fixed assets activity | | | | | | | |
| Safeguard assets | | | | | | | |
| Process payroll | | | | | | | |

# Example Inquiries to Identify Changes to Internal Control

## PURPOSE

This form has been designed to

- Help you identify changes to internal control that should be considered when planning your assessment of internal control effectiveness

## INSTRUCTIONS

When planning your assessment of internal control effectiveness, you should identify changes to internal control that have been made (or should have been made) since your last assessment. The guidelines and example inquiries presented here may be used to help you identify these changes.

### EXAMPLE INQUIRIES TO IDENTIFY CHANGES TO INTERNAL CONTROL

As part of planning an assessment of internal control effectiveness you should update your understanding of significant processes and major transactions. Determine whether your previous understanding of the company's information processing stream remains relevant and, if not, make any required changes to the company's documentation of internal control to reflect your updated knowledge. Your primary method for gathering information will be inquiries of company personnel. When making these inquiries

- Expand your inquiries to include those outside of management. Ask people who perform control procedures and process information as part of their daily job requirements.
- Make inquiries of those outside of the accounting department, for example, individuals involved in operations.

  Your inquiries should be designed to gather information about

- Changes in the company's business activities that have resulted in new or increased risks
- Whether and how specific information processes and related controls were changed in response to new or increased risks

- Changes to information processes or controls that should have been made based on previously identified internal control deficiencies
- Other changes to processes, controls, or transactions

## EXAMPLE INQUIRIES

Consider asking the following questions of company personnel or business process owners.

- Over the past year, what have been the most significant changes to the following?
    - The business environment in which the company operates
    - Company personnel, especially those with information processing or control duties
    - Information technology
    - Lines of business
    - Accounting and financial reporting standards that affect the company
- What effect have these changes had on the company's
    - Operations
    - Types of transactions entered into or counterparties to those transactions
    - Ability to capture, process, or report financial information
- How has company growth or retrenchment affected
    - Operations
    - Types of transactions entered into or counterparties to those transactions
    - Ability to capture, process, or report financial information
- How has the company modified its information processing and controls to respond to new financial reporting risks?
- What internal control deficiencies were identified as part of previous assessments of internal control effectiveness? During the past year, what additional weaknesses has management identified?
- What actions has management taken in response to known internal control weaknesses, those identified both by the auditors and by management?[1]
- What kinds of accounting system or financial reporting errors
    - Persist
    - Have surfaced in the past year
- What other changes, not yet discussed, has management made to its
    - Financial information processing system and related controls
    - Internal control
- Why were these changes made?

[1] *You should consider management's response to known internal control weaknesses, or lack of a response, when evaluating the entity's control environment.*

# Senior Management Review Checklist

## PURPOSE

This form has been designed to

- Guide the principal executive officer and principal financial officer in their participation, supervision, and review of the company's assessment of internal control effectiveness
- Provide documentation of the nature, timing, and extent of senior management's active involvement in the company's process for evaluating internal control

## INSTRUCTIONS

The company's principal executive officer and principal financial officer bear the ultimate responsibility for the effectiveness of the company's internal control over financial reporting. In addition, these officers must take responsibility for

- The evaluation of the effectiveness of the company's internal control
- The sufficiency of the evidence supporting the evaluation of internal control effectiveness
- The preparation of the written assessment of internal control effectiveness as of year-end.

This checklist will help the company's principal executive and financial officers fulfill these responsibilities.

To indicate that the step was completed, initial in the "Done by" space provided and indicate the date when the step was performed. To perform the steps, the program will require you to

- Review relevant documentation
- Make inquiries of the project team leader
- Observe the work of the project team

You also will be required to understand and evaluate key decisions *throughout the entire assessment process.*

# ASSESSMENT OF INTERNAL CONTROL EFFECTIVENESS
# SENIOR MANAGEMENT REVIEW CHECKLIST

Company: _____        Reporting Date: _____

Prepared by: _____

This form summarizes the nature and timing of the involvement of the company's principal executive officer and its principal financial officer in the company's process for assessing internal control effectiveness.

|  | Done By | Date |
|---|---|---|

## *Project Planning*

1. Review the composition of the project team and satisfy yourself that

   a. The team as a whole has the skills to perform the work competently.                          _____   _____

   b. The project manager has sufficient status within the company to ensure sufficient internal control testing coverage and adequate consideration of, and actions on, the findings and recommendations of the individuals performing the testing.                          _____   _____

2. Determine that the resources allocated to the project are adequate.                          _____   _____

3. Review the list of information sources used by the project team and determine that all internal control–related matters of which you are aware (e.g., communications from external auditors) have been made available to the project team.                          _____   _____

4. Determine that all entity-level controls required to be tested have been included within the project scope.                          _____   _____

5. Consider the company's major transactions or business processes. Determine that all of these have been included within the scope of the project.                          _____   _____

6. Obtain an understanding of the process used to select individual business units or locations and third-party information processing organizations (i.e., service organizations) that have been included within the scope of the project.                          _____   _____

| | Done By | Date |
|---|---|---|

7. Consider other events or circumstances that posed significant project scoping issues, for example, business acquisitions or new information systems. Determine that these issues were resolved appropriately. _____ _____

8. Review the project schedule and assess whether

   a. The planned timetable is reasonably attainable, given the project scope and resources assigned. _____ _____

   b. The scheduled completion dates will allow for the remediation of any identified control deficiencies and the testing by external auditors. _____ _____

9. Review and monitor the communication between the project team and the company's external auditors regarding significant planning matters. _____ _____

## Documentation and Testing of Internal Control

10. Obtain an understanding of how the company's internal control documentation is created, stored, protected from unauthorized changes, and maintained. _____ _____

11. Obtain an understanding of the procedures performed by the project team to assess the adequacy of the company's documentation of internal control and whether

   a. Controls related to *all* significant business processes and entity-level controls have been documented. _____ _____

   b. The content of the documentation contained all required elements to assess control design. _____ _____

   c. Control documentation reflects current operating practices. _____ _____

12. Obtain an overall understanding of the project team's tests of *entity-level* control effectiveness, including

   a. The nature of the tests performed. _____ _____

   b. The date as of which the tests were performed and the time period covered by the tests. _____ _____

   c. The extent or scope of the tests. _____ _____

|  | Done By | Date |
|---|---|---|

13. Obtain an overall understanding of the project
    team's tests of *activity-level* control effectiveness,
    including

     a. The nature of the tests performed.           _____    _____

     b. The date as of which the tests were
    performed and the time period covered
    by the tests.                                   _____    _____

     c. The extent of the tests, for example, the
    number of items selected for testing.       _____    _____

## *Review Findings and Evaluate*

*[Note: These procedures related to the review and evaluation of findings should be performed continuously, as significant phases of the project, starting with the documentation phase, are completed.]*

14. Review all test results and findings of the project
    team, distinguishing between

    • Isolated instances of noncompliance with
      stated procedures

    • Control deficiencies that are
      - Inconsequential
      - Significant
      - Material weaknesses                         _____    _____

15. Review the evidence supporting the conclusions
    reached in step 14 regarding the classification of
    testing exceptions and findings. Determine that the
    evidence adequately supports the conclusions
    reached.                                      _____    _____

16. Read all subcertifications received from business
    process owners. Determine that all issues raised by
    business process owners have been resolved
    appropriately.                             _____    _____

17. Determine that all material weaknesses have been
    communicated on a timely basis to the external
    auditors.                                    _____    _____

18. Review the project team's plans for remediating
    material weaknesses and other control deficiencies
    and assess the adequacy and achievability of these
    plans.                                      _____    _____

|  | Done By | Date |
|---|---|---|

19.  Determine that all changes to internal control to remediate material weaknesses have been disclosed, if necessary, in the company's quarterly SEC filings.  _____  _____

## *Final Evaluation*

20.  Review the project team's plans for updating tests of controls performed in advance of year-end.  _____  _____

21.  Understand the procedures performed to evaluate the effectiveness of control procedures implemented since the testing date, including newly designed controls to remediate control deficiencies. Assess the adequacy of those procedures.  _____  _____

22.  Review the written representation letter on internal control matters to be provided to the company's external auditors. Assess the adequacy of procedures performed to support representations made, if applicable.  _____  _____

## *Conclusion*

I have participated in the planning and performance of the company's process for evaluating internal control effectiveness. The results of the testwork performed support a conclusion that the company's internal control over financial reporting is _____ [*effective/ not effective*] as of _____ [*fiscal year-end*]. We have retained sufficient evidence, including documentation, to support this evaluation.

_____ _____
Signed Date

# Checklist for Preparation of Management's Report on Internal Control Effectiveness

## PURPOSE

This form has been designed to

• Help ensure that management's report on internal control effectiveness complies with SEC requirements and other suggestions

## INSTRUCTIONS

Use this checklist during the preparation or review of management's report on internal control effectiveness.

*Footnoted comments in italics are additional instructions to the preparer of the form and should be removed before the form is considered final.*

## CHECKLIST FOR MANAGEMENT'S REPORT ON THE EFFECTIVENESS OF INTERNAL CONTROL OVER FINANCIAL REPORTING

Company: _____     Reporting Date: _____

Prepared by: _____     Date Prepared: _____

## REQUIRED REPORTING MATTERS

|  | Yes | No | N/A |
|---|---|---|---|
| 1. Does the report include a statement that management is responsible for establishing and maintaining adequate internal control over financial reporting? | ❑ | ❑ | ❑ |

|  | Yes | No | N/A |
|---|---|---|---|

2. Does the report identify the framework (e.g., the COSO Internal Control Integrated Framework) used by management to evaluate the effectiveness of the company's internal control over financial reporting?  ❏ ❏ ❏

3. Does a material weakness in internal control over financial reporting exist as of year-end?  ❏ ❏ ❏

   a. If a material weakness in internal control does *not* exist at year-end, does the report include a statement that

      i. as of year-end . . .  ❏ ❏ ❏

      ii. internal control over financial reporting is effective . . .  ❏ ❏ ❏

      iii. based on the criteria in the identified framework  ❏ ❏ ❏

   b. If a material weakness in internal control *exists as of year-end,* does the report include

      i. The definition of a material weakness, as provided  ❏ ❏ ❏

      ii. A discussion of the material weakness that includes specific information about the nature of the material weakness and its actual and potential effect on the presentation of the company's financial statements issued during the existence of the weakness  ❏ ❏ ❏

      iii. A statement that as of year-end, internal control over financial reporting is not effective based on the criteria in the identified framework  ❏ ❏ ❏

4. Does the report include adequate disclosure (see 3.b.i and 3.b.ii) of material weaknesses identified by management that were corrected during the period?  ❏ ❏ ❏

|  | Yes | No | N/A |
|---|---|---|---|
| 5. Does the report include a statement that the registered accounting firm that audited the company's financial statements has issued an assessment of the company's internal control over financial reporting and make reference to where that report can be found? | ❑ | ❑ | ❑ |
| 6. If the company has disclosed matters related to entities that are included in the company's consolidated financial statements, but *not* included within the scope of management's assessment of internal control (see items 1 and 3 in the section titled "Disclosure Matters"), does management's report on internal control make appropriate reference to these disclosures? | ❑ | ❑ | ❑ |

## OPTIONAL REPORTING MATTERS

Indicate which of the following optional items have been included in management's report on internal control over financial reporting. Reference the applicable documentation supporting each disclosure.

|  | Included | Not Included | Reference |
|---|---|---|---|
| 1. Disclosures about corrective actions taken by the company after the date of management's assessment | ❑ | ❑ | _____ |
| 2. The company's plans to implement new controls | ❑ | ❑ | _____ |
| 3. A statement that management believes the cost of correcting a material weakness would exceed the benefits to be derived from implementing new controls | ❑ | ❑ | _____ |

Describe all other optional matters included in management's report on internal control effectiveness.

_____

_____

_____

_____

## DISCLOSURE MATTERS

SEC rules may require the disclosure of internal control–related matters outside of management's report on internal control over financial reporting.

|  | Yes | No | Reference |
|---|---|---|---|
| 1. Do the company's consolidated financial statements include a variable-interest entity (VIE) that meets all of the following conditions? |  |  |  |
|   a. The VIE was in existence prior to December 15, 2003. | ❑ | ❑ | _____ |
|   b. It is consolidated by virtue of FASB Interpretation No. 46 (i.e., it would *not* have been consolidated in the absence of application of that guidance). | ❑ | ❑ | _____ |
|   c. The company does not have the right or authority to assess the internal controls of the VIE and also lacks the ability, in practice, to make that assessment. | ❑ | ❑ | _____ |
| 2. For VIEs that meet all of the conditions specified in item 1, has the company disclosed in the body of its Form 10-K or 10-KSB |  |  |  |
|   a. That management has not evaluated the internal controls of the VIE | ❑ | ❑ | _____ |
|   b. That management's conclusion regarding the effectiveness of its internal control over financial reporting does not extend to the internal controls of the VIE | ❑ | ❑ | _____ |
|   c. Key subtotals, such as total and net assets, revenues, and net income that result from consolidation of the entity(ies) that have not been assessed | ❑ | ❑ | _____ |
|   d. That the financial statements include the accounts of certain entities consolidated pursuant to FIN 46 (or via proportionate consolidation in accordance with EITF 00-1) but that management has been unable to assess the effectiveness of internal control at those entities due to the fact that the company does not have the ability to dictate or modify the controls of the entities and does not have the ability, in practice, to assess those controls | ❑ | ❑ | _____ |
| 3. Has the company *excluded* from the scope of its assessment the controls at a newly acquired business? | ❑ | ❑ | _____ |

|  | Yes | No | Reference |
|---|---|---|---|

4. If the company has excluded a newly acquired
   business from the scope of its assessment, does the
   Form 10-K or 10-KSB include disclosure of the
   following?

   a. A statement noting that management excluded
      the acquired business from management's report
      on internal control over financial reporting ☐ ☐ _____

   b. The identity of the acquired business ☐ ☐ _____

   c. An indication of the significance of the acquired
      business to the company's consolidated financial
      statements ☐ ☐ _____

5. Has the company disclosed in its Form 10-K or
   10-KSB all changes in its internal control over
   financial reporting that occurred during the last
   fiscal quarter that have materially affected, or are
   reasonably likely to materially affect, the company's
   internal control over financial reporting? ☐ ☐ _____

   a. If so, has the company made appropriate
      disclosure of information about the
      circumstances surrounding the change that are
      necessary to make the disclosure about the
      change to internal control not misleading? ☐ ☐ _____

Describe all other internal control–related matters the company disclosed in its Form
10-K or 10-KSB.

_____

_____

_____

_____

# PART II
# Documentation of Internal Control Design

# Work Program for the Review of Documentation of Entity-Level Controls

## PURPOSE

This form has been designed to

- Document your overall approach to the review of internal control documentation of entity-level controls
- Document the work performed and conclusions reached regarding the adequacy of the company's documentation of entity-level controls

## INSTRUCTIONS

The work program on form DOC-1b assumes that you have already performed steps 15 and 16 of the General Work Program or otherwise satisfied yourself as to

- *Documentation completeness.* Documentation exists for all entity-level controls included within the scope of the project.
- *Documentation currency.* The company's internal control documentation has been properly maintained to ensure that
  - All changes to entity-level policies and procedures have been reflected in the related documentation
  - Access to entity-level documentation has been controlled effectively and *only* authorized changes to the documentation have been made

Once you have established the completeness of the company's entity-level documentation and the continued integrity of the documentation that was prepared previously, your review of internal control documentation may be limited to the changes made since the last assessment of internal control.

Form DOC-1a allows you to summarize your overall approach to reviewing the company's entity-level control documentation, that is

- The procedures performed to establish the completeness and currency of the documentation
- The new documentation selected for review

Form DOC-1b is a series of worksheets that should be prepared for each entity-level group of controls selected for review. These worksheets correspond to the entity-level controls that are required to be included in the company's assessment of internal control, as indicated on form ADM-2. All control deficiencies identified during your review should be carried forward to your summary of control deficiencies (e.g., form ADM-3).

## Determining Whether the Documentation Is Adequate

Unlike the guidance for the documentation of activity-level controls, the requirements for documenting entity-level controls are much less definitive. In general, the documentation of entity-level controls should be sufficiently detailed and clear enough to

- Indicate that management has identified the significant elements of each entity-level control group that are necessary to create an environment that enables the effective functioning of activity-level controls
- Communicate effectively the policies and procedures throughout the organization
- Monitor the effective operation of controls
- Allow the project team to fulfill its responsibilities to
  - Evaluate the effectiveness of the design of the policy or procedure and
  - Design tests of operating effectiveness

## Summary of Source Materials

Like any checklist, the checklist for reviewing the documentation of entity-level controls is a distillation of guidance provided elsewhere. For additional information and clarification of the items presented on these worksheets, you should refer to that guidance, which is summarized in the following table.

| Entity-Level Control | Source for Additional Information |
|---|---|
| Control Environment | See Chapter 2 of the COSO Internal Control Integrated Framework. |
| Risk Assessment | See Chapter 3 of the COSO Internal Control Integrated Framework. |
| Monitoring | See Chapter 6 of the COSO Internal Control Integrated Framework. |
| Period-End Financial Reporting Process | See paragraph 26 of PCAOB Auditing Standard No. 5. |
| Selection and Application of Accounting Policies | • AICPA Statement on Auditing Standards No. 61, *Communication with Audit Committees* (AICPA, *Professional Standards,* vol. 1, AU Section 380), particularly paragraph .07 |

| Entity-Level Control | Source for Additional Information |
|---|---|
| | • Practice Issues Task Force Alert 2000-2, *Quality of Accounting Principles—Guidance for Discussions with Audit Committees,* item 3.7, nonauthoritative guidance provided by the SEC Practice Section of the AICPA<br>• SEC release No. 33-8040, *Cautionary Advice Regarding Disclosure about Critical Accounting Policies* |
| IT General Controls | See *IT Control Objectives for Sarbanes-Oxley,* published by the Information Technology Governance Institute in conjunction with the Information Systems Audit and Control Association.[1] |
| Nonroutine Transactions | The guidance presented in this section is the suggestions of the author and not derived from other sources. |

[1] *This document can be downloaded from either the ITGI Web site at www.itgi.org or the ISACA Web site at www.isaca.org.*

*Footnoted comments in italics are additional instructions to the preparer of the form and should be removed before the form is considered final.*

# Assessment of Internal Control Effectiveness: Overall Approach to Review of the Documentation of Entity-Level Controls

## PURPOSE

This form has been designed to

- Document the procedures you performed to assess the completeness, currency, and content of entity-level controls
- Document the results of your review
- Describe the actions you took to correct identified entity-level control deficiencies

## INSTRUCTIONS

In step 1 of the form you should describe the procedures you performed to determine that documentation exists for all entity-level controls included within the scope of the project. The matrix included on form ADM-2 may be helpful for this purpose.

In step 2 you should document the methods used by the company to maintain the integrity of its documentation of internal control design. For example, the company's electronic database of control descriptions may be protected by logical and physical access controls. You then should describe the procedures you performed to conclude that these controls were operating effectively throughout the year. Once you establish that the integrity of previously documented controls has been maintained, then you may rely on that documentation in the current period, assuming that the control policies and procedures remain the same.

In step 3 you should identify all changes to entity-level control policies and procedures made since the last assessment. You can now restrict your review of entity-level control documentation to those changed elements, which are documented in step 4.

In steps 5 and 6 you should document the findings of your review, whether any control deficiencies were noted, and if so, the corrective action taken.

Company: _____ Reporting Date: _____

Prepared by: _____ Date Prepared: _____

# SUMMARY OF INTERNAL CONTROL DOCUMENTATION

Paragraph 42 of PCAOB Auditing Standard No. 2 requires the company to document all five components of internal control over financial reporting. Our compliance with that requirement is summarized in this form, which focuses on entity-level controls, and form DOC-2, which summarizes the documentation of activity-level controls. The following table maps the COSO internal control components to these two forms.

| Internal Control Component | Entity-Level (DOC-1) | Activity-Level (DOC-2) |
|---|---|---|
| Control environment | X | |
| Risk assessment | X | |
| Information | | X |
| Communication | X | X |
| Control activities | | X |
| Monitoring | X | |

# REVIEW OF DOCUMENTATION OF ENTITY-LEVEL CONTROLS

This form describes our overall approach for reviewing the documentation of entity-level controls.

1. *Documentation completeness.* We determined that the company's documentation included all entity-level controls within the scope of the project by performing the following procedures.

   _____

   _____

   _____

   _____

   _____

2. *Maintenance of previously created documentation.* We reviewed the company's method for ensuring the continued integrity of the documentation of entity-level controls in those instances where the company's policies and procedures have remained unchanged since the last assessment of internal control effectiveness. The following summarizes these methods and their adequacy, which served as a basis for concluding

that a review of the documentation of unchanged policies and procedures was not necessary.

_____

_____

_____

_____

_____

_____

3. *Changes to internal control procedures.* We identified all changes to entity-level control policies and procedures that have been made since the last assessment of internal control and determined that these changes were properly reflected in the internal control documentation. The procedures we performed to achieve this objective are as follows.

_____

_____

_____

_____

_____

4. *Entity-level controls selected for documentation review.* Our review of entity-level control documentation was limited to changes in that documentation that occurred since our last assessment of internal control effectiveness. We reviewed the documentation related to the following entity-level controls.

_____

_____

_____

_____

_____

5. *Findings.* We noted the following control deficiencies during our review of entity-level control documentation.[1]

_____

_____

_____

_____

_____

6. *Corrective action.* As a result of the control deficiencies summarized in step 5, we took the following actions.

_____

_____

_____

_____

_____

[1] *In addition to listing the control deficiencies, you also may want to indicate which deficiencies are considered significant deficiencies and which are material weaknesses.*

# Assessment of Internal Control Effectiveness: Checklist for the Review of the Documentation of Entity-Level Controls

## PURPOSE

Use this form to

- Determine whether the company's documentation of entity-level controls includes all relevant matters at an appropriate level of detail and clarity
- Document and assess the company's methods for communicating entity-level control policies and procedures throughout the organization

## INSTRUCTIONS

This form contains a series of worksheets that should be prepared for each entity-level group of controls selected for review. These worksheets correspond to the entity-level controls that are required to be included in the company's assessment of internal control, as indicated on form ADM-2. All control deficiencies identified during your review should be carried forward to your summary of control deficiencies (e.g., form ADM-3).

Each worksheet provides a listing of the key elements that should be described by the relevant document. As you read each document, determine whether it contains the required element and mark the corresponding checkbox.

Company: _____     Reporting Date: _____

Prepared by: _____     Date Prepared: _____

## CONTROL ENVIRONMENT

|  | Yes | No | N/A | Ref. |
|---|---|---|---|---|
| **Documentation Content**<br>Does the documentation include the following policies and procedures with sufficient clarity and detail so that they can be understood by all those who are affected by them? |  |  |  |  |
| 1. The company's values | ❑ | ❑ | ❑ |  |
| 2. Acceptable workplace behavior | ❑ | ❑ | ❑ |  |
| 3. Unacceptable workplace behavior | ❑ | ❑ | ❑ |  |
| 4. The responsibility of management to periodically review and, if necessary, modify policies relating to company values and workplace behavior | ❑ | ❑ | ❑ |  |
| 5. The responsibility of management to act in ways that are consistent with and reinforce stated policies | ❑ | ❑ | ❑ |  |
| 6. Management's responsibility to identify compensation policies or other incentives that may motivate unethical behavior by employees | ❑ | ❑ | ❑ |  |
| 7. Actions taken by management, if any, to mitigate the risks posed by policies or incentives identified as a result of item 6 | ❑ | ❑ | ❑ |  |
| 8. The procedures to be followed by management or the board of directors when it becomes aware of<br>a. Internal control deficiencies<br>b. Overly aggressive or other accounting policies that are of poor quality | ❑<br>❑ | ❑<br>❑ | ❑<br>❑ |  |
| 9. The company's organizational structure and lines of reporting | ❑ | ❑ | ❑ |  |
| 10. Management's responsibility to appropriately consider internal control and financial reporting risks when determining the organizational structure of the company | ❑ | ❑ | ❑ |  |

|  | Yes | No | N/A | Ref. |
|---|---|---|---|---|
| 11. The process for allocating resources to employees/employee groups that are necessary to enable them to perform their assigned responsibilities. Resources include<br>a. Budget/funding<br>b. Personnel<br>c. Training | ❑<br>❑<br>❑ | ❑<br>❑<br>❑ | ❑<br>❑<br>❑ |  |
| 12. Policies for establishing adequate segregation of duties |  |  |  |  |
| 13. Human resource policies relating to the following matters<br>a. Hiring<br>b. Compensation<br>c. Performance evaluations<br>d. Terminations<br>e. Responsibilities for adhering to ethical and behavioral policies<br>f. Consequences of failing to adhere to ethical or behavioral standards | ❑<br>❑<br>❑<br>❑<br>❑<br><br>❑ | ❑<br>❑<br>❑<br>❑<br>❑<br><br>❑ | ❑<br>❑<br>❑<br>❑<br>❑<br><br>❑ |  |
| 14. Independence requirements for members of the board | ❑ | ❑ | ❑ |  |
| 15. Financial accounting and other expertise required of the board of directors | ❑ | ❑ | ❑ |  |
| 16. Policies and procedures followed by the board of directors to<br>a. Oversee the company's financial reporting process<br>b. Participate in management's risk assessment process<br>c. Monitor the effectiveness of internal control | <br>❑<br><br>❑<br><br>❑ | <br>❑<br><br>❑<br><br>❑ | <br>❑<br><br>❑<br><br>❑ |  |

## Communication

We reviewed the ways in which the company communicates its control environment–related policies throughout the organization. Our findings and conclusions are as follows.

_____

_____

_____

## RISK ASSESSMENT

|  | Yes | No | N/A | Ref. |
|---|---|---|---|---|
| **Documentation Content** |  |  |  |  |
| Does the documentation include the following policies and procedures with sufficient clarity and detail so that they can be understood by all those who are affected by them? |  |  |  |  |
| 1. Management's process for assessing risk, including |  |  |  |  |
|    a. The overall financial reporting objective of the publishing of reliable financial statements | ❏ | ❏ | ❏ |  |
|    b. The identification of risks that may prevent the company from achieving its stated financial reporting objective | ❏ | ❏ | ❏ |  |
|    c. The analysis of risk for all key business processes where potential exposures of some consequence may exist | ❏ | ❏ | ❏ |  |
| 2. The mechanisms in place to identify changes that could create new risks to achieving stated financial reporting objectives. These changes include |  |  |  |  |
|    a. Changed operating environment | ❏ | ❏ | ❏ |  |
|    b. New personnel | ❏ | ❏ | ❏ |  |
|    c. New or revamped information technology (IT) systems | ❏ | ❏ | ❏ |  |
|    d. Rapid growth | ❏ | ❏ | ❏ |  |
|    e. New lines, products, or business activities | ❏ | ❏ | ❏ |  |
|    f. Restructurings | ❏ | ❏ | ❏ |  |
|    g. Foreign operations | ❏ | ❏ | ❏ |  |
|    h. New accounting principles or other financial reporting requirements | ❏ | ❏ | ❏ |  |

### *Communication*

We reviewed the ways in which the company communicates its risk assessment policies and procedures to affected individuals and groups. Our findings and conclusions are as follows.

_____

_____

_____

# MONITORING

|  | Yes | No | N/A | Ref. |
|---|---|---|---|---|
| **Documentation Content** |  |  |  |  |
| Does the documentation include the following policies and procedures with sufficient clarity and detail so that they can be understood by all those who are affected by them? |  |  |  |  |
| 1. Process for ensuring that *all* communications from external and internal parties relating to internal control effectiveness are considered by management | ❏ | ❏ | ❏ |  |
| 2. Policies and procedures for taking appropriate action with respect to identified control deficiencies | ❏ | ❏ | ❏ |  |
| 3. Policies and procedures regarding the comparison of amounts recorded by the accounting system with physical assets | ❏ | ❏ | ❏ |  |
| 4. Protocols for determining what information about internal control is needed at a particular time for decision making | ❏ | ❏ | ❏ |  |
| 5. Policies and procedures relating to whether personnel are asked periodically to state whether they understand and comply with the company's code of conduct and regularly perform critical control activities | ❏ | ❏ | ❏ |  |

## *Communication*

We reviewed the ways in which the company communicates its internal control monitoring policies and procedures to affected individuals and groups. Our findings and conclusions are as follows.

_____

_____

_____

_____

_____

## PERIOD-END FINANCIAL REPORTING

|  | Yes | No | N/A | Ref. |
|---|---|---|---|---|
| **Documentation Content** |  |  |  |  |
| Does the documentation include the following policies and procedures with sufficient clarity and detail so that they can be understood by all those who are affected by them? |  |  |  |  |
| 1. The procedures used to enter transaction totals into the general ledger | ❏ | ❏ | ❏ |  |
| 2. The procedures related to journal entries, including<br>  a. The initiation of journal entries<br>  b. The authorization of journal entries<br>  c. The recording of journal entries<br>  d. The processing of journal entries in the general ledger | ❏<br>❏<br>❏<br>❏ | ❏<br>❏<br>❏<br>❏ | ❏<br>❏<br>❏<br>❏ |  |
| 3. Other procedures used to record recurring and nonrecurring adjustments to the annual and quarterly financial statements, for example<br>  • Consolidating adjustments<br>  • Report combinations<br>  • Classifications | ❏ | ❏ | ❏ |  |
| 4. Procedures for drafting<br>  a. Financial statements<br>  b. Related disclosures | ❏<br>❏ | ❏<br>❏ | ❏<br>❏ |  |
| *Developing Significant Accounting Estimates* |  |  |  |  |
| 5. The significant estimates required to prepare the company's financial statements | ❏ | ❏ | ❏ |  |
| 6. Procedures for communicating the need for proper accounting estimates | ❏ | ❏ | ❏ |  |
| 7. Procedures for accumulating relevant, sufficient, and reliable data on which to base the accounting estimate | ❏ | ❏ | ❏ |  |
| 8. Procedures for the preparation of the estimate, including<br>  a. Who is responsible for preparing the estimate<br>  b. When the estimate is to be prepared | <br>❏<br><br>❏ | <br>❏<br><br>❏ | <br>❏<br><br>❏ |  |

| | Yes | No | N/A | Ref. |
|---|---|---|---|---|
| 9. Procedures for the review and approval of the estimate, including<br>a. Review of sources of relevant factors | ❑ | ❑ | ❑ | |
| b. Review of development of assumptions | ❑ | ❑ | ❑ | |
| c. Review of reasonableness of assumptions and resulting estimates | ❑ | ❑ | ❑ | |
| d. Consideration of the need to use the work of specialists | ❑ | ❑ | ❑ | |
| e. Consideration of changes in previously established methods to arrive at accounting estimates | ❑ | ❑ | ❑ | |
| 10. Policies relating to the comparison of prior accounting estimates with subsequent results to assess the reliability of the process used to develop estimates | ❑ | ❑ | ❑ | |
| 11. The responsibility of management to consider whether the final accounting estimate is consistent with the operational plans of the entity | ❑ | ❑ | ❑ | |

### Communication

We reviewed the ways in which the company communicates its period-end financial reporting policies and procedures to affected individuals and groups. Our findings and conclusions are as follows.

_____

_____

_____

## SELECTION AND APPLICATION OF ACCOUNTING POLICIES

| | Yes | No | N/A | Ref. |
|---|---|---|---|---|
| **Documentation Content** | | | | |
| Does the documentation include the following policies and procedures with sufficient clarity and detail so that they can be understood by all those who are affected by them? | | | | |

|  | Yes | No | N/A | Ref. |
|---|---|---|---|---|
| 1. Informing the audit committee of the initial selection of and subsequent changes to significant accounting policies or their application <br> a. The initial selection and application of significant accounting policies <br> b. Subsequent changes to significant accounting policies <br> c. Subsequent changes to the application of significant accounting policies | ❑ <br><br> ❑ <br><br> ❑ | ❑ <br><br> ❑ <br><br> ❑ | ❑ <br><br> ❑ <br><br> ❑ |  |
| 2. Informing the audit committee about the methods used to account for significant unusual transactions, which may include <br> • Bill-and-hold transactions <br> • Self-insurance <br> • Multielement arrangements contemporaneously negotiated <br> • Sales of assets or licensing arrangements with continuing involvement of the enterprise | ❑ | ❑ | ❑ |  |
| 3. Informing the audit committee about the effect of significant accounting policies in controversial or emerging areas for which there is a lack of authoritative accounting guidance or consensus, for example <br> • Revenue recognition <br> • Off-balance-sheet financing <br> • Accounting for equity investments <br> • Research and development activities <br> • Special-purpose financing structures that affect ownership rights (such as leveraged recapitalizations, joint ventures, and preferred stock subsidiaries) | ❑ | ❑ | ❑ |  |

## Communication

We reviewed the ways in which the company communicates its policies and procedures for the selection and application of significant accounting policies to affected individuals and groups. Our findings and conclusions are as follows.

_____

_____

_____

# IT GENERAL CONTROLS

|  | Yes | No | N/A | Ref. |
|---|---|---|---|---|
| **Documentation Content** |  |  |  |  |
| Does the documentation include the following policies and procedures with sufficient clarity and detail so that they can be understood by all those who are affected by them? |  |  |  |  |
| *Plan and Organize* |  |  |  |  |
| 1. An overall IT strategic plan | ❑ | ❑ | ❑ |  |
| 2. Information architecture, including issues such as<br>• Controls relating to the capture, processing, and reporting of information<br>• Security policies<br>• Privacy policies | ❑ | ❑ | ❑ |  |
| 3. Policies and procedures that define the IT organization and relationships. These policies and procedures might address issues such as<br>• The identification of key systems and data<br>• Roles and responsibilities of IT personnel<br>• The periodic evaluation of IT personnel | ❑ | ❑ | ❑ |  |
| 4. Policies and procedures that ensure compliance with external reporting requirements that address issues such as<br>• The identification of changes to external reporting requirements that require IT changes<br>• The identification of internal events that affect reporting requirements | ❑ | ❑ | ❑ |  |
| 5. Risk assessment policies and procedures that address issues such as<br>• Technology reliability<br>• Information integrity<br>• IT personnel<br>• Security assessments for all significant systems and locations | ❑ | ❑ | ❑ |  |

|  | Yes | No | N/A | Ref. |
|---|---|---|---|---|
| 6. Policies and procedures that ensure quality, for example<br>• IT systems documentation standards<br>• Data integrity, ownership, and responsibilities | ❏ | ❏ | ❏ | |
| *Acquire and Implement* | | | | |
| 7. Software acquisition and implementation policies and procedures, which address issues such as<br>• The systems development life cycle<br>• The acquisition of software<br>• The installation of new and modified software | ❏ | ❏ | ❏ | |
| 8. Hardware acquisition and implementation policies and procedures, which address issues such as<br>• Acquisition<br>• Implementation<br>• Maintenance | ❏ | ❏ | ❏ | |
| 9. User reference and support manuals or other documentation that helps ensure the long-term sustainability of the system | ❏ | ❏ | ❏ | |
| 10. Testing procedures for new or modified systems, including<br>a. Unit, system, integration, and user acceptance<br>b. Load and stress testing<br>c. Interfaces with other systems<br>d. Data conversion | ❏<br>❏<br>❏<br>❏ | ❏<br>❏<br>❏<br>❏ | ❏<br>❏<br>❏<br>❏ | |
| 11. Change management policies and procedures that address issues such as<br>• The override of established procedures, for example, in an emergency situation<br>• Plans for the timely change to systems and applications | ❏ | ❏ | ❏ | |

|  | Yes | No | N/A | Ref. |
|---|---|---|---|---|
| *Delivery and Support* | | | | |
| 12. Policies and procedures relating to the use of third-party service providers, which may include<br>• Vendor policies for selection of outsourced services<br>• Key performance indicators for managing service-level agreements<br>• Selection process for third-party service providers<br>• Third-party service contracts<br>• Policies and procedures for monitoring third-party service levels, including reviews of security, availability, and processing integrity | ❑ | ❑ | ❑ | |
| 13. Policies and procedures for monitoring the performance and capacity levels of the IT systems and, if measures are less than optimal, taking appropriate action | ❑ | ❑ | ❑ | |
| 14. A business continuity plan that may include policies and procedures for<br>• Testing the plan<br>• Updating the plan<br>• Testing offsite storage and recovery facilities<br>• System recovery procedures necessary to ensure the timely reporting of financial information | ❑ | ❑ | ❑ | |
| 15. System security policies and procedures, which address issues such as<br>• The development, updating, and maintenance of a security plan<br>• Methods used to authenticate users to the system<br>• Maintaining the effectiveness of authentication and access mechanisms<br>• The requesting, establishing, issuing, suspending, and closing of user accounts<br>• The prevention of unauthorized access to the network<br>• The performance of security assessments<br>• The monitoring of security activity and security violations | ❑ | ❑ | ❑ | |

| | Yes | No | N/A | Ref. |
|---|---|---|---|---|
| 16. Policies and procedures related to the education and training of all personnel using IT services | ❑ | ❑ | ❑ | |
| 17. Configuration management policies and procedures that address issues such as<br>• Software that is authorized for use by employees<br>• The configuration of system infrastructure<br>• The configuration of application software<br>• The configuration of data storage<br>• Mitigation of risks posed by computer viruses<br>• Testing software and network infrastructure to ensure it is properly configured | ❑ | ❑ | ❑ | |
| 18. Policies and procedures relating to the management of problems and incidents, which may address issues such as<br>• Operational events that are not part of the standard operation<br>• Emergency program changes<br>• Methods used to trace from the operational incident to its underlying cause | ❑ | ❑ | ❑ | |
| 19. Data management policies and procedures that address issues such as<br>• Data processing controls, including those related to<br>  - The completeness of transaction processing<br>  - The accuracy of transaction processing<br>  - The authorization of transactions<br>  - The validity of transactions<br>• Controls over data input<br>• The handling, distribution, and retention of data and reporting output<br>• The protection of sensitive information during its storage and transmission<br>• The retention and storage of<br>  - Data<br>  - Programs<br>  - Reports<br>  - Documentation<br>• Physical security and accountability for data<br>• Changes in data structures | ❑ | ❑ | ❑ | |

| | Yes | No | N/A | Ref. |
|---|---|---|---|---|
| 20. Facilities management policies and procedures, such as<br>• Controlled access to facilities<br>• Environmental controls at physical facilities | ❑ | ❑ | ❑ | |
| 21. IT operations management policies and procedures, including those that address issues such as<br>• Standard procedures for IT operations<br>• Processing continuity during operator shift changes<br>• Metrics used to manage daily activities of the IT department<br>• The retention of system event data that allows for the reconstruction, review, and examination of the time sequences of processing | ❑ | ❑ | ❑ | |
| *Monitoring* | | | | |
| 22. Policies and procedures related to the monitoring of IT processes that address issues such as<br>• Benchmarks used to monitor IT processes<br>• The processes used to identify IT weaknesses and take appropriate action<br>• The ongoing monitoring of IT controls and the reporting of deficiencies to senior management<br>• The periodic monitoring of IT services and activities by an independent individual(s) | ❑ | ❑ | ❑ | |

## Communication

We reviewed the ways in which the company communicates its IT general control policies and procedures to affected individuals and groups. Our findings and conclusions are as follows.

_____

_____

_____

_____

# NONROUTINE TRANSACTIONS

|  | Yes | No | N/A | Ref. |
|---|---|---|---|---|
| **Documentation Content** | | | | |
| Does the documentation include the following policies and procedures with sufficient clarity and detail? | | | | |
| 1. The nature of the transaction, including the terms that were most significant in determining the accounting treatment for the transaction | ❏ | ❏ | ❏ | |
| 2. The counterparty(ies) to the transaction | ❏ | ❏ | ❏ | |
| 3. The business reason for entering into the transaction | ❏ | ❏ | ❏ | |
| 4. The process followed by the company to authorize the transaction and its accounting treatment | ❏ | ❏ | ❏ | |
| 5. How the transaction was accounted for and disclosed in the financial statements | ❏ | ❏ | ❏ | |

## *Communication*

We reviewed the ways in which the company communicates its policies and procedures related to nonroutine transactions to affected individuals and groups. Our findings and conclusions are as follows.

_____

_____

_____

_____

# Work Program for the Review of Documentation of Activity-Level Controls

## PURPOSE

This form has been designed to

- Document your overall approach to the review of internal control documentation of activity-level controls
- Document the work performed and conclusions reached regarding the adequacy of the company's documentation of activity-level controls

## INSTRUCTIONS

The work program on form DOC-2b assumes that you have already performed steps 15 and 16 of the General Work Program or otherwise satisfied yourself as to

- *Documentation completeness.* Documentation exists for all significant processes, business units, or locations to be included within the scope of the project.
- *Documentation currency.* The company's internal control documentation has been properly maintained to ensure that
  - All changes to internal control procedures at the company have been reflected in its internal control documentation
  - Access to the documentation database has been controlled effectively and *only* authorized changes to the documentation have been made

Once you have established the completeness of the company's documentation and the continued integrity of the documentation that was prepared previously, your review of the internal control documentation may be limited to the changes made since the last assessment of internal control.

Form DOC-2a allows you to summarize your overall approach to reviewing the company's internal control documentation, that is

- The procedures performed to establish the completeness and currency of the documentation
- The new documentation selected for review, and if only a sample of the new documentation was reviewed, how you determined that sampling was appropriate and how you selected the items for review

Form DOC-2b is a worksheet that should be prepared for each significant process or business unit/location selected for review. All control deficiencies identified during your review should be carried forward to your summary of control deficiencies (e.g., form ADM-3). Note that this form includes *only* the consideration of routine transactions. Nonroutine transactions and accounting estimates are considered as part of the review of entity-level controls.

*Footnoted comments in italics are additional instructions to the preparer of the form and should be removed before the form is considered final.*

# Assessment of Internal Control Effectiveness: Overall Approach to Review of the Documentation of Activity-Level Controls

## PURPOSE

This form has been designed to

- Document the procedures you performed to assess the completeness, currency, and content of activity-level controls
- Document the results of your review
- Describe the actions you took to correct identified activity-level control deficiencies

## INSTRUCTIONS

In step 1 of the form you should describe the procedures you performed to determine that documentation exists for all activity-level controls included within the scope of the project.

In step 2 you should document the methods used by the company to maintain the integrity of its documentation of internal control design. For example, the company's electronic database of control descriptions may be protected by logical and physical access controls. You then should describe the procedures you performed to conclude that these controls were operating effectively throughout the year. Once you establish that the integrity of previously documented controls has been maintained, then you may rely on that documentation in the current period, assuming that the control policies and procedures remain the same.

In step 3 you should identify all changes to activity-level control policies and procedures made since the last assessment. You can now restrict your review of activity-level control documentation to those changed elements, which are documented in step 4.

In steps 5 and 6 you should document the findings of your review, whether any control deficiencies were noted, and if so, the corrective action taken.

Company: _____    Reporting Date: _____

Prepared by: _____    Date Prepared: _____

This form describes our overall approach for reviewing the internal control documentation of significant routine transactions and related controls. (The review of the documentation of controls relating to nonroutine transactions and accounting estimates was performed in conjunction with our review of entity-level controls, as documented on form DOC-1.)

1. *Documentation completeness.* We determined that the company's internal control documentation encompasses all significant transactions and business units/locations by performing the following procedures.

_____

_____

_____

_____

_____

2. *Maintenance of previously created documentation.* We reviewed the company's method for ensuring the continued integrity of the documentation of internal control in those instances where the company's control procedures have remained unchanged since the last assessment of internal control effectiveness. The following summarizes these methods and their adequacy, which served as a basis for concluding that a review of the documentation of unchanged controls was not necessary.

_____

_____

_____

_____

_____

3. *Changes to internal control procedures.* We identified all changes to business processes and internal control procedures that have been made since the last assessment of internal control and determined that these changes were properly reflected in the internal control documentation. The procedures we performed to achieve this objective are as follows.

_____

_____

_____

_____

_____

4. *Processes selected for review.* Our review of internal control documentation was limited to changes in that documentation that occurred since our last assessment of internal control effectiveness. We reviewed the following significant transactions and business units/locations.

_____

_____

_____

_____

_____

5. *Findings.* We noted the following control deficiencies during our review of internal control documentation.[1]

_____

_____

_____

_____

_____

6. *Corrective Action.* As a result of the control deficiencies summarized in step 5, we took the following actions.

_____

_____

_____

_____

_____

---

[1] *In addition to listing the control deficiencies, you also may want to indicate which deficiencies are considered significant deficiencies and which are material weaknesses.*

# Assessment of Internal Control Effectiveness: Checklist for the Review of the Documentation of a Significant Transaction or Business Unit/Location

## PURPOSE

Use this form to

- Determine whether the company's documentation of activity-level controls includes all relevant matters at an appropriate level of detail and clarity
- Document and assess the company's methods for communicating activity-level control policies and procedures throughout the organization

## INSTRUCTIONS

This form should be completed for each significant transaction or the significant accounts of individually important business units/locations included within the scope of the project. All control deficiencies identified during your review should be carried forward to your summary of control deficiencies (e.g., form ADM-3).

The form provides a listing of the key elements that should be described by the relevant document. As you read the documentation pertaining to the transaction or business unit, determine whether the documentation contains the required element and mark the corresponding checkbox.

Company: _____      Reporting Date: _____

Prepared by: _____      Date Prepared: _____

Transaction or Business Unit: _____

|  | Yes | No | N/A |
|---|---|---|---|
| **Documentation Content** |  |  |  |
| Does the documentation include the following elements? |  |  |  |
| 1. A description of the control procedure that is sufficiently detailed to allow an employee to understand and apply the procedure | ❏ | ❏ | ❏ |
| 2. An indication of the following items to which the control procedure relates<br>a. The control objective<br>b. The financial statement account or disclosure<br>c. The relevant assertion(s) | ❏<br>❏<br>❏ | ❏<br>❏<br>❏ | ❏<br>❏<br>❏ |
| 3. The person responsible for performing the control procedure | ❏ | ❏ | ❏ |
| 4. How frequently the procedure is to be performed | ❏ | ❏ | ❏ |
| 5. Whether and how the performance of the procedure is documented (or other information that will allow for the performance of tests to determine that the control procedure was performed properly) | ❏ | ❏ | ❏ |
| 6. Information about how the significant transaction is<br>a. Initiated<br>b. Authorized<br>c. Recorded<br>d. Processed<br>e. Reported | ❏<br>❏<br>❏<br>❏<br>❏ | ❏<br>❏<br>❏<br>❏<br>❏ | ❏<br>❏<br>❏<br>❏<br>❏ |
| 7. Sufficient information about the flow of transactions to identify the points at which material misstatements due to error or fraud could occur | ❏ | ❏ | ❏ |
| *Communication* |  |  |  |
| 8. Has the control procedure been communicated to the person responsible for its performance? | ❏ | ❏ | ❏ |
| *Ongoing Monitoring* |  |  |  |
| 9. Has an individual at an appropriate level of authority been assigned to periodically review the ongoing performance of the control procedure? | ❏ | ❏ | ❏ |

# Documentation Techniques and Selected Examples for Routine Transactions

## PURPOSE

Use this form to help you design internal control documentation. Design techniques include flowcharts, narratives, and matrixes.

## INSTRUCTIONS

This form provides only examples and guidance. It is not necessary to complete any section of this form or to include it in your documentation of internal control or the internal control assessment.

## HOW TO DESIGN INTERNAL CONTROL DOCUMENTATION

The way in which you document your company's routine transactions is entirely up to you. The only requirement is that the documentation meet the following objectives.

- The documentation of controls contains all the elements required by paragraph 42 of PCAOB Auditing Standard No. 5 (see form DOC-2b).
- The documentation of controls is sufficiently detailed and clear to allow
  - Those affected by the procedure to understand it and either perform the procedure or monitor its performance
  - The project team to (1) assess design effectiveness and (2) design tests of operating effectiveness

   Designing a documentation architecture that meets these two objectives will allow you to meet your compliance obligations. However, you may decide to go beyond mere compliance.

   Documentation—though not one of the COSO components—is an integral part of the internal control structure. High-quality documentation enables the effective communication of prescribed control procedures across the organization and over time. Documentation allows for the consistent performance and monitoring of controls, which allows internal control to be institutionalized, become part of a *system,* and be less reliant on the competency and diligence of individual employees. As you design your control documentation, consider whether it is capable of achieving these broader objectives.

There are three basic documentation techniques:

- Flowcharts
- Narratives
- Matrixes

Each technique has its relative strengths and weaknesses. Typically, a combination of two or all three techniques is used to document a given transaction or business process. Occasionally, for example, to document one of the company's less significant transactions, one technique may suffice.

The process followed to design internal control documentation typically involves the following steps.

1.  Decide on objective(s) for the documentation. For example, is the documentation being prepared solely for the project team to comply with the requirements of the internal control assessment? Or do you want the documentation to be distributed widely at the company to communicate control procedures and responsibilities?

2.  Determine the content necessary to achieve your objective.

3.  Decide which documentation techniques are best suited to communicate your content and serve either necessary function (see below).

4.  Design individual documents and overall document architecture. Regardless of which documentation technique you use, you will need to design individual documents or set basic guidelines for their creation. You also should determine how the individual documents relate to each other—that is, the overall documentation architecture. This design of individual documents and overall architecture is a fluid process in which the design of one will affect the design of the other.

### Functional Considerations in Structuring a Documentation Architecture

When designing your documentation of internal control, consider the following functional features that should be included.

- *Maintainability.* Your documentation should facilitate easy updating and maintenance as business processes and controls change over time.
- *Ease of review.* The documentation of internal control should be designed in a user-friendly fashion. For compliance purposes, the project team and the external auditors are the primary users, and so the documentation should allow for these individuals to
  - Easily assess the effectiveness of the design of internal control
  - Facilitate the design of tests of controls
- *Information gathering.* To create new or update existing documentation will require people to gather information about the company's business processes and controls. Your documentation methods should recognize this need and, to the extent possible, make it easy to gather and input the information required to create appropriate documentation.

- *Scalability.* Your documentation techniques should be equally adept at handling processes with many control points and those with only a few.

    In addition to the preceding, which are the minimum features you should consider for complying with the requirement to document internal control, you also may consider the following *optional* features.

- Whether your documentation allows individual employees to easily understand their responsibilities and to facilitate the communication of business processes and controls and roles and responsibilities throughout the organization

### Documentation Content Considerations

Paragraph 42 of PCAOB Auditing Standard No. 2 requires the following information to be included in your documentation of routine transactions.

- The design of controls over all relevant assertions related to all significant accounts and disclosures in the financial statements. The documentation should include the five components of internal control over financial reporting.
- Information about how significant transactions are initiated, authorized, recorded, processed, and reported.
- Sufficient information about the flow of transactions to identify the points at which material misstatements due to error or fraud could occur.
- Controls designed to prevent or detect fraud, including who performs the controls and the related segregation of duties.

    In addition to the required content elements, you may find that documenting the following information will help improve the overall effectiveness of the company's internal control documentation architecture.

- *Labels for control procedures, control objectives, or other information.* By assigning a unique label to information (e.g., one control procedure may be labeled "C-1" another "C-2", etc.), you allow for the easy linking or cross-referencing between individual documents.
- *Links to tests of operating effectiveness.* When evaluating the results of tests of controls, you should consider the control objective that the control procedure was designed to achieve. Providing that link in your documentation of internal control will facilitate the effective review of test results.
- *Links to overall conclusion on design effectiveness.* This evaluation typically is done for the transaction or business process as a whole and not for individual control procedures.
- *Date prepared or modified, date reviewed, and by whom.* This information will help assess the currency or continued accuracy of the documentation.

## FLOWCHARTING

Flowcharting allows you to describe graphically the overall information processing stream for a transaction or groups of transactions. Markers on the flowchart may then be used to indicate the point in the stream where control procedures are performed and to reference a description of the control procedure itself. Flowcharts may be embedded within a narrative to provide the reader with a high-level, more general depiction of the details described in the narrative.

## Strengths and Weaknesses

### STRENGTHS OF FLOWCHARTING AS A DOCUMENTATION METHOD FOR ROUTINE ACTIVITY-LEVEL CONTROLS

- It is easy to recognize the point in the processing stream at which errors could be introduced and control procedures should be located. This information aids in evaluating design effectiveness and determining which controls should be tested.
- It is highly effective at capturing the overall flow of information.
- For visual-based learners, flowcharts are the most effective means of communicating information about information processes and controls.
- It is a scalable and highly flexible format.

### WEAKNESSES OF FLOWCHARTING AS A DOCUMENTATION METHOD FOR ROUTINE ACTIVITY-LEVEL CONTROLS

- By itself, it is not capable of capturing all required documentation elements or the necessary detailed description of control procedures. It must be supplemented with other types of documentation.

## Tips for Flowcharting[1]

### FOLLOW THE FLOW OF INFORMATION

Accounting manuals and other traditional means of documenting accounting processes frequently focus on the flow of documents through the system. For example, if a four-part receiving form is completed to document the receipt of raw materials, one approach to documentation would be to track the processing and eventual disposition of each of the four copies of the form. For the purpose of understanding activity-level controls, it usually is more effective to track the flow of *information* rather than the flow of documents. By tracking the flow of information, you are better able to identify the processes that change that information. Whenever information is changed, the risk of error enters the system, and that risk must be controlled.

To focus on the flow of information, you should consider working *backwards*, beginning with the posting to the general ledger. Obtain answers to a series of questions that seek to determine what *information* is created throughout the process and *how it is processed.* For example:

---

[1] *A slightly different version of this section originally appeared in* How to Comply with Sarbanes-Oxley Section 404, *by Michael Ramos, published by John Wiley and Sons, 2004.*

*What is posted as a debit to inventory and a credit to accounts payable?*

Monthly purchases.

*How is this information created?*

It is an accumulation of individual transactions throughout the month.

*How is the information related to individual transactions created?*

Invoices are matched with receiving reports and purchase orders and entered into the system on a real-time basis.

In this short example, you have quickly determined how information is created and processed, from initiation through posting. The fact that one copy of the purchase order is sent to the vendor or that production managers receive updates on raw material receipts is not considered.

## DEFINE THE BOUNDARIES OF THE SYSTEM

Accounting systems have limits, and it is important that you clearly define them. The entity's control procedures start at the perimeter of its accounting system.

For example, an entity's purchase of raw materials may begin when the entity orders raw materials. The process continues through the vendor's selection, packing, and shipment of the product. Ultimately, the entity receives the materials it ordered.

In this scenario, the entity's controls begin when it receives the goods. It would be unreasonable to extend the control system any further upstream, for example, to the vendor's procedures for selecting and packing the materials.

For our purposes, the boundary of the activity-level accounting system is defined as the point at which the transaction information is approved and authorized and is in a format that is usable for accounting purposes (i.e., allows for the posting of debits and credits).

This definition of the accounting system boundary has several important implications. As a gatekeeper to the system, the system boundary must include control policies and procedures to ensure that

- Only valid, authorized transactions are allowed to enter the processing stream
- *All* valid, authorized transactions are captured for processing
- The accounting information that is captured accurately reflects the terms of the transaction

Your documentation of the activity-level controls should include a description of the control policies and procedures that meet these boundary control objectives.

## TRANSACTIONS VERSUS EVENTS

Accounting information can be generated from either transactions or events. So far we have discussed the control implications related to business transactions, for example, the purchase of raw materials. But what about the recording of depreciation expense? The process of calculating and posting depreciation expense is initiated not from a transaction with an external party, but rather with an event—namely, the passage of time.

Like transactions, events occur at the perimeter of the accounting system. The gatekeeper control objectives relating to events are the same as those relating to transactions. However, the way in which those objectives are achieved usually varies.

At the boundary, *transactions* usually are controlled in real time, on a transaction-by-transaction basis. Proper authorization of each transaction is critical. *Events* can be triggered merely by the passage of time. For example, the recording of depreciation expense is initiated by the arrival of the end of the month. Authorization of each individual event is not as critical. The processing of the event may be initiated by the system itself. The control procedures usually are performed after the fact, not at the time the event is processed. For example, the controller may scan the general ledger to ensure that depreciation expense was recorded once and only once.

## PREVENTIVE VERSUS DETECTIVE CONTROLS

Controls can be designed to either

- Identify errors as they occur and prevent them from further processing
- Detect and correct errors that already have entered the system

There are trade-offs for each approach. *Preventive* controls are more timely and help ensure that errors are never recorded in the accounting records to begin with. However, to design and perform preventive controls at each step in the processing stream may be costly. *Detective* controls may be cheaper to design and perform. For example, performing a reconciliation once a month between the general ledger and a subsidiary ledger may be more efficient than performing preventive controls on each transaction at each step in the process. However, the drawback to detective controls is that they are performed after the fact, sometimes well after the fact. The lack of timely performance of a detective control could mean that errors remain in the accounting records for extended periods of time. Most systems rely on a combination of preventive and detective controls, and it is common to build some redundancy into the system, in which more than one control meets the same objective.

Preventive and detective controls have one important thing in common. Both types of controls contain both an error detection and a correction component. The fact that a control procedure can identify an error does not make the control effective. It is the process of communicating identified errors to individuals who can then make corrections that makes the control complete.

## INFORMATION STORAGE AND RETRIEVAL

It is common for systems to capture data, store it, and then retrieve it for later use. For example, an entity may maintain a database of approved vendors. This database is updated regularly as vendors are added or removed. When the time comes to authorize a payment, the control procedure requires someone to access the database and determine whether the vendor has been approved. If the vendor is in the database, then payment is authorized; if not, then the matter is brought to someone of appropriate authority to take follow-up action.

Databases and other types of information storage repositories should be considered part of the activity-level processing stream and therefore protected by the control boundary. All of the boundary control objectives should be addressed for gaining access to the information storage repository. In this example, controls should exist to ensure that

- All approved vendors are in the database
- No unapproved vendors are in the database
- Only authorized users have the ability to access and modify the information maintained in the database

## COMPUTER APPLICATION CONTROLS

Many control procedures are programmed into the entity's computer system. For example, the process of matching a vendor to a database of preapproved vendors may be completely computerized. A user may submit an invoice for payment, the computer performs the match, and, if the vendor is on the list, processing is allowed to continue. The user is informed only when the computer detects an error, namely, that the vendor has not been preapproved. It is then the user's responsibility to take the appropriate follow-up action. Again, the follow-up of the identified errors is a critical component of the control.

Ultimately, the effectiveness of computer application controls will depend on the effectiveness of relevant computer general controls, including

- *Systems development.* The application was properly developed and tested to make sure that the control functions as designed.
- *Access.* Access to the program is monitored to ensure that unauthorized changes to the program cannot be made.

The control objectives for computer application controls are the same as the objectives for manual controls—information must remain complete and accurate at all phases, from initiation (data input) through processing.

## *Example Flowchart*

### BACKGROUND INFORMATION

The example company is a real estate investment trust (REIT) that is involved in the acquisition, ownership, management, and leasing of shopping malls. The company's revenue stream has two different components: base rent (i.e., the minimum, fixed monthly rental paid by tenants) and percentage rent (i.e., additional rent calculated as a percentage of the tenant's gross sales).

### *Base Rent*

Leases are negotiated at the local, property manager level, under broad guidelines provided by the corporate entity. Leases must be approved at the corporate level before they become final. A lease abstract is used to capture leasing information, and this information is entered into a database that is maintained at the property level. Monthly, the system runs reports showing all changes to the lease information database, and these reports are reviewed by the property managers to ensure that all information was captured properly.

Monthly billing for base rent is handled locally and is totally automated. The billing application program accesses the database and prepares the monthly rent statements for the tenants. The program updates the rent receivable subledger. It also prepares a report that provides information on each space in the mall, including

- Tenant name
- Lease information summary, including base rent, scheduled rent adjustments, rent concessions, and the like
- Current month and prior month base rent

The property manager uses this report to check to see that all tenants got billed and at the right amount.

Cash receipts are physically received in the property manager's office. The process for capturing and reporting the information is largely manual.

- A receipt is prepared for each tenant.
- The receipts are batched and periodically input into the accounting system.
- The system processes the information by updating the accounts receivable ledger and posting a debit to cash.

At month end, the bank account is reconciled. The property manager reviews a printout of the accounts receivable subledger to identify large, unexpected receivables balances that may indicate that a rent payment was not processed properly. The accounts receivable subledger is reconciled to the general ledger account on a monthly basis.

### Percentage Rent

Most tenants are required to pay additional rent based on an agreed-upon percentage of gross sales. This percentage rent is paid quarterly.

Quarterly, each tenant submits a report that shows gross sales, the percentage rent, and the total amount due. A check for the amount due usually is provided at the same time. The percentage rent reports are entered into the system. The program performs two checks on the data:

1. It compares reported quarterly gross sales to the comparable period for each of the last two years and calculates percentage changes in the reported amounts. It then prepares a report of this analysis for review by the property manager.

2. It compares the percentage used to calculate the amount due to the percentages maintained in the property management database. Any differences are identified and reported on an exception report.

### Month-End Reporting

Each mall prepares a standardized month-end reporting package, which it then submits to the corporate accounting office. The process for combining these reports at the corporate level is not yet fully automated. Some manual processing still is required to enter information into the system for updating the corporate accounting records. Clerical-level staff performs the input. In addition to updating the accounting records, the system also provides a number of operating reports that provide both financial and nonfinancial data. These reports group the malls by geographic region. The asset manager for each region reviews these reports for anomalies and possible errors by comparing rental income and cash flow to budget and looking for large, unusual accounts receivable balances.

*Internal Audit Activities*

Internal auditors perform two important control activities at the property management level:

1. Compare lease information maintained in the property management database to signed lease agreements

2. "Audit" percentage rent reports by comparing gross sales information reported to the landlord to the sales records maintained by the client

## DOCUMENTATION

The documentation of this system consists of two elements: a flowchart and an accompanying description of the related controls.

## EXAMPLE COMPANY LEASING REVENUE DESCRIPTION OF CONTROLS

| Ref. No. | Description |
|---|---|
| **Entity-Level Controls** | |
| 1 | The entity maintains access control software to monitor and limit unauthorized access to the database of lease information. |
| 2 | Internal auditors periodically compare the lease information in the database to signed lease agreements. |
| 3 | Month-end base rent calculations are performed automatically by the computer system. Systems development and program change controls ensure that the program functions properly. Access to the program is controlled to protect against unauthorized changes. |
| 4 | Periodically, internal auditors audit percentage rent reports by comparing gross sales information to tenant records. |
| **Authorization Controls** | |
| 1 | New leases and lease modifications and changes are reviewed, authorized, and approved by asset managers at the corporate level. |

| Ref. No. | Description |
|----------|-------------|
| **Activity-Level Controls** | |
| 1d | The property manager reviews a month-end report to ensure that all tenants got billed at their proper amount. |
| 2d | The property manager reviews month-end receivables to identify unexpected balances. |
| 3d | The bank account is reconciled monthly. |
| 4d | The accounts receivable general ledger account is reconciled to the subsidiary ledger on a monthly basis. |
| 5d | Monthly, the property manager reviews the changes made to the lease information database. |
| 1p | Computerized controls compare quarterly sales to historical activity. Monthly, the property manager reviews reports to identify possible errors in the reporting of percentage rent. |
| 2p | The percentage used by the tenant to calculate percentage rent is compared to the lease information database. Control is computerized—all exceptions are printed to a report for follow-up by a property management accountant on a monthly basis. |

## UNDERSTANDING THE FLOWCHART

- *Organization.* At the top of the flowchart are T-accounts, which represent the general ledger accounts affected by revenue transactions. At the bottom of the chart is the initiation of the transactions. In between the general ledger and the initiation are the various information processing steps.

- *Controls and processes.* Processes manipulate data. When data is changed, errors can occur. For example, one of the processes described on the flowchart is the batching of individual base-rent bills. In this process, it is possible that some individual bills could inadvertently be left out of the batch. Thus, each process should have related controls to ensure that the integrity of the information (i.e., its completeness and accuracy) is maintained during processing.

- *Referencing control descriptions.* This flowchart has identified four different types of controls.
  1. Authorization controls, which are designed to ensure that only valid, authorized transactions are entered into the processing stream.
  2. Entity-level controls.
  3. Activity-level controls, which may be either preventive or detective.
  4. Corporate controls, which are controls performed at the corporate level, not the property management level. By their nature, these are detective controls.

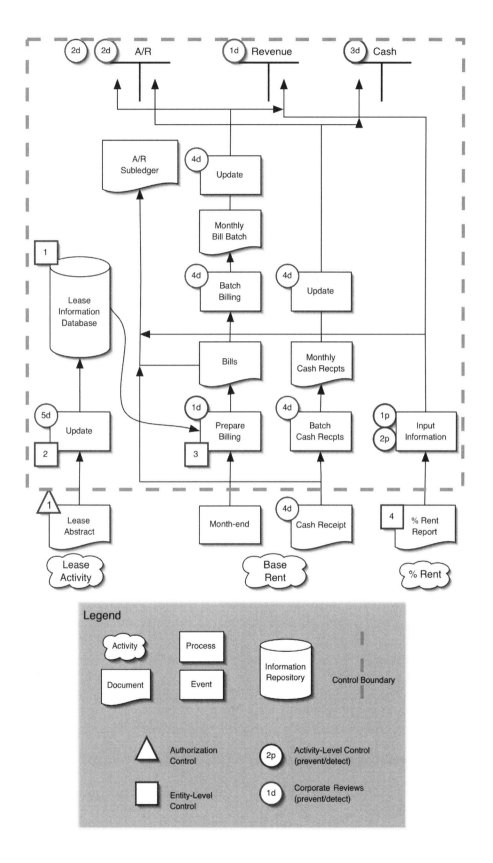

- *Information repository.* This system includes an information repository, which is the database of lease information. This database is used to prepare billings and possibly other information used to monitor activities. As described in this chapter, the information repository should reside within the boundary of the system and be protected from unauthorized access and changes.

# NARRATIVES

A narrative is simply a description of the information processing steps and related controls. Typically, this information is presented as a linear text, although it is possible to include nontext elements (e.g., multimedia files, flowcharts) or to construct an overall documentation architecture that is nonlinear.

## *Strengths and Weaknesses*

### STRENGTHS OF NARRATIVES AS A DOCUMENTATION METHOD FOR ROUTINE ACTIVITY-LEVEL CONTROLS

- On one hand, this is the most flexible of the primary documentation methods. The overall structure of the narrative can serve a variety of primary objectives. For example, it can be organized to trace the flow of transactions or track the relationship of risks to control objectives.
- For text-based learners, narratives are a highly effective means of communicating information about processing streams and controls.
- Well-written narratives about how information is processed and controlled will provide a natural lead-in to a discussion of your assessment of the overall design effectiveness of the system.

### WEAKNESSES OF NARRATIVES AS A DOCUMENTATION METHOD FOR ROUTINE ACTIVITY-LEVEL CONTROLS

- On the other hand, narratives can be relatively *inflexible* and rigid. Once the organizational scheme of a narrative is set, it is difficult to reengineer that scheme to achieve a different purpose. For example, a narrative written to help the external auditors evaluate control design effectiveness may not be useful for employees who need to know what procedures they are responsible for performing unless the narrative is completely rewritten.
- Because of the static nature of the medium, narratives may be difficult to maintain and update as processes and controls change.
- It is easy for narratives to become bloated, which reduces their effectiveness. Narratives can be used to capture any and all information, but too much information and the text loses focus and becomes confusing.
- Narratives are a good way to communicate information, but the form does not readily lend itself to capturing information from operational personnel about information processes and controls.

## *Tips for Preparing Narratives*

There are two basic ways you can use narratives in your documentation of internal control.

1. As the primary documentation means, supplemented by flowcharts, matrixes, or both

2. As a supplement to other forms of documentation

### NARRATIVES AS THE PRIMARY DOCUMENTATION MEANS

The best way to prepare effective and efficient narrative documentation of internal controls is to develop *one* general format for the narrative and use it repeatedly to document all significant transactions. This consistency will benefit

- Documentation preparers, who will become more adept at documenting internal control if they are required to master only one general narrative structure
- Project team members and external auditors, who review internal control documentation and who will quickly appreciate reviewing a consistent format and approach
- Operations personnel who provide the information on processes and controls necessary to create good documentation

Additionally, with one standard narrative format, the company will be better able to ensure that all documentation contains each of the elements required by PCAOB Auditing Standard No. 2, and they will be able to more quickly modify documentation as changes to processes or controls change.

In developing a standard narrative structure, the main requirements are that

- The narrative structure includes all required documentation elements
- The narration is logically organized and easy to follow

The following is an example outline that achieves these objectives.

---

### EXAMPLE OUTLINE: NARRATIVE DOCUMENTATION OF INTERNAL CONTROLS

I. Overview
   A. Description of transaction being described
   B. General ledger accounts affected and relevant assertions
   C. Business process owner and groups involved in the process
   D. Subledger and subsidiary accounting records involved in the process
   E. IT systems and electronic files involved in the process
II. Transaction initiation
   A. The process for initiating the transaction
   B. Whether, and if so how, the process is documented

  C. The financial reporting–related risks inherent in the process (i.e., "what could go wrong?")

  D. Description of the controls in place to address the issues raised in C
   1. Who performs the control procedure
   2. How frequently and when the procedure is performed
   3. Whether, and if so how, the control procedure is documented
   4. Whether the control is computerized, manual, or a combination of both
   5. If applicable, an indication of which control(s) are key controls most responsible for ensuring that the financial reporting objectives related to the transaction are met

III. Transaction authorization

  A. The policies and procedures followed for authorizing the transaction

  B. Whether, and if so how, the performance of the authorization procedures is documented

  C. The financial reporting–related risks inherent in the process (i.e., "what could go wrong?")

  D. Description of the controls in place to address the issues raised in C
   1. Who performs the control procedure
   2. How frequently and when the procedure is performed
   3. Whether, and if so how, the control procedure is documented
   4. Whether the control is computerized, manual, or a combination of both
   5. If applicable, an indication of which control(s) are key controls most responsible for ensuring that the financial reporting objectives related to the transaction are met

IV. Recording the transaction

  A. The process for initially recording the transaction

  B. Whether, and if so how, the recording of the transaction is documented

  C. The financial reporting–related risks inherent in the initial recording of the transaction (i.e., "what could go wrong?")

  D. Description of the controls in place to address the issues raised in C
   1. Who performs the control procedure
   2. How frequently and when the procedure is performed
   3. Whether, and if so how, the control procedure is documented
   4. Whether the control is computerized, manual, or a combination of both
   5. If applicable, an indication of which control(s) are key controls most responsible for ensuring that the financial reporting objectives related to the transaction are met

V. Transaction processing

  A. Once recorded, the information processing steps required to eventually post the transaction to the general ledger and any related subsidiary ledgers

  B. Whether, and if so how, each step of the information processing is documented

  C. The financial reporting–related risks inherent in each step of the information processing (i.e., "what could go wrong?")

  D. Description of the controls in place at each step to address the issues raised in C
   1. Who performs the control procedure
   2. How frequently and when the procedure is performed
   3. Whether, and if so how, the control procedure is documented

> 4. Whether the control is computerized, manual, or a combination of both
> 5. If applicable, an indication of which control(s) are key controls most responsible for ensuring that the financial reporting objectives related to the transaction are met

In reviewing the outline, note that

- After a brief overview of the transaction, the overarching structure follows the basic information processing stream and includes four of the five required elements of internal control documentation described in paragraph 42 of PCAOB Auditing Standard No. 2. This processing stream begins with the initiation of the transaction and ends with its posting to the general ledger. (The fifth required element, how the transaction is reported in the financial statements, is documented as part of the company's period-end financial reporting process.) This linear structure is logical and easy to follow.

- Within each section is the same information, organized in the same fashion. The organizational scheme described in the outline tracks with the COSO framework, which is echoed in PCAOB Auditing Standard No. 2. After describing how the information is processed, you discuss the financial reporting–related risks ("what could go wrong") and how the control procedures are designed to mitigate those risks.

- The documentation of the other information listed in the outline are suggestions that will help you plan your tests of operating effectiveness.

To prepare a narrative consider the following:

- Distinguish between information *processes* and *controls*. A *process* changes or manipulates the data, for example, by performing a mathematical or logical operation. Extending an invoice by multiplying the number of items shipped by their sales price is a process. When data is processed, errors can occur.

  A *control* is a procedure to prevent or detect the errors that can be introduced in the processing of data. Recalculating the extended invoice or otherwise is an example of a control.

  Your narratives will be much clearer and easier to understand if you clearly distinguish between the information processing steps and the control procedures related to those steps.

- When considering "what could go wrong," make sure to cover all relevant assertions for the affected account(s). Financial reporting–related risks are directly related to financial statement assertions. For example, there is a risk that not all authorized transactions will be recorded (completeness assertion) or that fictitious transactions will be processed (existence assertion). To make sure that you have considered all possible risks, review the relevant assertions and determine that each one has been addressed.

- When describing controls, check to make sure that at least one control has been identified to address each of the identified risks.

- When writing your narrative, use subheadings and bullet points to make the document more readable.

**NARRATIVES AS A SUPPLEMENT TO OTHER FORMS OF DOCUMENTATION**

Narratives can be used to supplement other forms of documentation such as a matrix or a flowchart. The most common ways to use narratives in this fashion include the following.

- Add analysis or higher-level understanding to a matrix. A matrix presents information at a high level of detail, and sometimes it is difficult for a user to absorb and understand its meaning. A narrative can be attached to a matrix to provide this type of analysis. For example, the narrative can provide an "executive summary" of your conclusions about design effectiveness or your approach to testing control effectiveness. The matrix itself would then serve the function of supporting detail that justifies your conclusions.

- Add detail and "walk the reader through" a flowchart. A flowchart presents highly summarized information. Narratives frequently are attached to flowcharts as a way to add details about the processing steps or related control procedures. In addition, some readers may find flowcharts vague or confusing (should they be read left to right? top to bottom? bottom to top?). A narrative can be added as a way to walk the reader through the sequencing of the processing steps to make sure there are no misunderstandings.

# MATRIXES

A matrix is a spreadsheet of rows and columns. It is a two-dimensional worksheet that links a set of independent variables with a set of dependent variables. Typically, the control procedures comprise the independent variables, while the dependent variables are the various data about the control procedures that are required to be documented.

## *Strengths and Weaknesses*

**STRENGTHS OF MATRIXES AS A DOCUMENTATION METHOD
FOR ROUTINE ACTIVITY-LEVEL CONTROLS**

- They are highly effective at showing relationships or links between elements, for example, the link between the control procedure and the related financial statement assertion.
- They are an effective way to structure both the capture and the communication of information about information processes and controls.
- They are capable of capturing and relating a great deal of information.
- They are relatively easy to maintain and update.
- They are scalable and flexible.

**WEAKNESSES OF MATRIXES AS A DOCUMENTATION METHOD
FOR ROUTINE ACTIVITY-LEVEL CONTROLS**

- They make it difficult to see the overall transaction flow and evaluate the effectiveness of control design.
- It is easy to document too much detail, making the matrix cumbersome to work with and confusing.

## Tips for Preparing Matrixes

When preparing a matrix, the main problem you want to guard against is creating a matrix that tries to do *everything,* capturing or summarizing every conceivable detail about a control procedure. The result is an overload of information that is hard to understand. It is better to create a series of worksheets, each with just a few columns, rather than a worksheet with 30 columns.

A matrix is a simple database, and it helps to think of preparing a matrix in the same way that you would work with a database.

Each row in the matrix is like an input form in a database. The row is used to gather all the relevant information about your subject, for example, the control objective or control procedure. A database separates the information *gathering* function from the information *communication* function. A database has a report writer function that allows the user to choose selected data and present them in a concise, easily understandable format for the reader.

When preparing a matrix to document transactions and controls, you should consider a similar approach. Create a matrix to help capture the required elements and other information. From that master matrix, create a series of derivative tables, each of which is designed to achieve one objective.

## Example Matrixes

The following are examples of individual matrixes you might consider. If you use a database program to warehouse control descriptions, then these matrixes describe the reports that you should consider writing from this database. If you use a spreadsheet program to create these matrixes, then common information between individual spreadsheets may be linked.

### INFORMATION GATHERING MATRIX

#### Purpose

The purpose of this matrix is to facilitate the easy gathering of information about each control procedure. If you are working with a database, then this is the information that should be captured in your form to be stored in the database.

#### Creating the Matrix

The independent variable is the control number. The dependent variables are all of the relevant pieces you will need later to evaluate control design and track the testing of design and operating effectiveness. The following is a highly summarized example of the matrix—space constraints prevent us from showing all the details. A more detailed description of each dependent variable follows.

| Financial Statement Information | | | | | Control Information | | | Control Number | Control Testing Information | | |
|---|---|---|---|---|---|---|---|---|---|---|---|
| | | | | | | | | 001 | | | |
| | | | | | | | | 002 | | | |
| | | | | | | | | 003 | | | |

### Information to Capture

The following are some suggestions on what information you should capture about each control, that is, the titles for each column in your matrix.

### Financial Statement Information

- *Description of the transaction.* Examples of information that would be entered in this column are "sales," "cash disbursements," or "payroll."
- *IT system.* This column would capture the name of the IT system involved in processing the transaction. This information is helpful when planning your IT-related tests, such as testing IT general or application controls or reviewing an SAS 70 report.
- *Electronic files.* Use this column to capture the name(s) of the electronic file(s) involved in processing. Again, this information will be useful when planning IT-related tests.
- *General ledger/accounts.* List the general ledger accounts that are affected as a result of this transaction, for example, "revenue" and "accounts receivable."
- *Relevant assertions.* Describe the relevant assertions for the general ledger accounts affected by the transaction. "Completeness" is an example of a relevant assertion for sales transactions.

### Control Information

- *Processing stage.* The PCAOB Auditing Standard requires documentation of each of the following stages of transaction processing:
  - Initiation
  - Authorization
  - Recording
  - Processing

Capturing this information will help you evaluate design effectiveness.

- *Control objective.* Control objectives are related to the financial statement assertions and stage of processing. For example, "To ensure that all valid sales transactions are captured at initiation" is an objective related to the completeness assertion at the initiation of the transaction.
- *Control description.* This is where you document your description of the control procedure. In addition to describing the procedure performed, you also may want to capture
  - The name of the responsible person or department
  - If or how the performance of the control procedure is documented

- Whether the control procedure is manual or automated
- How frequently the control procedure is performed
- Whether you consider the control procedure to be a "key control" for achieving the stated control objective, a determination that should be made only after evaluating the design effectiveness over the group of controls for a given transaction

*Control Number*

• Assign a unique control number to each control procedure.

*Testing Information*

• *Design effectiveness.* Use this column to track your conclusion as to whether the control procedure is designed effectively.

• *Operating effectiveness test procedure.* Describe, summarize, or cross-reference to the planned test(s) of operating effectiveness of the control.

• *Date test performed.* Track the date as of which the tests of operating effectiveness were performed. This information will help in determining whether and how tests will be updated to year-end.

• *Operating effectiveness conclusion.* Indicate your conclusion about whether the control is operating effectively.

## EVALUATE CONTROL DESIGN BY PROCESSING STAGE

### *Purpose*

Paragraph 42 of PCAOB Auditing Standard No. 5 requires the company to document "Sufficient information about the flow of transactions to identify the points at which material misstatements due to error or fraud could occur." Technically, that requirement may be met by including this information in the information gathering matrix described earlier. However, an important purpose of the requirement is to allow you to assess the design effectiveness of the controls over the transaction. The following matrix will help you make this assessment.

### *How to Prepare the Matrix*

Prepare a separate matrix for each significant transaction. If you are using a spreadsheet, sort your main information gathering spreadsheet first by transaction type and then by processing stage.

*Example Matrix*

| Transaction: Sales | | | | | |
|---|---|---|---|---|---|
| **Processing Stage** | **Assertion** | **Control Number** | **Control Description** | **Key Control?** | |
| | | | | **Y** | **N** |
| | Complete | 002 | Describe | ❑ | ❑ |
| Initiation | Complete | 014 | Describe | ❑ | ❑ |
| | Exist | 005 | Describe | ❑ | ❑ |
| | | 016 | Describe | ❑ | ❑ |
| | | 017 | Describe | ❑ | ❑ |
| | Accurate | 004 | Describe | ❑ | ❑ |
| | | 010 | Describe | ❑ | ❑ |
| Authorization | Complete | 002 | Describe | ❑ | ❑ |
| Etc. | | | | | |

*How to Use the Matrix*

For each transaction you should ascertain that controls exist for each relevant assertion for each of the four processing stages: initiation, authorization, recording, and processing (the reporting stage described in the Auditing Standard is covered in your review of entity-level controls). If there are no controls for an assertion or for a processing stage, then a flaw exists in the design of the controls for this transaction.

Next, review the description of each control procedure to determine whether it would be effective at addressing the stated assertion. Look at the group of controls aimed at the same assertion and determine which ones are "key controls" that should be tested.

## EVALUATE CONTROL DESIGN BY ASSERTION

*Purpose*

Paragraph 42 of PCAOB Auditing Standard No. 5 requires the company to document "Controls over all relevant assertions." Technically, that requirement may be met by including this information in the information gathering matrix described earlier. However, an important purpose of the requirement is to allow you to assess the design effectiveness of the controls over the transaction. The following matrix will help you make this assessment.

*How to Prepare the Matrix*

Prepare a separate matrix for each significant transaction. If you are using a spreadsheet, sort your main information gathering spreadsheet by transaction type and then by control number.

*Example Matrix*

| | | | Transaction: Sales | | | | | |
|---|---|---|---|---|---|---|---|---|
| Ctrl. No. | Control Description | Key | Assertions | | | | | |
| | | | Complete | Exist | Val. | Auth. | Rights | Disclose |
| 001 | Describe | Y | X | X | | X | | |
| 002 | Describe | Y | | | | X | | X |
| 003 | Describe | N | | | | | | X |
| 004 | Describe | Y | X | X | X | X | | |
| 005 | Describe | Y | | | | X | | |
| Etc. | | | | | | | | |

*How to Use the Matrix*

Review each control and determine which assertion the control relates to. When all controls for the transaction have been evaluated, review each column of assertions. A preponderance of controls for one assertion indicates that there probably is some control redundancy. Chances are that some of these controls are more significant than others—these should be your key controls. Reevaluate your planned tests of controls to make sure your testing plan focuses on these key controls. You may not have to test the others.

Conversely, if your analysis reveals a dearth of controls for a given assertion, that may indicate that a control deficiency exists because there are no controls to cover the assertion.

Finally, this matrix can help in evaluating the significance of control deficiencies. A deficient control related to an assertion for which redundant controls exist may not be considered significant if the redundant controls operate effectively. On the other hand, a deficiency in a control that is the only control for a given assertion probably will be at least a significant deficiency.

## SUMMARIZE IT-RELATED CONTROLS TO PLAN SCOPE OF TESTS

### *Purpose*

Coordinating the tests of IT controls can be challenging. One of the most important considerations in testing IT controls is making sure that the scope of the IT testwork is adequate—that it includes all the IT general and application controls that are relevant to internal control over financial reporting. This matrix can be used to help communicate with an IT specialist about the controls that should be included within the scope of his or her work.

### *How to Prepare the Matrix*

If you are using a spreadsheet, sort your main information gathering spreadsheet by transaction IT system and then by general ledger account.

### *Example Matrix*

| IT System | G/L Account | Transaction Type | Ctrl. No. | Control Description |
|---|---|---|---|---|
| | | | 001 | Description |
| | Revenue | Sales | 002 | Description |
| | | | 005 | Description |
| | | | 001 | Description |
| | | | 002 | Description |
| Sales and Billing | Accts. Rec. | Sales | 005 | Description |
| | | | 023 | Description |
| | | | 024 | Description |
| | Sales Return | Sales Returns | 037 | Description |
| Etc. | | | | |

### How to Use the Matrix

Use this matrix to communicate with the IT specialist important information about the scope of his or her work. From this matrix, the IT specialist will know which IT systems need to be included within the scope of the engagement and, for each system, which specific controls should be tested.

# Checklist for Evaluating
# SOX 404 Software[1]

## PURPOSE

This form has been designed to

- Help evaluate the relative merits of different software tools to determine which tool is the best fit for your company

## INSTRUCTIONS

1. Listed in the first column are the various criteria you might use in selecting a software tool. Review this list and modify it (add or delete criteria) to suit the needs of the entity.

2. Use the second column to weight each of the criteria according to how important it is to the entity. Use a five-point scale:
   5 = critically important
   1 = not at all important

3. Across the top row, list all of the software products the entity is considering.

4. Evaluate each product according to each criterion listed. Use a three-point scale:
   3 = excellent
   2 = good
   1 = fair

5. In each cell of the matrix, enter the product of the value assigned to each column and row. For example, if a given product was rated excellent (3) for a criterion that was considered critically important (5), enter 15 in the related cell.

6. Total each column and compare the results for the various products.

| Selection Criteria | Criteria Weight 5 = Critical | Products | | | | |
|---|---|---|---|---|---|---|
| | | A | B | C | D | E |
| Product features | | | | | | |
|     Compliance with documentation requirements | | | | | | |
|     Consistency with COSO | | | | | | |
|     Ability to handle company-level controls | | | | | | |
|     Ease of use | | | | | | |
|     Security | | | | | | |
|     Quality of preloaded database of risks and controls | | | | | | |
|     Reporting capabilities | | | | | | |
|     Project management features | | | | | | |
| Vendor's continued viability | | | | | | |
| Vendor support | | | | | | |
| Product compatibility with existing systems | | | | | | |
| Product scalability | | | | | | |
| Web-based interface | | | | | | |
| Availability and quality of training | | | | | | |
| Availability and quality of customization and implementation services | | | | | | |
| Price | | | | | | |
|     Initial cost | | | | | | |
|     Ongoing charges | | | | | | |
| **Total** | | | | | | |

# PART III
# Internal Control Testing Programs

# Entity-Level Controls Testing Tools

The tools in this section are designed to help you plan, perform, and document your tests of entity-level control operating effectiveness.

- *Plan.* In order to successfully plan the tests of entity-level controls, you will need to have a good understanding of the company's stated policies and procedures. You should have obtained this understanding through your review of the relevant documentation, which may have been summarized on form DOC-1. Planning the tests of operating effectiveness will require you to make decisions regarding

  - The nature or types of tests you will perform

  - The timing of those tests

  - The extent of the testwork, for example, the number and names of the people who will be interviewed or surveyed

- *Perform.* The tool set in this section provides a variety of tools that will facilitate the collection of information about the operating effectiveness of entity-level controls. One of these tools is a work program, which is organized according to the types of tests you should consider performing. In general, there are four types of tests you may perform to test operating effectiveness:

  1. Inquiry of appropriate personnel
  2. Inspection of relevant documentation
  3. Observation of operations
  4. Reperformance of the test

  The SEC requires you to obtain evidential matter that provides reasonable support for your assessment of internal control effectiveness.

- *Documentation.* Paragraph 20 of PCAOB Auditing Standard No. 2 requires you to support your evaluation of internal control with "sufficient evidence, including documentation," but no further guidance is provided on what you should document other than the results of your tests. (See paragraph 42 of the standard.)

  The external auditors will review your documentation of the tests of controls. This review will allow them to determine that you

  - Performed the necessary procedures

  - Obtained sufficient evidence regarding the operating effectiveness of controls

  - Reached appropriate conclusions

The tool set that follows will allow you to provide sufficient documentation of your tests by requiring you to document

- What you did
- What you found
- What you concluded

## ORGANIZATION OF THE TOOL SET

The tool set has been organized into four main levels of documentation, as indicated in the diagram that follows.

- *Summary of conclusions.* The worksheet at this level summarizes your conclusions about the key requirements of each entity-level control. By itself, the completion of this summary does *not* constitute sufficient evidence because it provides no indication of the tests performed or the results of these tests. The purpose of this summary is to enable the project team to assess the results of their tests and reach conclusions on the operating effectiveness of entity-level controls. It is intended that this worksheet be completed only after performing all the planned tests for the control.

- *Nature and timing of tests.* This work program provides example test procedures you can perform to obtain evidence about the operating effectiveness of entity-level controls. By completing this work program, you will document effectively the nature of the tests you performed and the timing of those tests.

- *Extent of tests.* These worksheets summarize the extent of your test procedures and, if necessary, allow you to document the factors you considered to determine that your extent of testing was sufficient. These worksheets also provide an index or table of contents to the detailed documentation that follows.

- *Evidence of performance and results.* These worksheets provide an easy-to-follow, standardized method for you to document the tests you performed, for example, the name of the person you made inquiries of, the questions you asked, and their responses.

This documentation scheme is designed to clearly provide the details necessary to support your conclusion about entity-level control effectiveness. The top-most level in the hierarchy—the conclusions reached about entity-level control effectiveness—is supported by the three levels beneath it. In order to reach a supportable conclusion about control effectiveness, you are required to

- Perform proper tests (Level II, nature of tests)
- Perform the tests within a time frame that allows you to draw a conclusion as of year-end (Level II, timing)
- Perform enough tests to reasonably support an opinion (Level III, extent of tests)
- Obtain results from tests that are consistent with the conclusions reached (Level IV, evidence of performance and results)

# TESTS OF ENTITY-LEVEL CONTROLS DOCUMENTATION HIERARCHY

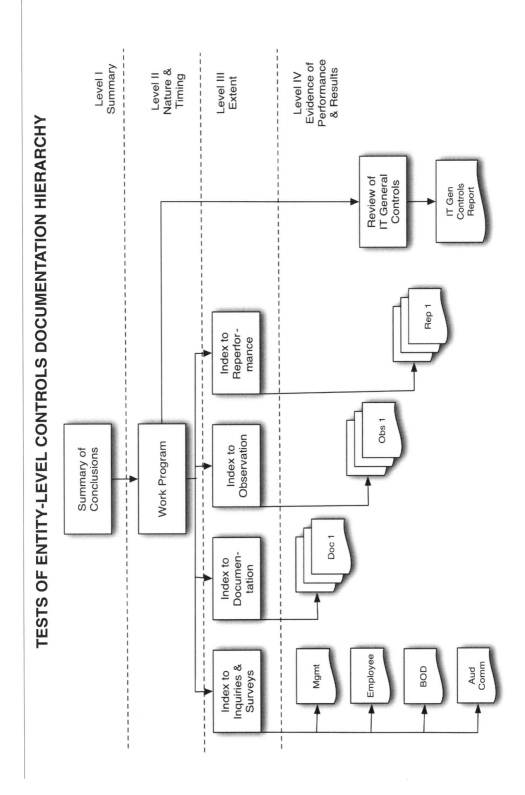

## MAP TO COSO

The control environment is one of several entity-level controls included in this tool set. The tools included encompass all of the control environment elements described in the COSO framework, but in a slightly reorganized fashion. The following table summarizes how the organization scheme of this document maps to the COSO framework.

| COSO Component | Corporate Culture | Personnel |
|---|---|---|
| Integrity and Ethical Values | X | |
| Commitment to Competence | | X |
| Board of Directors or Audit Committee | X | |
| Management's Philosophy and Operating Style | X | |
| Organizational Structure | | X |
| Assignment of Authority and Responsibility | | X |
| Human Resource Policies and Practices | X | X |

# Summary of Observations and Conclusions about Entity-Level Control Effectiveness

## PURPOSE

This form has been designed to

- Pull together the results of your procedures to test the operating effectiveness of entity-level controls and reach an overall conclusion as to their effectiveness
- Provide intermediate-level documentation on entity-level controls that is suitable for review by senior management, external auditors, or others with an interest in understanding the basis for your conclusions about entity-level controls

## INSTRUCTIONS

This is a summary-level document. The conclusions documented on this form should be supported by the documentation of the results of your tests of entity-level controls. For each control you will perform a variety of tests, such as

- Inquiry of appropriate personnel
- Inspection of relevant documentation
- Observation of operations
- Reperformance of the control

Once you have completed all tests for a particular control, you should be able to complete the questions in the attached summary.

After completing the questions for each entity-level control, you should document your considerations of identified control testing exceptions (i.e., indications that an identified control is operating effectively nearly "always"). This documentation of testing exceptions should include

- A description of the exceptions
- A conclusion as to whether the testing exception indicates a control deficiency and
  - If so, an evaluation of the significance of the deficiency
  - If not, an explanation of the evidence gathered to support your conclusions that the testing exception does not indicate a control deficiency

# ENTITY-LEVEL CONTROL TESTS

Company: _____     Reporting Date: _____

Prepared by: _____     Date Prepared: _____

This form summarizes our observations and conclusions about the operating effectiveness of the company's entity-level controls. This is a summary document only. The documentation of the nature, timing, and extent of the test procedures and the results of those procedures can be found where indicated in the column marked "Ref."

For each consideration listed, we indicated our observation and/or conclusion by placing an X along a continuum ranging from "Never" (or "none") to "Always" (or "all").

| Considerations | Observations and Conclusions | Ref. |
|---|---|---|

### Control Environment

| **CORPORATE CULTURE** | Never | Sometimes | Always |
|---|---|---|---|

The company prepares written communications to document the entity's values, norms, and acceptable behaviors. These documents include

- Code of conduct

- Charters for the board and other senior executive committees

- Other human resource policies

Management periodically reviews and modifies the company's documentation of its values, norms, and acceptable behaviors.

Management effectively communicates its expectations for ethical conduct and acceptable behavior throughout the organization.

Employees receive training on ethical conduct and standards of acceptable behavior.

Senior management has

- Identified compensation policies or other incentives that may motivate unethical behavior by employees

- Taken action to mitigate the risks posed by these policies or incentives                 └_____│_____┘

When management becomes aware of any of the following, it takes appropriate action.

- Internal control deficiencies                 └_____│_____┘

- Overly aggressive or otherwise poor-quality accounting policies                 └_____│_____┘

Employees believe that those who

- Violate established codes of conduct and ethical behavior will be punished                 └_____│_____┘

- Adhere to the company's code of conduct and standards for ethical behavior will be looked upon favorably by management                 └_____│_____┘

Employees believe that the performance of the control activities to which they have been assigned is a top priority.                 └_____│_____┘

Employees believe that the company generally is ethical and that management acts with integrity.                 └_____│_____┘

## ENTITY PERSONNEL AND ORGANIZATION

The entity's organizational structure facilitates the overall effective functioning of control policies and procedures.                 └_____│_____┘

Management appropriately considers internal control and financial reporting risks when determining the organizational structure of the company.                 └_____│_____┘

Management appropriately delegates responsibilities to lower levels.                 └_____│_____┘

Employees know which control-related activities they are required to perform.                 └_____│_____┘

Employees know how to perform the control activities to which they have been assigned.                 └_____│_____┘

Employees are provided with the resources necessary to perform their assigned responsibilities, including

- Information                 └_____│_____┘

- Training        L_____|_____J

- Funding/budget      L_____|_____J

- Personnel        L_____|_____J

- Supervision and performance feedback    L_____|_____J

Employee competence is ensured through personnel
policies such as

- Hiring        L_____|_____J

- Compensation      L_____|_____J

- Performance evaluation    L_____|_____J

- Termination       L_____|_____J

## BOARD OF DIRECTORS OVERSIGHT

The board of directors

- Functions independently from management    L_____|_____J

- Has the level of financial and other expertise neces-    L_____|_____J
  sary to effectively oversee the financial reporting
  process

The board of directors and/or audit committee is actively
involved in

- Oversight of the financial reporting process    L_____|_____J

- Management's risk assessment process    L_____|_____J

- Monitoring the effectiveness of all elements of in-   L_____|_____J
  ternal control, including the control environment

## ASSESSMENT OF CONTROL TESTING EXCEPTIONS—CONTROL ENVIRONMENT

Our tests of the control environment revealed the following control exceptions, which we have evaluated as follows.[1]

| Description of Testing Exception | Evaluation of Testing Exception | | | | |
| --- | --- | --- | --- | --- | --- |
| | Control Deficiency | | | Test Exception Not a Deficiency | |
| | Material Weakness | Significant Deficiency | Incon-sequential | No Deficiency | Ref. |
| | ❑ | ❑ | ❑ | ❑ | |
| | ❑ | ❑ | ❑ | ❑ | |
| | ❑ | ❑ | ❑ | ❑ | |
| | ❑ | ❑ | ❑ | ❑ | |
| | ❑ | ❑ | ❑ | ❑ | |
| | ❑ | ❑ | ❑ | ❑ | |
| | ❑ | ❑ | ❑ | ❑ | |
| | ❑ | ❑ | ❑ | ❑ | |
| | ❑ | ❑ | ❑ | ❑ | |

| *Considerations* | *Observations and Conclusions* | | | *Ref.* |
| --- | --- | --- | --- | --- |
| *Risk Assessment* | Never | Sometimes | Always | |
| Management identifies risks that can prevent the company from publishing reliable financial statements. | ⌊_____⌁_____⌋ | | | |
| Identified financial reporting–related risks are analyzed and assessed. | ⌊_____⌁_____⌋ | | | |

[1]See instructions to form TST-ENT-1 for guidance on how to complete this section of the form. Use the column marked "Ref." to reference to your documentation of the additional work performed to determine that the testing exception does not indicate a control deficiency.

Management identifies changes that could create
  new risks to publishing reliable financial statements.
  These changes include

- Changed operating environment
- New personnel
- New or revamped IT systems
- Rapid growth
- New lines, products, or business activities
- Restructurings
- Foreign operations
- New accounting principles or other financial
  reporting requirements

## ASSESSMENT OF CONTROL TESTING EXCEPTIONS— RISK ASSESSMENT

Our tests of the risk assessment component of internal control revealed the following control exceptions, which we have evaluated as follows.[2]

| Description of Testing Exception | Evaluation of Testing Exception | | | | |
| | Control Deficiency | | | Test Exception Not a Deficiency | |
| | Material Weakness | Significant Deficiency | Incon-sequential | No Deficiency | Ref. |
| --- | --- | --- | --- | --- | --- |
| | ❑ | ❑ | ❑ | ❑ | |
| | ❑ | ❑ | ❑ | ❑ | |
| | ❑ | ❑ | ❑ | ❑ | |
| | ❑ | ❑ | ❑ | ❑ | |
| | ❑ | ❑ | ❑ | ❑ | |
| | ❑ | ❑ | ❑ | ❑ | |
| | ❑ | ❑ | ❑ | ❑ | |

[2]See instructions to form TST-ENT-1 for guidance on how to complete this section of the form. Use the column marked "Ref." to reference to your documentation of the additional work performed to determine that the testing exception does not indicate a control deficiency.

| Description of Testing Exception | Evaluation of Testing Exception | | | | |
|---|---|---|---|---|---|
| | Control Deficiency | | | Test Exception Not a Deficiency | |
| | Material Weakness | Significant Deficiency | Incon-sequential | No Deficiency | Ref. |
| | ❑ | ❑ | ❑ | ❑ | |
| | ❑ | ❑ | ❑ | ❑ | |

*Considerations*      *Observations and Conclusions*      *Ref.*

*Monitoring*                          Never      Sometimes      Always

Management receives all communication from external and internal parties relating to internal control effectiveness.      └──────────┴──────────┘

Management appropriately considers all communication received relating to internal control effectiveness.      └──────────┴──────────┘

Management takes appropriate action with respect to internal control deficiencies.      └──────────┴──────────┘

Periodically, physical assets are compared to the related accounting records.      └──────────┴──────────┘

Periodically, personnel confirm that they understand and have complied with the company's code of conduct.      └──────────┴──────────┘

Periodically, personnel responsible for performing critical control functions confirm that they have regularly performed these functions.      └──────────┴──────────┘

## ASSESSMENT OF CONTROL TESTING EXCEPTIONS— MONITORING

Our tests of the monitoring component of internal control revealed the following control exceptions, which we have evaluated as follows.[3]

---

[3]*See instructions to form TST-ENT-1 for guidance on how to complete this section of the form. Use the column marked "Ref." to reference to your documentation of the additional work performed to determine that the testing exception does not indicate a control deficiency.*

| Description of Testing Exception | Evaluation of Testing Exception | | | | |
| --- | --- | --- | --- | --- | --- |
| | Control Deficiency | | | Test Exception Not a Deficiency | |
| | Material Weakness | Significant Deficiency | Incon-sequential | No Deficiency | Ref. |
| | ❏ | ❏ | ❏ | ❏ | |
| | ❏ | ❏ | ❏ | ❏ | |
| | ❏ | ❏ | ❏ | ❏ | |
| | ❏ | ❏ | ❏ | ❏ | |

*Considerations*      *Observations and Conclusions*      *Ref.*

*Period-End Financial Reporting*      Never    Sometimes    Always

Controls related to journal entries provide reasonable assurance that material misstatements will be prevented or detected.

Controls related to the procedures used to record recurring and nonrecurring adjustments to the financial statements provide reasonable assurance that material misstatements will be prevented or detected.

Controls over the drafting of the financial statements and related disclosures provide reasonable assurance that material misstatements will be prevented or detected.

Management identifies significant estimates required to prepare the company's financial statements.

Accounting estimates are based on relevant, sufficient, and reliable data.

Accounting estimates, including the support for the underlying assumptions, are appropriately reviewed and approved.

Significant accounting estimates are compared to subsequent results to assess the reliability of the estimation process.

Significant accounting estimates are consistent with
the operational plans of the company.

| └──────────┴──────────┘ |

## ASSESSMENT OF CONTROL TESTING EXCEPTIONS— PERIOD-END FINANCIAL REPORTING

Our tests of the controls over the period-end financial reporting process revealed the following control exceptions, which we have evaluated as follows.[4]

| Description of Testing Exception | Evaluation of Testing Exception | | | | |
| --- | --- | --- | --- | --- | --- |
| | Control Deficiency | | | Test Exception Not a Deficiency | |
| | Material Weakness | Significant Deficiency | Incon-sequential | No Deficiency | Ref. |
| | ❑ | ❑ | ❑ | ❑ | |
| | ❑ | ❑ | ❑ | ❑ | |
| | ❑ | ❑ | ❑ | ❑ | |
| | ❑ | ❑ | ❑ | ❑ | |
| | ❑ | ❑ | ❑ | ❑ | |
| | ❑ | ❑ | ❑ | ❑ | |
| | ❑ | ❑ | ❑ | ❑ | |
| | ❑ | ❑ | ❑ | ❑ | |
| | ❑ | ❑ | ❑ | ❑ | |

| *Considerations* | *Observations and Conclusions* | *Ref.* |
| --- | --- | --- |

*Selection and Application of Accounting Policies*

Never  Sometimes  Always

The audit committee is informed about

a. The initial selection and application of significant accounting policies

| └──────────┴──────────┘ |

---

[4]*See instructions to form TST-ENT-1 for guidance on how to complete this section of the form. Use the column marked "Ref." to reference to your documentation of the additional work performed to determine that the testing exception does not indicate a control deficiency.*

    b.  Subsequent changes to the selection of signific-
       ant accounting policies                  |_____|_____|_____|

    c.  Subsequent changes to the application of sig-
       nificant accounting policies              |_____|_____|_____|

The audit committee is informed about the methods
   used to account for significant unusual transactions.   |_____|_____|_____|

The audit committee is informed about the effect of
   significant accounting policies in controversial or
   emerging areas for which there is a lack of authori-
   tative accounting guidance or consensus.          |_____|_____|_____|

## ASSESSMENT OF CONTROL TESTING EXCEPTIONS—
## SELECTION AND APPLICATION OF ACCOUNTING PRINCIPLES

Our tests of the controls over the selection and application of accounting principles revealed the following control exceptions, which we have evaluated as follows.[5]

| | Evaluation of Testing Exception | | | | |
| | Control Deficiency | | | Test Exception Not a Deficiency | |
| Description of Testing Exception | Material Weakness | Significant Deficiency | Incon-sequential | No Deficiency | Ref. |
|---|---|---|---|---|---|
| | ❏ | ❏ | ❏ | ❏ | |
| | ❏ | ❏ | ❏ | ❏ | |
| | ❏ | ❏ | ❏ | ❏ | |
| | ❏ | ❏ | ❏ | ❏ | |

[5]See instructions to form TST-ENT-1 for guidance on how to complete this section of the form. Use the column marked "Ref." to reference to your documentation of the additional work performed to determine that the testing exception does not indicate a control deficiency.

| *Considerations* | *Observations and Conclusions* | | | *Ref.* |
|---|---|---|---|---|

## *IT General Controls*

| | Never | Sometimes | Always |
|---|---|---|---|

The company develops and maintains an overall IT strategic plan.

| L_____|_____| _____| |
|---|

The company develops and maintains policies and procedures related to information architecture.

| L_____|_____| _____| |
|---|

The company develops and maintains policies and procedures that define the IT organization and relationships.

| L_____|_____| _____| |
|---|

The company develops and maintains policies and procedures that ensure compliance with external reporting requirements.

| L_____|_____| _____| |
|---|

The IT department develops and maintains risk assessment policies and procedures that address issues such as

- Technology reliability
- Information integrity
- IT personnel
- Security assessments for all significant systems and locations

| L_____|_____| _____| |
|---|

The IT department develops, maintains, communicates, and monitors policies and procedures that ensure quality, including

a. IT systems documentation standards

| L_____|_____| _____| |
|---|

b. Data integrity, ownership, and responsibilities

| L_____|_____| _____| |
|---|

## ACQUIRE AND IMPLEMENT

The IT department establishes, maintains, communicates, and monitors compliance with software acquisition and implementation policies and procedures.

| L_____|_____| _____| |
|---|

The IT department establishes, maintains, communicates, and monitors compliance with hardware acquisition and implementation policies and procedures.

| L_____|_____| _____| |
|---|

User reference and support manuals or other documentation help ensure the long-term sustainability of the IT system.

| L_____|_____| _____| |
|---|

The IT department tests new or modified systems, including

   a.  Unit, system, integration, and user acceptance      └──────┴──────┘

   b.  Load and stress testing      └──────┴──────┘

   c.  Interfaces with other systems      └──────┴──────┘

   d.  Data conversion      └──────┴──────┘

The IT department establishes, maintains, communi-     └──────┴──────┘
cates, and monitors compliance with change man-
agement policies and procedures that address issues
such as

- The override of established procedures, for
  example, in an emergency situation
- Plans for the timely change to systems and
  applications

## DELIVERY AND SUPPORT

The IT department establishes, maintains, communi-     └──────┴──────┘
cates, and monitors compliance with policies and
procedures relating to the use of third-party service
providers. These policies and procedures may include

- Vendor policies for selection of outsourced services
- Key performance indicators for managing service-
  level agreements
- Selection process for third-party service providers
- Third-party service contracts
- Policies and procedures for monitoring third-
  party service levels, including reviews of security,
  availability, and processing integrity

The IT department monitors the performance and      └──────┴──────┘
capacity levels of the IT systems and, if measures
are less than optimal, takes appropriate action.

The IT department establishes, updates, and tests a      └──────┴──────┘
business continuity plan

The IT department establishes, maintains, communi-     └──────┴──────┘
cates, and monitors compliance with system secu-
rity policies and procedures, which address issues
such as

- The development, updating, and maintenance
  of a security plan

- Methods used to authenticate users to the system
- Maintaining the effectiveness of authentication and access mechanisms
- The requesting, establishing, issuing, suspending, and closing of user accounts
- The prevention of unauthorized access to the network
- The performance of security assessments
- The monitoring of security activity and security violations

Personnel using IT services are educated and trained on the proper use of those services.

The IT department establishes, maintains, communicates, and monitors compliance with configuration management policies and procedures that address issues such as

- Software that is authorized to be used by employees
- The configuration of system infrastructure
- The configuration of application software
- The configuration of data storage
- Mitigation of risks posed by computer viruses
- Testing software and network infrastructure to ensure it is properly configured

The IT department establishes, maintains, communicates, and monitors compliance with policies and procedures relating to the management of problems and incidents.

The IT department establishes, maintains, communicates, and monitors compliance with data management policies and procedures that address issues such as

- Data processing controls, including those related to
  - The completeness of transaction processing
  - The accuracy of transaction processing
  - The authorization of transactions
  - The validity of transactions
- Controls over data input
- The handling, distribution, and retention of data and reporting output

- The protection of sensitive information during its storage and transmission
- The retention and storage of
  - Data
  - Programs
  - Reports
  - Documentation
- Physical security and accountability for data
- Changes in data structures

The IT department establishes, maintains, communi-        |_____|_____|_____|
cates, and monitors compliance with facilities man-
agement policies and procedures, such as
- Controlled access to facilities
- Environmental controls at physical facilities

The IT department establishes, maintains, communi-        |_____|_____|_____|
cates, and monitors compliance with operations
management policies and procedures.

### MONITORING

Significant IT processes are monitored.                    |_____|_____|_____|

## ASSESSMENT OF CONTROL TESTING EXCEPTIONS—IT GENERAL CONTROLS

Our tests of IT general controls revealed the following control exceptions, which we have evaluated as follows.[8]

| | Evaluation of Testing Exception | | | | |
| --- | --- | --- | --- | --- | --- |
| | Control Deficiency | | | Test Exception Not a Deficiency | |
| Description of Testing Exception | Material Weakness | Significant Deficiency | Incon-sequential | No Deficiency | Ref. |
| | ❏ | ❏ | ❏ | ❏ | |
| | ❏ | ❏ | ❏ | ❏ | |

[8]*See instructions to form TST-ENT-1 for guidance on how to complete this section of the form. Use the column marked "Ref." to reference to your documentation of the additional work performed to determine that the testing exception does not indicate a control deficiency.*

| Description of Testing Exception | Evaluation of Testing Exception | | | | |
| --- | --- | --- | --- | --- | --- |
| | Control Deficiency | | | Test Exception Not a Deficiency | |
| | Material Weakness | Significant Deficiency | Incon-sequential | No Deficiency | Ref. |
| | ❏ | ❏ | ❏ | ❏ | |
| | ❏ | ❏ | ❏ | ❏ | |
| | ❏ | ❏ | ❏ | ❏ | |
| | ❏ | ❏ | ❏ | ❏ | |
| | ❏ | ❏ | ❏ | ❏ | |
| | ❏ | ❏ | ❏ | ❏ | |
| | ❏ | ❏ | ❏ | ❏ | |

*Considerations*              *Observations and Conclusions*              *Ref.*

*Nonroutine Transactions*                          Never     Sometimes     Always

Management identifies nonroutine transactions.          └————————┴————————┘

The consummation of nonroutine transactions is
  authorized appropriately.                             └————————┴————————┘

The accounting treatment for nonroutine transactions
  is authorized appropriately.                          └————————┴————————┘

## ASSESSMENT OF CONTROL TESTING EXCEPTIONS— NONROUTINE TRANSACTIONS

Our tests of the controls over nonroutine transactions revealed the following control exceptions, which we have evaluated as follows.[9]

---

[9]See instructions to form TST-ENT-1 for guidance on how to complete this section of the form. Use the column marked "Ref." to reference to your documentation of the additional work performed to determine that the testing exception does not indicate a control deficiency.

| Description of Testing Exception | Evaluation of Testing Exception | | | | |
|---|---|---|---|---|---|
| | Control Deficiency | | | Test Exception Not a Deficiency | |
| | Material Weakness | Significant Deficiency | Incon-sequential | No Deficiency | Ref. |
| | ❏ | ❏ | ❏ | ❏ | |
| | ❏ | ❏ | ❏ | ❏ | |
| | ❏ | ❏ | ❏ | ❏ | |
| | ❏ | ❏ | ❏ | ❏ | |
| | ❏ | ❏ | ❏ | ❏ | |
| | ❏ | ❏ | ❏ | ❏ | |
| | ❏ | ❏ | ❏ | ❏ | |
| | ❏ | ❏ | ❏ | ❏ | |
| | ❏ | ❏ | ❏ | ❏ | |

# Checklist for Small Business Entity-Level Controls

## PURPOSE

This form has been designed to—

- Facilitate the effective organization of an efficient process for performing a review of IT general controls.
- Document the work performed to evaluate IT general controls

## INSTRUCTIONS

Use this form to guide the design and performance of the review of IT general controls. As the steps in program are completed, the person responsible for performing the step should initial and date in the indicated column on the worksheet. If the step is not applicable, indicate that by noting "N/A." Use the "Notes" column to cross reference to where the performance of the procedure is documented, or to make other notations.

*Notations in italics are additional instructions to the preparer of the form and should be removed before the form is considered final.*

# CHECKLIST FOR SMALL BUSINESS
# ENTITY-LEVEL CONTROLS

Company: _____    Reporting Date: _____

Prepared by: _____    Date Prepared: _____

| Question | Yes | No | Partial | Notes |
|---|---|---|---|---|
| *Control Environment* | | | | |
| 1. Management has clearly articulated the company's ethical values and acceptable business practices. | ❏ | ❏ | ❏ | |
| 2. Management monitors adherence to stated ethical values and acceptable business practices. | ❏ | ❏ | ❏ | |
| 3. Behavior that is inconsistent with company's stated values or ethical business practices are identified and addressed in an appropriate manner. | ❏ | ❏ | ❏ | |
| *Board of Directors* | | | | |
| 4. The board of directors has a clearly defined set of responsibilities and the requisite authority. | ❏ | ❏ | ❏ | |
| 5. A significant number of board members are independent from management. | ❏ | ❏ | ❏ | |
| 6. The board actively evaluates and monitors the risk of management override of the system of internal control. | ❏ | ❏ | ❏ | |
| 7. One or more members of the board or audit committee possess a level of financial expertise that is appropriate given the size and relative complexity of the entity. | ❏ | ❏ | ❏ | |

| Question | Yes | No | Partial | Notes |
|---|---|---|---|---|
| 8. The board of directors actively monitors the effectiveness of the company's internal control and oversees the preparation of the company's financial statements. | ❏ | ❏ | ❏ | |
| 9. The board/audit committee oversees the annual financial statement audit. | ❏ | ❏ | ❏ | |
| 10. The board meets privately with the company's external auditors to discuss matters affecting the company's financial statements, financial reporting process, and/or internal control. | ❏ | ❏ | ❏ | |
| 11. The board actively evaluates and monitors the risk of management override of the system of internal control. | ❏ | ❏ | ❏ | |
| *Management Philosophy and Operating Style* | | | | |
| 12. Management's philosophy and operating style reinforce the importance of reliable financial reporting and internal control. | ❏ | ❏ | ❏ | |
| *Organizational Structure* | | | | |
| 13. The company's organizational structure facilitates effective financial reporting communication about financial reporting and internal control matters. | ❏ | ❏ | ❏ | |
| 14. The assignment of authority and responsibility includes appropriate limitations. | ❏ | ❏ | ❏ | |

| Question | Yes | No | Partial | Notes |
|---|---|---|---|---|
| 15. Management ensures that all employees understand their responsibilities relating to financial reporting and internal control. | ❏ | ❏ | ❏ | |
| *HR Policies* | | | | |
| 16. The company has identified necessary financial reporting competencies, and it has employed or otherwise engaged individuals who possess those competencies. | ❏ | ❏ | ❏ | |
| 17. The company takes action to maintain the financial reporting competencies needed. | ❏ | ❏ | ❏ | |
| 18. The company's HR policies and procedures are consistent with a commitment to integrity, ethical behavior, and competence. | ❏ | ❏ | ❏ | |
| 19. Management provides employees with the resources necessary to perform their financial reporting and/or internal control responsibilities. | ❏ | ❏ | ❏ | |
| 20. The company's hiring, compensation, and retention policies support the establishment and maintenance of an effective internal control and reliable financial reporting. | ❏ | ❏ | ❏ | |
| **Risk Assessment** | | | | |
| *Financial Reporting Objectives and Preparation* | | | | |
| 21. Management considers the requirements of GAAP as a basis for developing financial reporting objectives. | ❏ | ❏ | ❏ | |

| Question | Yes | No | Partial | Notes |
|---|:---:|:---:|:---:|---|
| 22. The company's accounting policies are appropriate and result in a fair presentation of the company's financial condition, results of operations, and cash flows. | ❏ | ❏ | ❏ | |
| 23. The financial statements are informative of matters that may affect their use, understanding, and interpretation. | ❏ | ❏ | ❏ | |
| 24. The level of summarization in the financial statements is appropriate. | ❏ | ❏ | ❏ | |
| 25. Management appropriately considers the concept of materiality when preparing the financial statements. | ❏ | ❏ | ❏ | |
| *Financial Reporting Risks* | | | | |
| 26. Management understands how the company's business processes impact it's financial statements, and they use this understanding to identify financial reporting risks. | ❏ | ❏ | ❏ | |
| 27. Management considers the competency of company personnel when identifying and assessing financial reporting risks. | ❏ | ❏ | ❏ | |
| 28. Management considers IT processes and related infrastructure when identifying and assessing financial reporting risks. | ❏ | ❏ | ❏ | |
| 29. Management's risk assessment process considers both internal and external factors. | ❏ | ❏ | ❏ | |

| Question | Yes | No | Partial | Notes |
|---|---|---|---|---|
| 30. When assessing risk, management considers both the likelihood and magnitude of a financial statement that may occur as a result of the risk. | ❑ | ❑ | ❑ | |
| 31. External and internal changes prompt management to reevaluate its risk assessments. | ❑ | ❑ | ❑ | |
| *Fraud Risks Assessment* | | | | |
| 32. Management's risk assessment process includes the consideration of:<br>a. The opportunity to commit fraud<br>b. Incentives/motivations to commit fraud<br>c. The ability of those committing fraud to rationalize their actions. | ❑ | ❑ | ❑ | |
| 33. Management has identified risk factors that affect the company's vulnerability to fraud. | ❑ | ❑ | ❑ | |
| 34. When assessing fraud risk, management considers the impact that a fraud may have on its financial statements. | ❑ | ❑ | ❑ | |
| 35. Management's consideration of fraud risk includes both defalcation/theft and financial reporting fraud. | ❑ | ❑ | ❑ | |
| **Information and Communication** | | | | |
| *Financial Reporting Information* | | | | |
| 36. The capture of transaction data is complete, accurate, and timely at the time the transaction occurs. | ❑ | ❑ | ❑ | |

| Question | Yes | No | Partial | Notes |
|---|---|---|---|---|
| 37. Information for all valid transactions is captured. | ❑ | ❑ | ❑ | |
| 38. Financial reporting information is developed using both internal and external sources. | ❑ | ❑ | ❑ | |
| 39. Information systems provide accurate information that is timely, current, and accessible. | ❑ | ❑ | ❑ | |
| *Internal Control Information* | | | | |
| 40. Data necessary to perform control activities and other control components (e.g., risk assessment, monitoring, etc.) is complete, accurate, timely, current, and accessible. | ❑ | ❑ | ❑ | |
| 41. A degradation in the quality of information produced by the system triggers an investigation into the root cause of the problem and an assessment of the effectiveness of related controls. | ❑ | ❑ | ❑ | |
| *Internal Communication* | | | | |
| 42. Personnel are informed of their responsibilities relating to financial reporting and/or internal control. | ❑ | ❑ | ❑ | |
| 43. Personnel with key financial reporting and/or internal control responsibilities receive the information they need on a timely basis to perform their job responsibilities. | ❑ | ❑ | ❑ | |

| Question | Yes | No | Partial | Notes |
|---|---|---|---|---|
| 44. Open communication between management and the board enables the board to have all the information necessary to fulfill their financial reporting oversight responsibilities. | ❏ | ❏ | ❏ | |
| *External Communication* | | | | |
| 45. The company maintains open communication channels with third parties that allow them to provide information that would allow management to identify internal control weaknesses. | ❏ | ❏ | ❏ | |
| 46. Observations about internal control made by the company's external auditors are communicated to management and the board of directors. | ❏ | ❏ | ❏ | |
| **Monitoring** | | | | |
| 47. Management receives regular feedback on the effectiveness of internal control. | ❏ | ❏ | ❏ | |
| 48. Internal control deficiencies are reported to management and to the individual who owns the process and related controls. | ❏ | ❏ | ❏ | |
| 49. Internal control deficiencies are reported to the audit committee and senior management as appropriate. | ❏ | ❏ | ❏ | |
| 50. Action to correct identified control deficiencies is taken as needed. | ❏ | ❏ | ❏ | |

# Work Program for Testing Entity-Level Control Effectiveness

## PURPOSE

This form has been designed to

- Provide a comprehensive list of tests you may perform to assess the operating effectiveness of entity-level controls
- Document the nature of the tests performed to gather information about the operating effectiveness of entity-level controls
- Track the progress the project team has made in testing entity-level controls

## INSTRUCTIONS

The horizontal axis of the form is a summary of all entity-level controls that should be included in the scope of your assessment, *except for* information technology general controls. The work program for IT general controls can be found at TST-ENT-7. These entity-level controls are

- *Control environment.* The company's control environment, divided into its corporate culture element and personnel policies element.
- *Risk assessment.* Management's process for identifying and assessing financial reporting–related risks.
- *Information and communication.* The information and communication component of internal control, which for entity-level controls consists primarily of the communication subcomponent.
- *Monitoring.* Controls to monitor other controls and the results of operations.
- *Period-end reporting.* Controls over the period-end financial reporting process.
- *Accounting policies.* Controls over the selection and application of accounting policies in accordance with generally accepted accounting principles.
- *Audit committee.* Tests designed to evaluate the effectiveness of the company's audit committee.
- *Antifraud.* Controls designed to prevent or detect fraud.
- *Nonroutine transactions.* Controls over significant nonroutine and nonsystematic transactions, such as accounts involving judgments and estimates.

The first column of the form is a list of recommended test procedures. Cells that are filled with gray indicate that the recommended test procedure most likely does not provide direct evidence about the operating effectiveness of the related entity-level control.

You may determine that some recommended procedures are not considered necessary under the circumstances. You should indicate this conclusion by entering "ncn" in the appropriate cell. When choosing the mix of procedures to perform, be aware that PCAOB Auditing Standard No. 2 states that inquiry alone does not provide sufficient evidence to support the operating effectiveness of a control (see the fifth bullet of paragraph 40 of the standard).

Use this form to track the project team's progress in testing entity-level controls. As a test procedure is completed, the person completing the test should initial and date the appropriate cell(s). You also may wish to provide a reference to where the performance of the test is documented.

---

## TESTS OF ENTITY-LEVEL CONTROL OPERATING EFFECTIVENESS

This worksheet summarizes the nature of the tests we performed to evaluate the operating effectiveness of entity-level controls. The collective objectives of these tests were to

- Confirm that stated policies are being consistently followed by company personnel.
- Determine that entity-level controls provide an overall environment that enables the effective functioning of activity-level controls. To make this determination, our tests were designed to gather information about
  - *Awareness.* Company personnel's awareness and understanding of relevant entity-level control policies.
  - *Attitude.* Company personnel's attitude toward internal control in general and the adherence to stated entity-level controls, in particular.
  - *Actions.* Whether management's actions and those of other personnel are consistent with stated company values and policies.
- Identify entity-level control deficiencies, to the extent such deficiencies exist.

Company: _____        Reporting Date: _____

Prepared by: _____        Date Prepared: _____

**Planning**

*These procedures may have been performed and documented on forms ADM-1 and ADM-2. If so, you should review this documentation before proceeding with your tests of controls.*

| Test Procedure | Entity-Level Control | | | | | | | |
|---|---|---|---|---|---|---|---|---|
| | Control Environment | | Risk Assess | Information and Communication | Monitoring | Period End Reporting | Accounting Policies | Nonroutine Transactions |
| | Culture | Personnel | | | | | | |
| 1. Determine which business units or locations are to be included within the scope of your testwork. | | | | | | | | |
| 2. Review other information sources to identify control deficiencies or other conditions or events that may indicate the existence of entity-level control deficiencies. | | | | | | | | |
| Consider sources such as <br>• The company's recent SEC filings <br>• Prior reports on entity-level control effectiveness, including those prepared by internal auditors | | | | | | | | |

## Entity-Level Control

| Test Procedure | Control Environment | | Risk Assess | Information and Communication | Monitoring | Period End Reporting | Accounting Policies | Nonroutine Transactions |
|---|---|---|---|---|---|---|---|---|
| | Culture | Personnel | | | | | | |
| • Communications from the external auditors, legal counsel, regulators, or other third parties<br>• Findings or recommendations of the company's disclosure committee | | | | | | | | |

### Understand Entity-Level Control Policies and Procedures

*These procedures may have been performed and documented on forms DOC-1 and DOC-1a. If so, you should review this documentation before proceeding with your tests of controls.*

| | | | | | | | | |
|---|---|---|---|---|---|---|---|---|
| 3. Review the documentation pertaining to the company's stated entity-level control policies and procedures. | | | | | | | | |

### Test Operating Effectiveness of Entity-Level Controls

*Inquiries or Written Surveys of Appropriate Personnel*

| | | | | | | | | |
|---|---|---|---|---|---|---|---|---|
| 4. Determine overall objective(s) of your inquiry procedures or written surveys. | | | | | | | | |

| Test Procedure | Entity-Level Control | | | | | | | | |
|---|---|---|---|---|---|---|---|---|---|
| | Control Environment | | Risk Assess | Information and Communication | Monitoring | Period End Reporting | Accounting Policies | Nonroutine Transactions |
| | Culture | Personnel | | | | | | |
| 5. Identify types of individuals who are most likely to be able to achieve stated inquiry objective(s). Consider<br>• Management<br>• Board members<br>• Audit committee members<br>• Financial personnel<br>• Nonfinancial personnel | | | | | | | | |
| 6. Determine the number of individuals from each category in step 5 who should be interviewed or surveyed to draw a reliable conclusion about the operating effectiveness of the tests. | | | | | | | | |
| 7. Determine the time period during which the interviews or surveys will be conducted and make necessary arrangements with interviewees. | | | | | | | | |
| 8. Conduct inquiries or surveys and document results. | | | | | | | | |

| Test Procedure | Entity-Level Control | | | | | | | |
| --- | --- | --- | --- | --- | --- | --- | --- | --- |
| | Control Environment | | Risk Assess | Information and Communication | Monitoring | Period End Reporting | Accounting Policies | Nonroutine Transactions |
| | Culture | Personnel | | | | | | |
| *Inspect Documentation*<br><br>The documentation to be reviewed in this section is that related to the *implementation and performance* of the control procedures and not the documentation of the company's policies, which was addressed in step 3. | | | | | | | | |
| Inspect relevant documentation that provides evidence that key documents related to company values and acceptable and unacceptable behavior were communicated broadly throughout the organizations. | | | | | | | | |
| 9. Key documents related to company values and acceptable and unacceptable behavior were communicated broadly throughout the organization. | | | | | | | | |

|  | Entity-Level Control | | | | | | | |
| | Control Environment | | Risk Assess | Information and Communication | Monitoring | Period End Reporting | Accounting Policies | Nonroutine Transactions |
| Test Procedure | Culture | Personnel | | | | | | |
|---|---|---|---|---|---|---|---|---|
| Key documents include<br>• Code of conduct<br>• Board of directors charter<br>• Audit committee charter<br>• Charters for other senior committees<br>• Other human resource policies | | | | | | | | |
| 10. Key documents identified in step 9 were received, read, and understood by company personnel. | | | | | | | | |
| 11. Management has taken appropriate action regarding | | | | | | | | |
| a. Mitigation of risks created by compensation policies or other incentive policies that may motivate unethical behavior by employees | | | | | | | | |
| b. Internal control deficiencies | | | | | | | | |

| Test Procedure | Entity-Level Control | | | | | | | |
|---|---|---|---|---|---|---|---|---|
| | Control Environment | | Risk Assess | Information and Communication | Monitoring | Period End Reporting | Accounting Policies | Nonroutine Transactions |
| | Culture | Personnel | | | | | | |
| c. Overly aggressive or other accounting policies that are of poor quality | | | | | | | | |
| d. The delegation of responsibility and organizational structure of the company | | | | | | | | |
| e. Violations of the code of conduct or other unethical or unacceptable behaviors | | | | | | | | |
| f. Reports of questionable accounting or auditing matters | | | | | | | | |
| Such support may come from a variety of documents, including<br>• Minutes of the board, the audit committee, or other committees<br>• Memos and e-mails circulated internally, within the company | | | | | | | | |

| Test Procedure | Control Environment | | Risk Assess | Information and Communication | Monitoring | Period End Reporting | Accounting Policies | Nonroutine Transactions |
| --- | --- | --- | --- | --- | --- | --- | --- | --- |
| | Culture | Personnel | | | | | | |
| • Written correspondence and e-mails with external third parties<br>• Compliance with the provisions of Section 302 of the Sarbanes-Oxley Act requiring procedures for submission by employees of concerns regarding questionable accounting or auditing matters | | | | | | | | |
| 12. Stated human resource policies relating to the following matters have been followed consistently. | | | | | | | | |
| a. Hiring | | | | | | | | |
| b. Compensation | | | | | | | | |
| c. Performance evaluations | | | | | | | | |
| d. Terminations | | | | | | | | |

151

**Entity-Level Control**

| Test Procedure | Control Environment — Culture | Control Environment — Personnel | Risk Assess | Information and Communication | Monitoring | Period End Reporting | Accounting Policies | Nonroutine Transactions |
|---|---|---|---|---|---|---|---|---|
| 13. Board members have complied with key provisions of the board charter, including those relating to the board's | | | | | | | | |
| a. Independence | | | | | | | | |
| b. Financial accounting and other expertise | | | | | | | | |
| 14. The board has been actively involved in | | | | | | | | |
| a. Oversight of the financial reporting process | | | | | | | | |
| b. Management's risk assessment process | | | | | | | | |
| c. Monitoring the effectiveness of internal control | | | | | | | | |

| Test Procedure | Entity-Level Control | | | | | | | |
| | Control Environment | | Risk Assess | Information and Communication | Monitoring | Period End Reporting | Accounting Policies | Nonroutine Transactions |
| | Culture | Personnel | | | | | | |
| Documentation of the active involvement of the board may be found in <br> • Board minutes <br> • Board meeting agendas and other materials circulated in advance of the meeting | | | | | | | | |
| 15. Management has adhered to its stated process for allocating necessary resources to employees, including funding, personnel, and training. | | | | | | | | |
| 16. Management has actively engaged in a risk assessment process that includes the identification and analysis of the financial reporting–related risks for all key business processes. | | | | | | | | |

| Test Procedure | Entity-Level Control | | | | | | | |
| --- | --- | --- | --- | --- | --- | --- | --- | --- |
| | Control Environment | | Risk Assess | Information and Communication | Monitoring | Period End Reporting | Accounting Policies | Nonroutine Transactions |
| | Culture | Personnel | | | | | | |
| 17. Management has identified and assessed risks related to changes in the company or its operating environment that create new risks to achieving its financial reporting objectives. | | | | | | | | |

These changes may include
- Changed operating environment
- New personnel
- New or revamped IT systems
- Rapid growth
- New lines, products, or business activities
- Restructurings
- Foreign operations
- New accounting principles or other financial reporting requirements

| Test Procedure | Entity-Level Control | | | | | | | |
| | Control Environment | | Risk Assess | Information and Communication | Monitoring | Period End Reporting | Accounting Policies | Nonroutine Transactions |
| | Culture | Personnel | | | | | | |
| 18. Physical assets, including inventory, have been compared to and reconciled with amounts recorded by the accounting system. | | | | | | | | |
| 19. Stated control procedures related to journal entries have been performed properly, consistently, and on a timely basis. These procedures include those relating to the way in which journal entries are | | | | | | | | |
| a. Initiated | | | | | | | | |
| b. Authorized | | | | | | | | |
| c. Recorded | | | | | | | | |
| d. Processed | | | | | | | | |

| | Entity-Level Control | | | | | | | |
| Test Procedure | Control Environment – Culture | Control Environment – Personnel | Risk Assess | Information and Communication | Monitoring | Period End Reporting | Accounting Policies | Nonroutine Transactions |
| --- | --- | --- | --- | --- | --- | --- | --- | --- |
| The performance of control procedures related to journal entries may be documented on the journal entry itself, if a paper-based copy of the journal entry exists. Inspecting a sample of journal entries may be sufficient to support an assessment that controls related to journal entries are effective. | | | | | | | | |
| 20. Stated control procedures related to adjustments to the financial statements (e.g., consolidating adjustments, report combinations, or classifications) have been performed properly, consistently, and on a timely basis. | | | | | | | | |
| 21. The need for preparing significant accounting estimates has been communicated to appropriate personnel. | | | | | | | | |

| | Entity-Level Control | | | | | | | |
| | Control Environment | | Risk Assess | Information and Communication | Monitoring | Period End Reporting | Accounting Policies | Nonroutine Transactions |
| Test Procedure | Culture | Personnel | | | | | | |
| 22. The person responsible for preparing an accounting estimate has accumulated relevant, sufficient, and reliable data on which to base the estimate. | | | | | | | | |
| 23. The process for preparing the accounting estimate has been reviewed. | | | | | | | | |
| 24. Management has reviewed the estimate to determine that it is consistent with | | | | | | | | |
| a. Subsequent results | | | | | | | | |
| b. The operational plans of the entity | | | | | | | | |
| 25. Audit committee members have complied with the company's stated independence policies. | | | | | | | | |

| Test Procedure | Entity-Level Control | | | | | | | |
|---|---|---|---|---|---|---|---|---|
| | Control Environment | | Risk Assess | Information and Communication | Monitoring | Period End Reporting | Accounting Policies | Nonroutine Transactions |
| | Culture | Personnel | | | | | | |
| 26. The audit committee has actively interacted with | | | | | | | | |
| a. External auditors | | | | | | | | |
| b. Internal auditors | | | | | | | | |
| c. Key members of financial management | | | | | | | | |
| Documentation of the active interaction of the audit committee with others may be found in<br>• Audit committee minutes<br>• Audit committee meeting agendas and other materials circulated in advance of the meeting | | | | | | | | |
| 27. The audit committee has | | | | | | | | |
| a. Been actively involved with and responded appropriately to significant internal control and financial reporting matters | | | | | | | | |

158

| Test Procedure | Entity-Level Control | | | | | | | |
| --- | --- | --- | --- | --- | --- | --- | --- | --- |
| | Control Environment | | Risk Assess | Information and Communication | Monitoring | Period End Reporting | Accounting Policies | Nonroutine Transactions |
| | Culture | Personnel | | | | | | |
| b. Provided oversight of the company's antifraud processes and controls | | | | | | | | |
| c. Been informed about the initial selection and application of accounting policies | | | | | | | | |
| d. Been informed about changes to the selection of accounting policies | | | | | | | | |
| e. Been informed about changes to the application of accounting policies | | | | | | | | |
| f. Been informed about the methods used to account for significant unusual transactions | | | | | | | | |

| Test Procedure | Entity-Level Control | | | | | | | |
|---|---|---|---|---|---|---|---|---|
| | Control Environment | | Risk Assess | Information and Communication | Monitoring | Period End Reporting | Accounting Policies | Nonroutine Transactions |
| | Culture | Personnel | | | | | | |
| g. Been informed about the effect of significant accounting policies in controversial or emerging areas for which there is a lack of authoritative accounting guidance or consensus | | | | | | | | |
| Documentation of the active interaction of the audit committee with others may be found in<br>• Audit committee minutes<br>• Audit committee meeting agendas and other materials circulated in advance of the meeting<br>• Correspondence with external auditors or other third parties | | | | | | | | |
| 28. Management has followed the company's stated policies and procedures relating to the identification and assessment of fraud risk. | | | | | | | | |

| Test Procedure | Entity-Level Control | | | | | | | |
| --- | --- | --- | --- | --- | --- | --- | --- | --- |
| | Control Environment | | Risk Assess | Information and Communication | Monitoring | Period End Reporting | Accounting Policies | Nonroutine Transactions |
| | Culture | Personnel | | | | | | |
| Documentation of the assessment of fraud risk may be found in the company's documentation of its overall risk assessment process. | | | | | | | | |
| 29. The consummation of and accounting for nonroutine transactions have been properly authorized. | | | | | | | | |
| Documentation relating to the authorization of and accounting for nonroutine transactions may be found in<br>• Minutes of the board of directors, audit committee, or other senior committees<br>• Internal memos and e-mail<br>• Correspondence with external parties such as the independent auditors, the staff of the SEC, or legal counsel | | | | | | | | |

| Test Procedure | Entity-Level Control | | | | | | | |
| --- | --- | --- | --- | --- | --- | --- | --- | --- |
| | Control Environment | | Risk Assess | Information and Communication | Monitoring | Period End Reporting | Accounting Policies | Nonroutine Transactions |
| | Culture | Personnel | | | | | | |
| *Observation of Operations* | | | | | | | | |
| 30. Observe a meeting of the board of directors in which one or more of the following topics is discussed. | | | | | | | | |
| a. Internal control deficiencies or other internal control matters, including communications from external parties on internal control effectiveness | | | | | | | | |
| b. The quality of the company's accounting policies | | | | | | | | |
| c. The operating budget or allocation of other resources such as personnel or training | | | | | | | | |
| d. Published financial reports | | | | | | | | |

| Test Procedure | Entity-Level Control | | | | | | | |
|---|---|---|---|---|---|---|---|---|
| | Control Environment | | Risk Assess | Information and Communication | Monitoring | Period End Reporting | Accounting Policies | Nonroutine Transactions |
| | Culture | Personnel | | | | | | |
| e. Management's assessment of risks facing the company, including fraud risks | | | | | | | | |
| f. Nonroutine transactions, including their accounting treatment | | | | | | | | |
| g. Disciplinary action taken with regard to violations of the code of conduct or other unethical behavior | | | | | | | | |
| 31. Observe a meeting of the audit committee in which one or more of the following topics is discussed. | | | | | | | | |
| a. Internal control–related matters, including control deficiencies | | | | | | | | |

| Test Procedure | Entity-Level Control | | | | | | | |
| | Control Environment | | Risk Assess | Information and Communication | Monitoring | Period End Reporting | Accounting Policies | Nonroutine Transactions |
| | Culture | Personnel | | | | | | |
| b. The initial selection of or subsequent changes to accounting policies | | | | | | | | |
| c. The accounting policies in controversial or emerging areas | | | | | | | | |
| d. Significant accounting estimates | | | | | | | | |
| e. Other matters raised by the external auditors, including the quality of the company's accounting policies | | | | | | | | |
| f. Nonroutine transactions, including their accounting treatment | | | | | | | | |
| 32. Observe a meeting of the audit committee in which one or more of the following participates. | | | | | | | | |

| | | Entity-Level Control | | | | | | |
|---|---|---|---|---|---|---|---|---|
| | **Control Environment** | | **Risk Assess** | **Information and Communication** | **Monitoring** | **Period End Reporting** | **Accounting Policies** | **Nonroutine Transactions** |
| **Test Procedure** | **Culture** | **Personnel** | | | | | | |
| a. External auditors | | | | | | | | |
| b. Internal auditors | | | | | | | | |
| c. Key members of financial management | | | | | | | | |
| 33. Observe a meeting of the company's compensation committee, if any, or others involved in implementing the company's stated compensation and other incentive policies. | | | | | | | | |
| 34. Observe a meeting of the company's budget committee, if any, or others responsible for allocating resources to employees. | | | | | | | | |

| | Entity-Level Control | | | | | | | | |
| Test Procedure | Control Environment | | Risk Assess | Information and Communication | Monitoring | Period End Reporting | Accounting Policies | Nonroutine Transactions |
| | Culture | Personnel | | | | | | |
|---|---|---|---|---|---|---|---|---|
| 35. Observe management's deliberations regarding the risks facing the company, including fraud risks. | | ▓ | | | ▓ | ▓ | ▓ | ▓ |
| 36. Observe the counting of physical assets, including inventory. | | | ▓ | | | | ▓ | ▓ |
| 37. Observe meetings held by company personnel to draft or review interim or annual financial statements and related disclosures. | | | ▓ | | | | ▓ | |
| 38. Observe the operation of computer application controls related to the initiation, authorization, recording, or processing of journal entries. | ▓ | ▓ | ▓ | ▓ | ▓ | | | ▓ |

| Test Procedure | Entity-Level Control | | | | | | | |
|---|---|---|---|---|---|---|---|---|
| | Control Environment | | Risk Assess | Information and Communication | Monitoring | Period End Reporting | Accounting Policies | Nonroutine Transactions |
| | Culture | Personnel | | | | | | |
| *Reperformance of the Control Procedure* | | | | | | | | |
| 39. On a test basis, reperform counts of physical assets. | | | | | | | | |
| 40. Assess the propriety of the adjustments to the financial statements such as consolidating adjustments, report combinations, and classifications. | | | | | | | | |
| 41. Determine that accounting estimates are consistent with data supporting the underlying assumptions used in the estimate. | | | | | | | | |

| Test Procedure | Control Environment | | Risk Assess | Information and Communication | Monitoring | Period End Reporting | Accounting Policies | Nonroutine Transactions |
| --- | --- | --- | --- | --- | --- | --- | --- | --- |
| | Culture | Personnel | | | | | | |
| 42. Compare significant accounting estimates to subsequent results and assess the reliability of the process used to develop the estimate. | | | | | | | | |
| 43. Determine that the assumptions underlying significant estimates are consistent with management's operational plans. | | | | | | | | |
| 44. Verify information used to support the independence and financial expertise of board or audit committee members. | | | | | | | | |

| Test Procedure | Entity-Level Control | | | | | | | | |
|---|---|---|---|---|---|---|---|---|---|
| | Control Environment | | Risk Assess | Information and Communication | Monitoring | Period End Reporting | Accounting Policies | Nonroutine Transactions |
| | Culture | Personnel | | | | | | |
| 45. Review current published financial statements and identify significant accounting policies or changes to those policies or their application. Determine that the audit committee was informed of these policies or changes. | | | | | | | | |
| 46. Review current published financial statements and identify the accounting policies related to significant unusual transactions or transactions in controversial or emerging areas. Determine that the audit committee was informed of these policies. | | | | | | | | |

| Test Procedure | Entity-Level Control | | | | | | | |
| --- | --- | --- | --- | --- | --- | --- | --- | --- |
| | Control Environment | | Risk Assess | Information and Communication | Monitoring | Period End Reporting | Accounting Policies | Nonroutine Transactions |
| | Culture | Personnel | | | | | | |
| **Summarize Results** | | | | | | | | |
| 47. Summarize the results and findings of tests of the operating effectiveness of entity-level controls. | | | | | | | | |

# Index to Tests of Entity-Level Controls: Inquiries and Surveys

## PURPOSE

This form has been designed to

- Summarize the extent of your inquiries and surveys of entity personnel and map these tests to the entity-level controls to which they relate
- Provide a centralized cross-reference to the documentation of the procedures performed and test results for entity-level controls

## INSTRUCTIONS

There are four separate forms here, one for each category of individual you may interview or survey: management, board members, audit committee members, and employees.

Provide the name and any other relevant information (e.g., title) and enter this into the second column. In the third column, note the date on which the interview took place. In the first column, you should assign this item an identifying number as a way to cross-reference the reviewer to your description of the test performed and its results.

Check the appropriate boxes to indicate the entity-level control(s) to which the test relates. It is common for inquiries to provide evidence about the operating effectiveness of more than one control. Columns that are filled with gray indicate that the inquiries of this category of individual usually are not designed to provide evidence about that particular control. However, if you modify your planned inquiries to address these controls, then you should adjust your summary accordingly.

To this index you should attach summaries of the inquiries or a copy of the survey and the results of those procedures. The forms TST-ENT-3a–3b may be used for this purpose. One form should be completed for each person interviewed.

# SUMMARY OF INTERVIEWS
## MANAGEMENT

| | | | Control Environment | | | | Entity-Level Control | | | | |
| --- | --- | --- | --- | --- | --- | --- | --- | --- | --- | --- |
| Ref. | Management Team Member Interviewed | Date | Culture | Personnel | Risk Assess | Information and Communication | Monitor | Period-End Reporting | Select Accounting Policies | Nonroutine Transactions |
| | | | ☐ | ☐ | ☐ | ☐ | ☐ | ☐ | ☐ | ☐ |
| | | | ☐ | ☐ | ☐ | ☐ | ☐ | ☐ | ☐ | ☐ |
| | | | ☐ | ☐ | ☐ | ☐ | ☐ | ☐ | ☐ | ☐ |
| | | | ☐ | ☐ | ☐ | ☐ | ☐ | ☐ | ☐ | ☐ |
| | | | ☐ | ☐ | ☐ | ☐ | ☐ | ☐ | ☐ | ☐ |
| | | | ☐ | ☐ | ☐ | ☐ | ☐ | ☐ | ☐ | ☐ |
| | | | ☐ | ☐ | ☐ | ☐ | ☐ | ☐ | ☐ | ☐ |

# SUMMARY OF INTERVIEWS
# MANAGEMENT

| Ref. | Management Team Member Interviewed | Date | Control Environment | | Risk Assess | Information and Communication | Entity-Level Control | | | Nonroutine Transactions |
|---|---|---|---|---|---|---|---|---|---|---|
| | | | Culture | Personnel | | | Monitor | Period-End Reporting | Select Accounting Policies | |
| | | | ☐ | | ☐ | ☐ | | | ☐ | ☐ |
| | | | ☐ | | ☐ | ☐ | | | ☐ | ☐ |
| | | | ☐ | | ☐ | ☐ | | | ☐ | ☐ |
| | | | ☐ | | ☐ | ☐ | | | ☐ | ☐ |
| | | | ☐ | | ☐ | ☐ | | | ☐ | ☐ |
| | | | ☐ | | ☐ | ☐ | | | ☐ | ☐ |
| | | | ☐ | | ☐ | ☐ | | | ☐ | ☐ |

# SUMMARY OF INTERVIEWS MANAGEMENT

| Ref. | Management Team Member Interviewed | Date | Control Environment | | Risk Assess | Information and Communication | Monitor | Period-End Reporting | Select Accounting Policies | Nonroutine Transactions |
|---|---|---|---|---|---|---|---|---|---|---|
| | | | Culture | Personnel | | | | | | |
| | | | ☐ | | | ☐ | | | ☐ | |
| | | | ☐ | | | ☐ | | | ☐ | |
| | | | ☐ | | | ☐ | | | ☐ | |
| | | | ☐ | | | ☐ | | | ☐ | |
| | | | ☐ | | | ☐ | | | ☐ | |
| | | | ☐ | | | ☐ | | | ☐ | |
| | | | ☐ | | | ☐ | | | ☐ | |

*Entity-Level Control*

## SUMMARY OF INTERVIEWS
## MANAGEMENT

| Ref. | Management Team Member Interviewed | Date | Control Environment | | Risk Assess | Information and Communication | Entity-Level Control | | | | Nonroutine Transactions |
|------|------|------|------|------|------|------|------|------|------|------|------|
| | | | Culture | Personnel | | | Monitor | Period-End Reporting | Select Accounting Policies | | |
| | | | ❑ | ❑ | | ❑ | | | | | |
| | | | ❑ | ❑ | | ❑ | | | | | |
| | | | ❑ | ❑ | | ❑ | | | | | |
| | | | ❑ | ❑ | | ❑ | | | | | |
| | | | ❑ | ❑ | | ❑ | | | | | |
| | | | ❑ | ❑ | | ❑ | | | | | |
| | | | ❑ | ❑ | | ❑ | | | | | |

# Entity-Level Tests of Operating Effectiveness: Inquiry Note Sheets—Management

## PURPOSE

This form has been designed to

- Help you prepare for an interview with management to assess the operating effectiveness of entity-level controls by providing you with example questions
- Document management's responses to your inquiries and your assessment of entity-level control operating effectiveness based on those responses

## INSTRUCTIONS

Part I of this form is example questions you may ask management to gather evidence supporting the operating effectiveness of entity-level controls. Generally, these questions are designed to gather information about the following.

- *Awareness.* Management's awareness and understanding of entity-level control policies and procedures will help determine their overall effectiveness. Individuals who are responsible for implementing these control policies and procedures may be ineffective if they possess only a rudimentary awareness (or none at all) of the policies' existence. On the other hand, when these individuals have an in-depth understanding of the policies and procedures, the control objectives they address, and the implications of control failure, implementation of the policies will be more effective. Formal, consistent, and regular communication of entity-level controls (including training) will improve awareness and understanding.
- *Attitude.* To be effective, management personnel should have a positive attitude toward internal control compliance. Negative attitudes can render good policies and procedures ineffective. Positive attitudes include the belief that the performance of control procedures is a priority and that adhering to stated control policies and procedures provides benefit to the organization.
- *Action.* The actions of management members should be consistent with stated policies and procedures.

   Part II of this form is a note sheet that you may use during your interview to document responses to your inquiries. Responses that provide evidence of the effective operation of controls should be separated from testing exceptions. Testing exceptions should be accumulated and evaluated to determine whether a control deficiency exists. You may use this form to take notes during your interview or to prepare a summary of your observations after the interview is completed.

*If you do not take notes contemporaneously with your interview, the documentation of your inquiries of management should be completed as soon as possible after the completion of the interview.*

## EXAMPLE QUESTIONS: MANAGEMENT (BOTH FINANCIAL AND NONFINANCIAL)

### *Control Environment—Culture*

#### ESTABLISH AND COMMUNICATE VALUES, NORMS, AND ACCEPTABLE BEHAVIORS THROUGHOUT THE ORGANIZATION

- What process was followed to develop the company's code of conduct?
- How often is the code reviewed and updated?
- What was the main reason for developing the code?
    - Has that objective been met?
        - -- If so, how can you tell?
        - -- If not, what have been the major barriers to achieving the objective?
- Have you participated in management discussions about the company's culture and "tone at the top" and how these affect the overall effectiveness of controls?
    - If so, what observations has management made?
    - If not, what prevents you from doing so?

#### TAKE ACTION TO REINFORCE STATED VALUES, NORMS, AND ACCEPTABLE BEHAVIORS

- If management becomes aware of an allegation of unacceptable behavior, what is the process for investigating the matter?
    - Do you have any specific examples?
        - -- How was the action of management in this matter perceived by the employees?
- What was the process followed to implement the requirements of section 302 of the Sarbanes-Oxley Act relating to the establishment of procedures for the anonymous reporting by employees of concerns regarding questionable accounting or auditing matters?
    - Do you have specific examples of how management has followed up on these concerns?
- Has management identified compensation policies or other incentives that may motivate unethical behavior by employees?
    - If so, what are they? How do you monitor these policies for possible unintended consequences?
    - If not, why not? What criteria are considered when setting incentive policies and programs?

- Have you become aware of any control deficiencies in the last three years?
  - How did you become aware?
  - What action was taken?

## *Control Environment—Entity Personnel*

### THE COMPANY'S ORGANIZATIONAL STRUCTURE FACILITATES THE EFFECTIVE FUNCTIONING OF INTERNAL CONTROL

- How did management determine the overall organization's structure for the company?
  - When was the last time the structure was reviewed for continued relevance and effectiveness?
  - How do you determine that the structure is effective?
  - How are internal control and financial reporting matters considered when evaluating the company's organizational structure?
- Is there a formal process used to determine which responsibilities should be delegated to lower levels?
  - How do you ensure that responsibility, authority, and accountability are linked and delegated together as a unit?
  - How do you provide for an adequate segregation of duties?

### HUMAN RESOURCE (HR) POLICIES CONTRIBUTE TO A CULTURE THAT IS COMMITTED TO COMPETENCE

- What is the process for determining the resources that are necessary for employees to perform their responsibilities effectively? Resources include
  - Training
  - Budget/funding
  - Personnel
  - Supervision and feedback
- Once management decides to pursue a certain strategy, what is the process for determining the human resource needs required to implement the strategy? Consider
  - Number of people needed
  - Required skills or competencies
  - Experience level
  - Training
- How successful has the company been at attracting and retaining the right number of qualified people necessary to achieve its goals? Which HR policies and programs have been most responsible for the company's success (or lack of success) in this area?

## *Control Environment—Overall Conclusion*

### OPINION ABOUT EFFECTIVENESS OF THE CONTROL ENVIRONMENT

- Do you believe that the company has established standards of behavior and a "tone at the top" that creates an effective control environment, one that reflects an appropriate level of control consciousness within the organization?
  - What have you observed that leads you to this conclusion?

## *Risk Assessment*

### DISCUSSION OF THE RISK ASSESSMENT PROCESS

- Describe the process used to identify the most significant business risks facing the company.
  - Who is involved in the process?
  - What criteria are used to determine the relative significance of the risks?
- How does the company decide how to manage identified risks?
- How is the board of directors involved in the risk management process?
  - What concerns and issues have they raised recently about the risks facing the entity?

### CHANGE MANAGEMENT AND THE ABILITY
### TO IDENTIFY NEW RISKS FACING THE COMPANY

- In the past three years, what have been the most significant changes to the company, its operations, or the business environment in which it operates?
  - What financial reporting challenges did these changes create?
  - Did management anticipate these challenges?
  - How quickly were you able to incorporate these changes into your financial reporting process?

## *Information and Communications*

### RECEIPT OF TIMELY, RELIABLE, AND COMPLETE INFORMATION

- What financial information do you rely on to manage the company/business unit/department? How do you use this information?
- Do you receive all the information needed to perform your job effectively?
  - If so, is it reliable? Timely?
  - If not, what is missing?

## *Systemwide Monitoring*

### DISCUSSION OF MANAGEMENT'S INVOLVEMENT IN MONITORING INTERNAL CONTROL EFFECTIVENESS AND TAKING CORRECTIVE ACTION

- How does management
  - Obtain information on internal control effectiveness (e.g., from external or internal auditors)
  - Obtain confirmation from employees on their regular compliance with stated policies
- How often do you obtain this information?
- How confident are you that this information is
  - Accurate
  - Complete
  - Timely
- What steps does management take to
  - Understand the internal control implications of errors in the company's financial statements or accounting records
  - Understand the underlying causes for identified internal control deficiencies
  - Take appropriate corrective action in response to identified deficiencies

### *Nonroutine Transactions*

### DESCRIBE RECENT SIGNIFICANT NONROUTINE TRANSACTIONS AND THE RELATED CONTROLS OVER THE ACCOUNTING FOR AND REPORTING OF THESE TRANSACTIONS

- What significant nonroutine transactions has the company entered into in the last year?
  - What was the business purpose of the transactions?
  - What procedures were followed to review the transactions and authorize their consummation?
  - How did the company decide on the proper accounting, reporting, and disclosure of these transactions?

# ADDITIONAL QUESTIONS FOR FINANCIAL MANAGEMENT

## *Period-End Financial Reporting Processes*

### CONTROLS OVER JOURNAL ENTRIES

- How would an inappropriate journal entry be detected if it was posted to the system (or an attempt was made to post it to the system?)

### CONTROLS OVER NONROUTINE TRANSACTIONS

- What is the process for structuring nonsystematic, nonroutine transactions?
  - What is driving these transactions, for example, are they necessary to
    -- Implement the entity's strategic plan
    -- Achieve forecasted financial results
  - At what point in the process does management receive input on the accounting treatment of these transactions?
    -- Who provides this input?
    -- What is the type and significance of the input received from external auditors?
  - What factors does the board consider when reviewing and approving these transactions?

### CONTROLS OVER ACCOUNTING ESTIMATES

- What process does the entity follow for making its most significant accounting estimates?
  - How is information relating to the underlying assumptions gathered?
  - How do you know the information is reliable?
  - What factors are considered when making significant assumptions about the estimate?
  - How is senior management and the board involved in the review and approval of significant estimates?
    -- In the company's most recent financial reporting cycle, what were the most significant issues raised by senior management or the board regarding the estimates or the estimation process?

## CONTROLS OVER THE PREPARATION
## OF THE FINANCIAL STATEMENTS

- Who has the primary responsibility for drafting the financial statements?
- Who else participates in the process?
  - What is the type and significance of the input received from the external auditors?

### *Selection and Application of Accounting Policies*

## CONTROLS OVER THE SELECTION AND APPLICATION
## OF ACCOUNTING POLICIES

- Describe the conversations you have had with the independent auditors regarding the quality of the entity's accounting principles?
  - What actions did the board take as a result of those discussions?
- What is the process used by management to
  - Identify emerging accounting issues or other circumstances or events that may require a consideration of accounting policies
  - Choose appropriate accounting policies

---

# NOTE SHEET
# INQUIRIES OF MANAGEMENT

Company: _____        Reporting Date: _____

Prepared by: _____        Date Prepared: _____

# ALL MANAGEMENT PERSONNEL

| Topic of Discussion | Evidence of Control Effectiveness | | | Testing Exception |
|---|---|---|---|---|
| | Awareness | Attitude | Action | |
| *Control Environment* | | | | |
| Establish, communicate values, norms, acceptable behavior<br>• Develop code of conduct.<br>• Discuss culture. | | | | |
| Action to reinforce policies<br>• Allegations of unacceptable behavior, questionable accounting practices.<br>• Review of and response to incentives that may motivate unethical behavior.<br>• Correction of control deficiencies. | | | | |
| Organizational structure facilitates internal control effectiveness.<br>• Consider financial reporting and control when determining organizational structure.<br>• Delegate responsibilities. | | | | |
| HR policies and commitment to competence<br>• Provide resources to employees.<br>• Identify number and type of people necessary to achieve objectives.<br>• HR policies allow company to attract and retain right number of qualified people. | | | | |
| Overall opinion on control environment effectiveness<br>• Standards of behavior and tone at top create appropriate level of control consciousness. | | | | |

| Topic of Discussion | Evidence of Control Effectiveness | | | Testing Exception |
|---|---|---|---|---|
| | **Awareness** | **Attitude** | **Action** | **Testing Exception** |
| *Risk Assessment* | | | | |
| Description of the risk assessment process<br>• Identification of risk<br>• Risk management strategies<br>• Active involvement of the board | | | | |
| Change management<br>• Identification of changes to business that create financial reporting challenges.<br>• Ability to make timely changes to financial reporting process and controls. | | | | |
| *Information and Communication* | | | | |
| Use of financial information to manage business | | | | |
| Adequate communication of information necessary to perform job<br>• Reliably<br>• Timely<br>• Completely | | | | |
| *Monitoring* | | | | |
| Management monitors internal control effectiveness and takes action.<br>• Establish a process for periodically gathering information on internal control effectiveness.<br>• Analyze and assess information received.<br>• Take appropriate corrective action. | | | | |

| Topic of Discussion | Evidence of Control Effectiveness | | | Testing Exception |
|---|---|---|---|---|
| | Awareness | Attitude | Action | |
| *Nonroutine Transactions* | | | | |
| Description of nonroutine transactions<br>• Description of transaction<br>• How transaction was reviewed and authorized<br>• Process for determining proper accounting and reporting | | | | |

## FINANCIAL MANAGEMENT

| Topic of Discussion | Evidence of Control Effectiveness | | | Testing Exception |
|---|---|---|---|---|
| | Awareness | Attitude | Action | |
| *Period-End Financial Reporting* | | | | |
| Controls over journal entries <br> • Detection of inappropriate journal entries | | | | |
| Controls over nonroutine transactions <br> • Process for structuring transactions <br> • How and when accounting treatment is considered <br> • Extent and significance of external auditor input <br> • Board involvement | | | | |
| Controls over accounting estimates <br> • Estimation process <br> • Involvement of senior management and board in reviewing estimates | | | | |
| Controls over the preparation of the financial statements <br> • Primary responsibility for drafting the financial statements <br> • Type and significance of external auditor involvement | | | | |
| *Selection and Application of Accounting Policies* | | | | |
| Controls over the selection and application of accounting policies <br> • Discussions with auditors regarding quality of accounting principles <br> • Management's actions in response to these discussions <br> • Process for choosing appropriate accounting policies | | | | |

# Entity-Level Tests of Operating Effectiveness: Inquiry Note Sheets—Board Members

## PURPOSE

This form has been designed to

- Help you prepare for an interview with board members to assess the operating effectiveness of entity-level controls by providing you with example questions
- Document the board member's responses to your inquiries and your assessment of entity-level control operating effectiveness based on those responses

## INSTRUCTIONS

Part I of this form is example questions you may ask management to gather evidence supporting the operating effectiveness of entity-level controls. Generally, these questions are designed to gather information about the following.

- *Awareness.* The board of directors' awareness and understanding of entity-level control policies and procedures will help determine their overall effectiveness. Individuals who are responsible for implementing these control policies and procedures may be ineffective if they possess only a rudimentary awareness (or none at all) of the policies' existence. On the other hand, when these individuals have an in-depth understanding of the policies and procedures, the control objectives they address, and the implications of control failure, implementation of the policies will be more effective. Formal, consistent, and regular communication of entity-level controls (including training) will improve awareness and understanding.
- *Attitude.* To be effective, management personnel and the board should have a positive attitude toward internal control compliance. Negative attitudes can render good policies and procedures ineffective. Positive attitudes include the belief that the performance of control procedures is a priority and that adhering to stated control policies and procedures provides benefit to the organization.
- *Action.* The actions of management and the board should be consistent with stated policies and procedures.

Part II of this form is a note sheet that you may use during your interview to document responses to your inquiries. Responses that provide evidence of the effective operation of controls should be separated from testing exceptions. Testing exceptions should be accumulated and evaluated to determine whether a control deficiency exists. You may use this form to take notes during your interview or to prepare a summary of your observations after the interview is completed.

*If you do not take notes contemporaneously with your interview, the documentation of your inquiries of management should be completed as soon as possible after the completion of the interview.*

## EXAMPLE QUESTIONS

### *Control Environment—Culture*

#### ESTABLISH AND COMMUNICATE VALUES, NORMS, AND ACCEPTABLE BEHAVIORS THROUGHOUT THE ORGANIZATION

- Have you read the company's code of conduct?
  - Do you believe it helps management and employees identify unacceptable business practices and behaviors?
- Have you participated in management discussions about the company's culture and "tone at the top" and how these affect the overall effectiveness of controls?
  - If so, what observations has management made?
  - If not, what prevents you from doing so?

#### TAKING ACTION TO REINFORCE STATED VALUES, NORMS, AND ACCEPTABLE BEHAVIORS

- If the board becomes aware of an allegation of unacceptable behavior, what is the process for investigating the matter?
  - Are you provided with sufficient and timely information on these allegations?
  - Do you have any specific examples of the board's involvement with an allegation of unacceptable behavior?
    -- What action did management take in this matter?
- What was the board's involvement with implementing the requirements of section 302 of the Sarbanes-Oxley Act relating to the establishment of procedures for the anonymous reporting by employees of concerns regarding questionable accounting or auditing matters?
  - Do you have specific examples of how management has followed up on these concerns?
- Have you become aware of any control deficiencies in the last three years?
  - How did you become aware?
  - What action was taken?

## BOARD STRUCTURE AND OVERSIGHT OF MANAGEMENT

- How do board members monitor and retain their independence from management?
- Are board members sufficiently independent that necessary questions are raised, even if the questions are difficult and probing?
  - What are some examples of these types of questions that have been raised recently?
- How does the board acquire and maintain an appropriate level of financial expertise?

## *Control Environment—Overall Conclusion*

## *Opinion about the Effectiveness of the Control Environment*

- Do you believe that the company has established standards of behavior and a "tone at the top" that creates an effective control environment, one that reflects an appropriate level of control consciousness within the organization?

## *Risk Assessment*

## BOARD INVOLVEMENT WITH THE RISK ASSESSMENT PROCESS

- How is the board of directors involved in the risk management process?
  - What concerns and issues have they raised recently about the risks facing the entity?

## *Information and Communication*

- Do you receive all the information needed to monitor management's objectives and strategies, the entity's financial position and operating results, and terms of significant agreements?
  - If so, is this information reliable? Timely? Sufficient?
  - If not, what is missing?

## *Selection and Application of Accounting Policies*

## CONTROLS OVER THE SELECTION AND APPLICATION OF ACCOUNTING POLICIES

- Describe the conversations the board has had with the independent auditors regarding the quality of the entity's accounting policies.
  - What actions did the board take as a result of those discussions?

## *Antifraud Programs and Controls*

### SPECIFIC KNOWLEDGE OF FRAUD

- Are you aware of any fraud or suspected fraud affecting the entity?
  - If so, describe
    - -- What happened
    - -- Who was involved
    - -- How it was discovered
    - -- How the company responded

### *Nonroutine Transactions*

### BOARD AWARENESS OF AND INVOLVEMENT WITH NONROUTINE TRANSACTIONS

- What significant nonroutine transactions has the company entered into in the last year?
  - What was the business purpose of the transactions?
  - What procedures were followed to review the transactions and authorize their consummation?
- To what extent was the board involved in the review and approval of
  - The transaction
  - The accounting for and reporting of the transaction

---

# NOTE SHEET INQUIRIES OF BOARD MEMBERS

Company: _____    Reporting Date: _____

Prepared by: _____    Date Prepared: _____

| Topic of Discussion | Evidence of Control Effectiveness | | | Testing Exception |
|---|---|---|---|---|
| | Awareness | Attitude | Action | |
| *Control Environment* | | | | |
| Establish and communicate values, norms, and acceptable behaviors.<br>• Reading of code of conduct<br>• Effectiveness of code of conduct | | | | |

| Topic of Discussion | Evidence of Control Effectiveness | | | Testing Exception |
|---|---|---|---|---|
| | Awareness | Attitude | Action | |
| *Control Environment* | | | | |
| • Board discussions on company culture | | | | |
| Take action to reinforce stated values, norms, and acceptable behaviors.<br>• Process for investigating allegations of unacceptable behavior<br>• Board involvement with procedures for investigating concerns about questionable accounting matters<br>• Board response to identified control deficiencies | | | | |
| Board structure and oversight of management<br>• Maintain independence.<br>• Board members ask difficult and probing questions of management.<br>• Maintain appropriate level of financial expertise. | | | | |
| Opinion about effectiveness of control environment<br>• Establishment of standards of behavior and tone at top that creates effective control environment | | | | |
| *Information and Communication* | | | | |
| Adequate communication of information necessary to perform job<br>• Reliably<br>• Timely<br>• Completely | | | | |

| Topic of Discussion | Evidence of Control Effectiveness | | | Testing Exception |
|---|---|---|---|---|
| | Awareness | Attitude | Action | |
| *Risk Assessment* | | | | |
| Board involvement with risk assessment process<br>• Process for ensuring board's involvement<br>• Board concerns about risks facing the company | | | | |
| *Selection and Application of Accounting Policies* | | | | |
| Board involvement with the selection and application of accounting policies<br>• Discussions regarding quality of accounting policies<br>• Board response to these discussions | | | | |
| *Antifraud Programs and Controls* | | | | |
| Specific knowledge of fraud<br>• Awareness of any fraud or suspected fraud at the entity<br>• If so, provide details | | | | |
| *Nonroutine Transactions* | | | | |
| Board awareness and involvement with nonroutine transactions<br>• Description of significant nonroutine transactions<br>• Board review and approval of transaction<br>• Board review and approval of related accounting and reporting | | | | |

# Entity-Level Tests of Operating Effectiveness: Inquiry Note Sheets—Audit Committee Members

## PURPOSE

This form has been designed to

- Help you prepare for an interview with audit committee members to assess the operating effectiveness of entity-level controls by providing you with example questions
- Document the audit committee members' responses to your inquiries and your assessment of entity-level control operating effectiveness based on those responses

## INSTRUCTIONS

Part I of this form is example questions you may ask management to gather evidence supporting the operating effectiveness of entity-level controls. Generally, these questions are designed to gather information about the following.

- *Awareness.* The audit committee's awareness and understanding of entity-level control policies and procedures will help determine their overall effectiveness. Individuals who are responsible for implementing these control policies and procedures may be ineffective if they possess only a rudimentary awareness (or none at all) of the policies' existence. On the other hand, when these individuals have an in-depth understanding of the policies and procedures, the control objectives they address, and the implications of control failure, implementation of the policies will be more effective. Formal, consistent, and regular communication of entity-level controls (including training) will improve awareness and understanding.
- *Attitude.* To be effective, management personnel and the audit committee should have a positive attitude toward internal control compliance. Negative attitudes can render good policies and procedures ineffective. Positive attitudes include the belief that the performance of control procedures is a priority and that adhering to stated control policies and procedures provides benefit to the organization.
- *Action.* The actions of management and the board should be consistent with stated policies and procedures.

Part II of this form is a note sheet that you may use during your interview to document responses to your inquiries. Responses that provide evidence of the effective operation of controls should be separated from testing exceptions. Testing exceptions should be accumulated and evaluated to determine whether a control deficiency exists. You may use this form to take notes during your interview or to prepare a summary of your observations after the interview is completed.

*If you do not take notes contemporaneously with your interview, the documentation of your inquiries of management should be completed as soon as possible after the completion of the interview.*

## EXAMPLE QUESTIONS

### Control Environment—Culture

#### TAKING ACTION TO REINFORCE STATED VALUES, NORMS, AND ACCEPTABLE BEHAVIORS

- What was the audit committee's involvement with implementing the requirements of section 302 of the Sarbanes-Oxley Act relating to the establishment of procedures for the anonymous reporting by employees of concerns regarding questionable accounting or auditing matters?
    - Do you have specific examples of how management and the audit committee have followed up on these concerns?
- Have you become aware of any control deficiencies in the last three years?
    - How did you become aware?
    - What action was taken?

### Information and Communication

- Do you receive all the information needed to carry out your responsibilities?
    - If so, is this information reliable? Timely? Sufficient?
    - If not, what is missing?

### Selection and Application of Accounting Policies

#### CONTROLS OVER THE SELECTION AND APPLICATION OF ACCOUNTING POLICIES

- What discussions has the audit committee had in the past year regarding
    - The initial selection and application of significant accounting policies
    - Subsequent changes to the selection of significant accounting policies
    - Subsequent changes to the application of significant accounting policies
    - The methods used to account for significant unusual transactions
    - The effect of significant accounting policies in controversial or emerging areas

- Do you believe that the audit committee is well informed of these matters?
    - If so, what steps are taken to ensure that you remain well informed?
    - If not, how could the process for informing the audit committee of matters affecting the selection or application of accounting policies be improved?
- Describe the conversations the audit committee has had with the independent auditors regarding the quality of the entity's accounting policies?
    - What actions did the board take as a result of those discussions?

## *Audit Committee Oversight*

### AUDIT COMMITTEE STRUCTURE AND OVERSIGHT OF MANAGEMENT

- How do audit committee members monitor and retain their independence from management?
- Are audit committee members sufficiently independent that necessary, even if difficult and probing, questions are raised?
    - What are some examples of these types of questions that have been raised recently?
- How does the audit committee acquire and maintain an appropriate level of financial expertise?

### UNDERSTANDING OF RESPONSIBILITIES

- How were your responsibilities as an audit committee member communicated to you?
- Do you believe that you have a sufficient understanding of these responsibilities?
    - If so, what steps did the company take to ensure that you obtained this understanding?
    - If not, how could the process for informing audit committee members of their responsibilities be improved?

### ACTIVE INVOLVEMENT OF THE AUDIT COMMITTEE IN SIGNIFICANT MATTERS

- In the past year, what significant issues has the committee become involved with? Consider
    - Internal control matters
    - Financial reporting matters
    - Antifraud processes and controls
- How would you describe the interactions the audit committee has with
    - The company's external auditors
    - Internal auditors
    - Key members of financial management

## *Antifraud Programs and Controls*

### SPECIFIC KNOWLEDGE OF FRAUD

- Are you aware of any fraud or suspected fraud affecting the entity?
  - If so, describe
    - -- What happened
    - -- Who was involved
    - -- How it was discovered
    - -- How the company responded

---

# NOTE SHEET INQUIRIES OF AUDIT COMMITTEE MEMBERS

Company: _____     Reporting Date: _____

Prepared by: _____     Date Prepared: _____

| | Evidence of Control Effectiveness | | | |
|---|---|---|---|---|
| **Topic of Discussion** | **Awareness** | **Attitude** | **Action** | **Testing Exception** |
| *Control Environment* | | | | |
| Action to reinforce stated values, norms, and acceptable behaviors<br>• Procedures for reporting by employees of concerns regarding questionable accounting matters and subsequent follow-up by management<br>• Audit committee awareness of control deficiencies<br>• Audit committee involvement in correcting control deficiencies | | | | |
| *Information and Communication* | | | | |
| Adequate communication of information necessary to perform job<br>• Reliable<br>• Timely<br>• Complete | | | | |

| Topic of Discussion | Evidence of Control Effectiveness | | | | |
|---|---|---|---|---|---|
| | Awareness | Attitude | Action | Testing Exception |
| *Selection and Application of Accounting Policies* | | | | |
| Audit committee involvement in the selection and application of accounting policies<br>• Initial selection and application<br>• Subsequent changes to selection or application<br>• Accounting for unusual transactions<br>• Accounting in controversial or emerging areas<br>• Conversations with auditors and subsequent response by company on quality of accounting policies | | | | |
| *Audit Committee Oversight* | | | | |
| Audit committee structure<br>• Maintain independence.<br>• Ask difficult and probing questions.<br>• Maintain financial expertise. | | | | |

| Topic of Discussion | Evidence of Control Effectiveness | | | |
| --- | --- | --- | --- | --- |
| | Awareness | Attitude | Action | Testing Exception |
| Understanding responsibilities<br>• Establish process for communicating responsibilities to audit committee members.<br>• Audit committee members have good understanding of their responsibilities. | | | | |
| Active involvement in significant matters<br>• Internal control<br>• Financial reporting<br>• Antifraud<br>• Interactions with external and internal auditors and financial management | | | | |
| *Antifraud Programs and Controls* | | | | |
| Specific knowledge of fraud<br>• Awareness of any fraud or suspected fraud at the entity<br>• If so, provide details | | | | |

# Entity-Level Tests of Operating Effectiveness: Inquiry Note Sheets—Employees

## PURPOSE

This form has been designed to

- Help you prepare for an interview with financial and nonfinancial employees to assess the operating effectiveness of entity-level controls by providing you with example questions
- Document the employees' responses to your inquiries and your assessment of entity-level control operating effectiveness based on those responses

## INSTRUCTIONS

Included in this form are example questions you may ask employees to gather evidence supporting the operating effectiveness of entity-level controls. Generally, these questions are designed to gather information about the following.

- *Awareness.* Company personnel awareness and understanding of entity-level control policies and procedures will help determine their overall effectiveness. Individuals who are responsible for following these control policies and procedures may do so ineffectively if they possess only a rudimentary awareness (or none at all) of the policies' existence. On the other hand, when these individuals have an in-depth understanding of the policies and procedures, the control objectives they address, and the implications of control failure, implementation of the policies will be more effective. Formal, consistent, and regular communication of entity-level controls (including training) will improve awareness and understanding.
- *Attitude.* For controls to be effective, company personnel should have a positive attitude toward compliance. Negative attitudes can render good policies and procedures ineffective. Positive attitudes include the belief that the performance of control procedures is a priority and that adhering to stated control policies and procedures provides benefit to the organization.
- *Action.* The actions of management members should be consistent with stated policies and procedures. Company personnel often are able to observe management actions and comment on the message such actions convey.

This form also includes a note sheet that you may use during your interview to document responses to your inquiries. Responses that provide evidence of the effective operation of controls should be separated from testing exceptions. Testing exceptions should be accumulated and evaluated to determine whether a control deficiency exists. You may use this form to take notes during your interview or to prepare a summary of your observations after the interview is completed.

*If you do not take notes contemporaneously with your interview, the documentation of your inquiries of management should be completed as soon as possible after the completion of the interview.*

## EXAMPLE QUESTIONS

### Control Environment—Culture

#### UNDERSTANDING AND ATTITUDES TOWARD THE COMPANY'S CODE OF CONDUCT

- Have you read the company's code of conduct?
  - If so, then do you find that it helps you identify unacceptable business practices and behaviors?
  - If not, why not?
- What happens (or what do you think will happen) if you observe unacceptable behavior on the job and report it to a member of senior management? Will the matter be investigated promptly? Thoroughly?
- What happens (or what do you think will happen) if someone raises concerns regarding questionable accounting or auditing matters? Will the matter be investigated promptly? Thoroughly?
- Are people in the company who demonstrate a commitment to high ethical standards of behavior rewarded (e.g., through compensation or advancement)?
- Are people who act in an unethical manner punished (e.g., through diminished compensation, lack of advancement, or termination)?

#### OBSERVABLE ACTIONS THAT REINFORCE OR CONTRADICT STATED VALUES, NORMS, AND ACCEPTABLE BEHAVIORS

- In the last three years, have you been asked by someone senior to you to take action that would be considered unethical?
- Do you know anyone at the company who, in the last three years, has been asked by someone senior to them to take action that would be considered unethical?
- For the most part, do company employees act in an ethical manner?
- For the most part, does company management act in an ethical manner? Do they set a good example of ethical behavior?

## *Control Environment—Personnel Policies*

### UNDERSTANDING OF JOB RESPONSIBILITIES AND APPROPRIATE SUPERVISION AND FEEDBACK

- Have your job responsibilities been communicated to you? How?
- Do you believe that you have a good understanding of your job responsibilities?
- Do you know how your performance will be evaluated?
- Does the feedback you receive on your job performance help you improve?
- Does the training you receive improve your job performance?

### AVAILABILITY OF RESOURCES TO PERFORM ASSIGNED DUTIES

- Have you been delegated the decision-making authority necessary to effectively perform your job?
- For the most part, have you been provided with the following resources necessary to perform your job effectively?
  - Budget/funding
  - Personnel
  - Supervisory guidance

## *Control Environment—Overall Conclusion*

### OPINION ABOUT EFFECTIVENESS OF CONTROL ENVIRONMENT

- Are there any other aspects of the company's culture or management policies that contribute to or detract from your performing your job effectively? If a family member or friend were considering employment at this company and asked, "What's it like working there?" how would you respond?

## *Information and Communication*

### RECEIPT OF TIMELY, RELIABLE, AND COMPLETE INFORMATION

- Is the information you need to perform your job communicated to you
  - Accurately
  - In a timely fashion
  - Completely

## *Antifraud Programs and Controls*

### KNOWLEDGE OF ANY FRAUD

- Are you aware of any fraud or suspected fraud affecting the entity?
  - If so, describe
    - -- What happened
    - -- Who was involved
    - -- How it was discovered
    - -- How the company responded

---

## NOTE SHEET
## INQUIRIES OF EMPLOYEES

Company: _____     Reporting Date: _____

Prepared by: _____     Date Prepared: _____

| | Evidence of Control Effectiveness | | | |
| --- | --- | --- | --- | --- |
| Topic of Discussion | Awareness | Attitude | Action | Testing Exception |
| *Control Environment* | | | | |
| Understanding and attitudes about stated values, norms, and acceptable behaviors<br>• Understanding of code of conduct<br>• Perceived consequences of unacceptable behavior<br>• Rewards and punishments for compliance with stated policies | | | | |
| Observable actions that reinforce or contradict stated values, norms, and acceptable behaviors<br>• Knowledge of management asking employee to take action considered unethical<br>• Perception of whether employees act ethically<br>• Perception of whether management acts ethically | | | | |

| Topic of Discussion | Evidence of Control Effectiveness | | | |
| --- | --- | --- | --- | --- |
| | Awareness | Attitude | Action | Testing Exception |
| Understanding job responsibilities<br>• Responsibilities have been communicated.<br>• Responsibilities are well understood.<br>• Performance is evaluated.<br>• Effective training is in place. | | | | |
| Availability of resources<br>• Delegation of authority<br>• Budget/financing<br>• Personnel<br>• Supervisory guidance | | | | |
| Overall opinion on control environment effectiveness<br>• Company culture or policies that contribute to or detract from job performance | | | | |
| *Information and Communication* | | | | |
| Adequate communication of information necessary to perform job<br>• Reliable<br>• Timely<br>• Complete | | | | |

| | Evidence of Control Effectiveness | | | |
|---|---|---|---|---|
| **Topic of Discussion** | **Awareness** | **Attitude** | **Action** | **Testing Exception** |
| *Antifraud Programs and Controls* | | | | |
| Specific knowledge of fraud<br>• Awareness of any fraud or suspected fraud at the entity<br>• If so, provide details | | | | |

# Example Employee Survey[1]

## PURPOSE

This example has been provided to help you

- Conduct a survey of employees to gather information about the operating effectiveness of entity-level controls
- Evaluate the results of those surveys

## INSTRUCTIONS

There are three separate tools that will help you in conducting employee surveys related to the operating effectiveness of entity-level controls. Included are

- Example Letter to Employees in Advance of Employee Survey
- Example Employee Survey of Corporate Culture and Personnel Policies
- Evaluation of Employee Survey Results

Each example provides a separate set of instructions for its use.

## EXAMPLE LETTER TO EMPLOYEES IN ADVANCE OF EMPLOYEE SURVEY

## INSTRUCTIONS

- This letter should be sent out a week or two in advance of sending the actual employee survey. The purpose of the letter is to prepare the employees for its arrival and to encourage them to complete it as soon as possible.
- The letter assumes that *all* employees will receive a survey. If that is not the case, then the letter should explain how the individual employee was selected; for example, "We are sending the survey to 50 percent of all our employees and management. Your name has been selected at random."
- To convey a proper sense of urgency and importance to the completion of the survey, the letter should be signed by a member of senior management, for example, the CEO.

---

[1] *These tools originally were published in a slightly different form in* How to Comply with Sarbanes-Oxley Section 404, *by Michael Ramos, published by John Wiley & Sons (2004).*

## EXAMPLE LETTER TO EMPLOYEES IN ADVANCE OF EMPLOYEE SURVEY

Dear _____,

We are required by law to annually review and report on the policies and procedures we use to manage and control our company. The scope of this review is quite broad and includes evaluating not just individual tasks you perform in your daily work assignments but also the environment in which you perform those assignments.

To help us perform our review we are conducting a survey of all employees to obtain their observations about the way in which our company is managed. Within the next two weeks you will be receiving this survey. We have tried hard to balance our need for comprehensive feedback with everyone's desire to keep the survey as short as possible. We believe we have reached a suitable compromise.

I urge you to complete this survey and return it as soon as possible to _____ _____. Your prompt attention to this matter is important, not only because it will allow us to comply with certain legal requirements, but also because it will help us to continually improve our management practices. All individual responses to the questionnaire will be kept strictly confidential.

/s/ Chief Executive Officer

---

## EXAMPLE EMPLOYEE SURVEY OF CORPORATE CULTURE AND PERSONNEL POLICIES

### INSTRUCTIONS

- Included with the example survey is a cover sheet to the employee/respondent, which explains the purpose of the survey, how to fill it out, and confidentiality policies.
- If you are an outside consultant who has been engaged by the company to conduct the survey, you should print the survey on your letterhead, as this will reinforce the message that responses are confidential and encourage more candid responses.
- All responses should be returned directly to you.
- Questions 4 through 9 make reference to "high ethical standards" and personal ethics, which may introduce an element of unreliability to the survey because what may be unacceptable to one person may be acceptable to another. Alternatively, the questions may be reworded to refer to the company's stated ethical policies or values. However, if you choose to refer to company policies in these questions, you should include these policies as part of the survey. Without easy, immediate access to the company's stated policies, most individuals will not be able to respond to the statement.
- The example behaviors listed in question 18 have been deliberately worded in a way that makes them all seem positive. If negative behaviors are noted in response to this question, then this could indicate the strong presence of negative elements in the entity's control environment. The question leads the respondent to consider only positive char-

acteristics. If the employee makes note of negative characteristics, it is probably because these characteristics have made a strong impression on the respondent.

# EXAMPLE SURVEY OF EMPLOYEES

## Purpose of the Survey

By law, XYZ Company is required to review and report on the policies and procedures used to manage and control the company. The scope of this review is broad and includes an evaluation of the overall environment in which individual employees perform their assigned responsibilities.

The purpose of this survey is to obtain input from all employees on how the company is managed.

## Confidentiality

Individual responses will not be disclosed. All responses will be evaluated as a group and reported to company management in a summarized fashion.

## Instructions

Please respond by indicating the degree to which you agree or disagree with the statements presented. When you are done, please mail your completed questionnaire to _____. A self-addressed, stamped envelope has been provided for your convenience.

## Survey of the Employees of ABC Corporation

| ETHICAL VALUES | Strongly Disagree | Disagree | Neither Agree nor Disagree | Agree | Strongly Agree |
|---|---|---|---|---|---|
| 1. I have read the company's code of conduct. | ❑ | ❑ | ❑ | ❑ | ❑ |
| 2. The company's code of conduct helps me identify unacceptable business practices. | ❑ | ❑ | ❑ | ❑ | ❑ |
| 3. If I observe unacceptable behavior on the job and report it to a member of the management team, I believe that the matter will be investigated. | ❑ | ❑ | ❑ | ❑ | ❑ |

| | Strongly Disagree | Disagree | Neither Agree nor Disagree | Agree | Strongly Agree |
|---|---|---|---|---|---|
| 4. I believe that people who demonstrate a commitment to high ethical standards of behavior will be rewarded (e.g., through compensation or advancement). | ❑ | ❑ | ❑ | ❑ | ❑ |
| 5. I believe that people who act in an unethical manner will be punished (e.g., through diminished compensation, lack of advancement, or termination). | ❑ | ❑ | ❑ | ❑ | ❑ |
| 6. In the last three years, I have been asked by someone senior to me to take action that would be considered unethical. | ❑ | ❑ | ❑ | ❑ | ❑ |
| 7. I know someone at the company who, in the last three years, has been asked by someone senior to them to take action that would be considered unacceptable. | ❑ | ❑ | ❑ | ❑ | ❑ |
| 8. For the most part, company employees act in an ethical manner. | ❑ | ❑ | ❑ | ❑ | ❑ |
| 9. For the most part, company management acts in an ethical manner. | ❑ | ❑ | ❑ | ❑ | ❑ |

**PERSONNEL POLICIES**

| | Strongly Disagree | Disagree | Neither Agree nor Disagree | Agree | Strongly Agree |
|---|---|---|---|---|---|
| 10. My job responsibilities have been communicated to me. | ❑ | ❑ | ❑ | ❑ | ❑ |

| ETHICAL VALUES | Strongly Disagree | Disagree | Neither Agree nor Disagree | Agree | Strongly Agree |
|---|---|---|---|---|---|
| 11. I understand my job responsibilities. | ❑ | ❑ | ❑ | ❑ | ❑ |
| 12. The criteria for assessing my performance have been communicated to me. | ❑ | ❑ | ❑ | ❑ | ❑ |
| 13. The feedback I receive on my performance helps me improve. | ❑ | ❑ | ❑ | ❑ | ❑ |
| 14. The information I need to perform my job is communicated to me | | | | | |
| • Accurately | ❑ | ❑ | ❑ | ❑ | ❑ |
| • In a timely fashion | ❑ | ❑ | ❑ | ❑ | ❑ |
| • Completely | ❑ | ❑ | ❑ | ❑ | ❑ |
| 15. The training I receive helps me do a better job. | ❑ | ❑ | ❑ | ❑ | ❑ |
| 16. I have been delegated the decision-making authority necessary to effectively perform my job. | ❑ | ❑ | ❑ | ❑ | ❑ |
| 17. For the most part, I have been provided with the following resources necessary to perform my job effectively. | | | | | |
| • Budget/funding | ❑ | ❑ | ❑ | ❑ | ❑ |
| • Personnel | ❑ | ❑ | ❑ | ❑ | ❑ |
| • Supervisory guidance | ❑ | ❑ | ❑ | ❑ | ❑ |

## COMPANY VALUES

18. Please list the behaviors that are most frequently rewarded (see question 4 for example rewards). Example behaviors might include customer service, profit maximization, innovation, team building, cost reduction, or business expansion.

_____

_____

_____

_____

## OTHER

19. Please comment on any other aspect of the company's culture or management policies that contributes to or detracts from your job responsibilities effectively. If a family member or friend were considering employment at ABC Company and asked, "What's it like working there?" how would you respond?

_____

_____

_____

_____

## EVALUATION OF EMPLOYEE SURVEY RESULTS

## INSTRUCTIONS

The example employee survey groups questions into categories: company culture and personnel policies. However, note that question 14 also provides evidence of the operating effectiveness of the information and communication component of internal control. The survey is designed to gather information about the effectiveness of each of these entity-level controls in three different areas. These areas are

1. Awareness/understanding

2. Action

3. Attitude

The following form can be used to summarize the results of the survey. You should complete the form by

- Assigning a numeric value to each of the five possible responses, for example, "strongly agree" = 5, and "strongly disagree" = 1.
- Calculating an average value of the response for each question.
- Entering that average in the form in the space provided. Note that the form distinguishes the category (awareness, action, attitude) that the question was to address.

| | Average Response | | |
|---|---|---|---|
| | **Awareness** | **Action** | **Attitude** |
| **Ethical Values** | | | |
| 1. I have read the company's code of conduct. | | | |
| 2. The company's code of conduct helps me identify unacceptable business practices. | | | |
| 3. If I observe unacceptable behavior on the job and report it to a member of the management team, I believe that the matter will be investigated. | | | |
| 4. I believe that people who demonstrate a commitment to high ethical standards of behavior will be rewarded (e.g., through compensation or advancement). | | | |
| 5. I believe that people who act in an unethical manner will be punished (e.g., through diminished compensation, lack of advancement, or termination). | | | |
| 6. In the last three years, I have been asked by someone senior to me to take action that would be considered unethical. | | | |
| 7. I know someone at the company who, in the last three years, has been asked by someone senior to them to take action that would be considered unacceptable. | | | |
| 8. For the most part, company employees act in an ethical manner. | | | |
| 9. For the most part, company management acts in an ethical manner. | | | |

| | Average Response | | |
| --- | --- | --- | --- |
| | **Awareness** | **Action** | **Attitude** |
| **Personnel Policies** | | | |
| 10. My job responsibilities have been communicated to me. | | | |
| 11. I understand my job responsibilities. | | | |
| 12. The criteria for assessing my performance have been communicated to me. | | | |
| 13. The feedback I receive on my performance helps me improve. | | | |
| 14. The information I need to perform my job is communicated to me<br>• Accurately<br>• In a timely fashion<br>• Completely | | | |
| 15. The training I receive helps me do a better job. | | | |
| 16. I have been delegated the decision-making authority necessary to effectively perform my job. | | | |
| 17. For the most part, I have been provided with the following resources necessary to perform my job effectively.<br>• Budget/funding<br>• Personnel<br>• Supervisory guidance | | | |

# Index to Tests of Entity-Level Controls: Inspection of Documentation

## PURPOSE

This form has been designed to

- Summarize the extent of your inspection of documents and map these tests to the entity-level controls to which they relate
- Provide a centralized cross-reference to the documentation of the procedures performed and test results for entity-level controls

## INSTRUCTIONS

Provide a brief description of the document you inspected and enter this into the second column. In the first column, you should assign this item an identifying number as a way to cross-reference the reviewer to your description of the test performed and its results.

Check the appropriate boxes to indicate the entity-level control(s) to which the test relates. It is common for the inspection of one document to provide evidence about the operating effectiveness of more than one control.

To this index you should attach descriptions of the procedures performed and the results of those procedures. The form TST-ENT-4a may be used for this purpose. One form should be completed for each document or group of related documents reviewed.

| Ref. | Description | Control Environment | | Risk Assess | Information and Communication | Monitor | Period-End Reporting | Select Accounting Policies | Audit Committee | Antifraud | Nonroutine Transactions |
| | | Culture | Personnel | | | | | | | | |
| --- | --- | --- | --- | --- | --- | --- | --- | --- | --- | --- | --- |
| | | ☐ | ☐ | ☐ | ☐ | ☐ | ☐ | ☐ | ☐ | ☐ | ☐ |
| | | ☐ | ☐ | ☐ | ☐ | ☐ | ☐ | ☐ | ☐ | ☐ | ☐ |
| | | ☐ | ☐ | ☐ | ☐ | ☐ | ☐ | ☐ | ☐ | ☐ | ☐ |
| | | ☐ | ☐ | ☐ | ☐ | ☐ | ☐ | ☐ | ☐ | ☐ | ☐ |
| | | ☐ | ☐ | ☐ | ☐ | ☐ | ☐ | ☐ | ☐ | ☐ | ☐ |
| | | ☐ | ☐ | ☐ | ☐ | ☐ | ☐ | ☐ | ☐ | ☐ | ☐ |
| | | ☐ | ☐ | ☐ | ☐ | ☐ | ☐ | ☐ | ☐ | ☐ | ☐ |

*Entity-Level Control*

# Worksheet to Document Inspection of Documentation of Performance of Entity-Level Controls

## PURPOSE

This form has been designed to

- Facilitate your inspection of documentation that provides evidence of the performance of entity-level controls
- Document the work performed and conclusions reached regarding the inspection of the company's documentation

## INSTRUCTIONS

This form should be used to document your inspection of documentation that provides evidence as to the performance of entity-level controls. The documentation of the performance of an entity-level control is different from the documentation of the control policy or procedure itself. Documentation of the company's stated entity-level control policies may be found on form DOC-1.

At the top right-hand corner, assign an identifying number to the form. This identifier should correspond to the reference number provided in the Index to Tests of Entity-Level Controls: Inspection of Documentation, form TST-ENT-4.

In the first part of the form, summarize the basic information about the document inspected. You then should indicate the entity-level control to which your test relates.

In part II of the form, you should describe the results of your tests that are relevant to assessing the operating effectiveness of the control tested. First, describe the evidence you observed that indicates that the control is operating as designed. Next, summarize any deviations from stated company policies. These testing deviations will be summarized and evaluated along with all other test results.

*Footnoted comments in italics are additional instructions to the preparer of the form and should be removed before the form is considered final.*

Reference No: _____

---

# ASSESSMENT OF INTERNAL CONTROL EFFECTIVENESS
## INSPECTION OF DOCUMENTATION
## OF CONTROL PERFORMANCE

Company: _____          Reporting Date: _____

Prepared by: _____          Date Prepared: _____

This form describes our inspection of relevant documentation indicating the performance of certain entity-level controls.

## PART I: BASIC INFORMATION

Title of Document Reviewed _____

Document Prepared by _____

Date Document Prepared _____

Reference to Original Document _____

Purpose of Document or Summary of Contents

_____

_____

_____

### *Test Objective*

This document provides evidence about the operating effectiveness of the following entity-level control(s).[1]

- ❏ Control environment
- ❏ Risk assessment
- ❏ Information and communication
- ❏ Monitoring
- ❏ Period-end financial reporting

- ❏ Selection and application of accounting policies
- ❏ Audit committee oversight
- ❏ Antifraud programs and controls
- ❏ Nonroutine transactions

[1] *Check all that apply.*

## PART II: SUMMARY OF RESULTS

My inspection of the document identified the following matters that are relevant to assessing the operating effectiveness of the above-indicated controls.

### *Evidence That Control Is Operating as Designed*

_____

_____

_____

_____

_____

_____

_____

_____

### *Control Deviations*

The document indicates the following deviations from stated company policies.

_____

_____

_____

_____

# Index to Tests of Entity-Level Controls: Observation of Operations

## PURPOSE

This form has been designed to

- Summarize the extent of your observation of operations and map these tests to the entity-level controls to which they relate
- Provide a centralized cross-reference to the documentation of the procedures performed and test results for entity-level controls

## INSTRUCTIONS

Provide a brief description of the operation you observed and enter this into the second column. In the first column, you should assign this item an identifying number as a way to cross-reference the reviewer to your description of the test performed and its results.

Check the appropriate boxes to indicate the entity-level control(s) to which the test relates. It is common for the observation of one operation to provide evidence about the operating effectiveness of more than one control.

To this index you should attach descriptions of the procedures performed and the results of those procedures. The form TST-ENT-5a may be used for this purpose. One form should be completed for each operation or group of related operations made.

| Ref. | Description | Control Environment | | Risk Assess | Information and Communication | Monitor | Period-End Reporting | Select Accounting Policies | Nonroutine Transactions |
| | | Culture | Personnel | | | | | | |
|---|---|---|---|---|---|---|---|---|---|
| | | ☐ | ☐ | ☐ | ☐ | ☐ | ☐ | ☐ | ☐ |
| | | ☐ | ☐ | ☐ | ☐ | ☐ | ☐ | ☐ | ☐ |
| | | ☐ | ☐ | ☐ | ☐ | ☐ | ☐ | ☐ | ☐ |
| | | ☐ | ☐ | ☐ | ☐ | ☐ | ☐ | ☐ | ☐ |
| | | ☐ | ☐ | ☐ | ☐ | ☐ | ☐ | ☐ | ☐ |
| | | ☐ | ☐ | ☐ | ☐ | ☐ | ☐ | ☐ | ☐ |
| | | ☐ | ☐ | ☐ | ☐ | ☐ | ☐ | ☐ | ☐ |

Entity-Level Control

# Worksheet to Document Observation of Operation of Entity-Level Controls

## PURPOSE

This form has been designed to

- Facilitate your observation of operations that provides evidence of the performance of entity-level controls
- Document the work performed and conclusions reached regarding the observation of operations

## INSTRUCTIONS

This form should be used to document your observation of an operation that provides evidence as to the performance of entity-level controls. The documentation of the performance of an entity-level control is different from the documentation of the control policy or procedure itself. Documentation of the company's stated entity-level control policies may be found on form DOC-1.

At the top right-hand corner, assign an identifying number to the form. This identifier should correspond to the reference number provided in the Index to Tests of Entity-Level Controls: Observation of Operations, form TST-ENT-5.

In the first part of the form, summarize the basic information about the operation you observed, for example, a meeting of the audit committee or board of directors. You then should indicate the entity-level control to which your test relates.

In part II of the form, you should describe what you observed that is relevant to assessing the operating effectiveness of the control tested. First, describe the observations that indicate that the control is operating as designed. Next, summarize any deviations from stated company policies. These testing deviations will be summarized and evaluated along with all other test results.

*Footnoted comments in italics are additional instructions to the preparer of the form and should be removed before the form is considered final.*

Reference No: _____

## ASSESSMENT OF INTERNAL CONTROL EFFECTIVENESS
## OBSERVATION OF OPERATIONS

Company: _____          Reporting Date: _____

Prepared by: _____          Date Prepared: _____

This form describes our observations of company operations related to the performance of certain entity-level controls

## PART I: BASIC INFORMATION

Operation Observed _____

Person(s) Involved in the Operation _____

_____

_____

Date the Operation Was Performed _____

Brief Description of the Operation

_____

_____

_____

### *Test Objective*

This observation provides evidence about the operating effectiveness of the following entity-level control(s).[1]

❏ Control environment                    ❏ Period-end financial reporting

❏ Risk assessment                         ❏ Selection and application
                                            of accounting policies

❏ Information and communication           ❏ Nonroutine transactions

❏ Monitoring

[1]*Check all that apply.*

## PART II: SUMMARY OF RESULTS

My observation identified the following matters that are relevant to assessing the operating effectiveness of the above-indicated controls.

### *Evidence That Control Is Operating as Designed*

I observed the following, which indicate that the control is operating as designed.

_____

_____

_____

_____

_____

_____

_____

### *Control Deviations*

I observed the following deviations from stated company policies.

_____

_____

_____

_____

# Index to Tests of Entity-Level Controls: Reperformance of Controls

## PURPOSE

This form has been designed to

- Summarize the extent of your reperformance of controls and map these tests to the entity-level controls to which they relate
- Provide a centralized cross-reference to the documentation of the procedures performed and test results for entity-level controls

## INSTRUCTIONS

Provide a brief description of the control you reperformed and enter this into the second column. In the first column, you should assign this item an identifying number as a way to cross-reference the reviewer to your description of the test performed and its results.

Check the appropriate boxes to indicate the entity-level control(s) to which the test relates. The reperformance of one control procedure may provide evidence about the operating effectiveness of more than one control.

To this index you should attach descriptions of the procedures performed and the results of those procedures. The form TST-ENT-6a may be used for this purpose. One form should be completed for each control or group of related controls reperformed.

| Ref. | Description | Entity-Level Control | | | | | | | |
| --- | --- | --- | --- | --- | --- | --- | --- | --- | --- |
| | | Control Environment | | Risk Assess | Information and Communication | Monitor | Period-End Reporting | Select Accounting Policies | Nonroutine Transactions |
| | | Culture | Personnel | | | | | | |
| | | ❏ | ❏ | ❏ | ❏ | ❏ | ❏ | ❏ | ❏ |
| | | ❏ | ❏ | ❏ | ❏ | ❏ | ❏ | ❏ | ❏ |
| | | ❏ | ❏ | ❏ | ❏ | ❏ | ❏ | ❏ | ❏ |
| | | ❏ | ❏ | ❏ | ❏ | ❏ | ❏ | ❏ | ❏ |
| | | ❏ | ❏ | ❏ | ❏ | ❏ | ❏ | ❏ | ❏ |
| | | ❏ | ❏ | ❏ | ❏ | ❏ | ❏ | ❏ | ❏ |
| | | ❏ | ❏ | ❏ | ❏ | ❏ | ❏ | ❏ | ❏ |

# Worksheet to Document Reperformance of Entity-Level Controls

## PURPOSE

This form has been designed to

- Facilitate your reperformance of an entity-level control(s)
- Document the work performed and conclusions reached regarding the inspection of the company's documentation

## INSTRUCTIONS

This form should be used to document your reperformance of an entity-level control(s). The documentation of the performance of an entity-level control is different from the documentation of the control policy or procedure itself. Documentation of the company's stated entity-level control policies may be found on form DOC-1.

At the top right-hand corner, assign an identifying number to the form. This identifier should correspond to the reference number provided in the Index to Tests of Entity-Level Controls: Reperformance of Controls, form TST-ENT-6.

In the first part of the form, summarize the basic information about the control you reperformed. You then should indicate the entity-level control to which your test relates.

In part II of the form, you should describe the results of your tests that are relevant to assessing the operating effectiveness of the control tested. First, describe the evidence you observed that indicates that the control is operating as designed. Next, summarize any deviations from stated company policies. These testing deviations will be summarized and evaluated along with all other test results.

*Footnoted comments in italics are additional instructions to the preparer of the form and should be removed before the form is considered final.*

Reference No: _____

---

## ASSESSMENT OF INTERNAL CONTROL EFFECTIVENESS
## REPERFORMANCE OF ENTITY-LEVEL CONTROL

Company: _____        Reporting Date: _____

Prepared by: _____        Date Prepared: _____

This form describes our reperformance of certain entity-level controls.

## PART I: BASIC INFORMATION

Description of Control Procedure

_____

_____

_____

_____

Control Performed by _____

Date Control Performed _____

Description of Procedures to Reperform the Original Test

_____

_____

_____

_____

### *Test Objective*

This test provides evidence about the operating effectiveness of the following entity-level control(s).[1]

❑ Control environment                    ❑ Selection and application
                                            of accounting policies

---

[1]*Check all that apply.*

❏ Risk assessment        ❏ Period-end financial reporting

❏ Information and communication        ❏ Nonroutine transactions

❏ Monitoring

## PART II: SUMMARY OF RESULTS

My reperformance of the control identified the following matters that are relevant to assessing the operating effectiveness of the above-indicated controls.

### *Evidence That Control Is Operating as Designed*

I obtained the following results, which indicate that the control is operating as designed.

_____

_____

_____

_____

_____

_____

_____

_____

### *Control Deviations*

The results of my tests indicate the following deviations from stated company policies.

_____

_____

_____

_____

# Work Program for Reviewing a Report on IT General Control Effectiveness

## PURPOSE

This form has been designed to

- Facilitate the effective review of a specialist's report on IT general control operating effectiveness

## INSTRUCTIONS

The testing of IT general control effectiveness requires specialized expertise. This work program assumes that the project team will engage an IT specialist to perform this work.

Engaging an IT specialist to test IT general controls does *not* relieve the project team of all responsibilities relating to IT controls. Although the IT specialist will have the primary responsibility for planning and performing the tests of controls and for discussing the results of these tests, the project team must assume the final responsibility for assessing IT control effectiveness. To fulfill this responsibility, the project team should obtain an understanding of the nature of the work performed by the IT specialist. Generally, this understanding should cover the following.

- The objective of the work
- The scope of the work
- The timing of the work
- The testing procedures and methods used
- The criteria used by the specialist to evaluate control testing exceptions, including a determination of the relative significance of any control deficiencies
- The form and content of the IT specialist's findings that will enable you to evaluate IT general control operating effectiveness

This work program is designed to help you meet these responsibilities.

*Notations in italics are additional instructions to the preparer of the form and should be removed before the form is considered final.*

# REVIEW OF REPORT ON IT GENERAL CONTROL OPERATING EFFECTIVENESS

Company: _____ Reporting Date: _____

Prepared by: _____ Date Prepared: _____

This form summarizes the procedures we performed to understand and evaluate the work performed by an IT specialist to test and evaluate the operating effectiveness of IT general controls

| Procedure Performed | N/A | Performed by | Date | Notes |
|---|---|---|---|---|
| **Planning** | | | | |
| 1. Determine the IT systems that should be included within the scope of the testwork. Identify all elements of the systems including<br>• Hardware<br>• Software<br>• Data<br>• Facilities | | | | |
| 2. Obtain a preliminary understanding of the IT general control objectives and control policies and procedures that should be included within the scope of the evaluations. | | | | |
| 3. Engage an IT specialist to plan, perform, assess, and report on the operating effectiveness of IT general controls. | | | | |
| 4. Obtain an understanding of the specialist's qualifications to perform the work. These qualifications may include<br>• Professional certification or licensing<br>• Reputation and standing in the views of peers and others familiar with the specialist's capability or performance | | | | |

| Procedure Performed | N/A Performed by | Date | Notes |
|---|---|---|---|
| • Experience in testing and reporting on IT general controls in conjunction with an overall evaluation of the effectiveness of internal control over financial reporting | | | |
| 5. Reach an understanding with the specialist regarding<br>a. The objective of the work<br>b. The scope of the work<br>c. The general nature, timing, and extent of the testwork<br>d. The criteria to be used to evaluate testing exceptions and control deficiencies<br>e. The form and content of the report to be issued | | | |
| **Read and Understand Report** | | | |
| Read and understand the IT specialist's report on IT general control effectiveness and evaluate the following. | | | |
| 6. Assess the scope of the specialist's engagement and determine that the engagement included<br>a. All IT systems that are part of the project team's internal control assessment project<br>b. All control objectives that were previously determined to be evaluated in order to conclude on the overall effectiveness of internal control over financial reporting | | | |
| 7. Evaluate the date as of which control effectiveness was assessed and determine that this timing is suitable to evaluate overall internal control effectiveness as of year-end. | | | |

| Procedure Performed | N/A Performed by | Date | Notes |
|---|---|---|---|
| a. If the timing of the tests of controls does not allow for a reasonable conclusion on the effectiveness of the company's internal control as of year-end, reach an understanding with the IT specialist about the nature, timing, and extent of tests necessary to update the conclusions on IT general control operating effectiveness. | | | |
| 8. Identify and assess the propriety of the specialist's conclusions regarding<br>a. Material weaknesses in IT general controls<br>b. Significant control deficiencies<br>c. Other control deficiencies<br>d. Testing exceptions not considered to be indicative of a control deficiency<br>e. The effect that identified IT general control deficiencies have on the operating effectiveness of associated application controls | | | |
| 9. Summarize all control deficiencies, significant deficiencies, and material weaknesses (carry these forward to form ADM-3). | | | |
| 10. Communicate findings to management and external auditors, as required. | | | |
| 11. Plan and implement corrective action to address all control deficiencies, significant deficiencies, and material weaknesses. | | | |

| | | | |
|---|---|---|---|
| 12. Identify compensating controls, if any, that address the same control objective(s) as the controls where deficiencies were determined to exist. | | | |
| 13. Assess the impact that IT general control deficiencies (including those identified as significant or material weaknesses) will have on the following.<br>a. The effectiveness of associated application controls<br>b. Tests of activity-level controls<br>c. Overall effectiveness of the company's internal control over financial reporting, after considering the effectiveness of any compensating controls | | | |

# Planning and Review of Scope of Tests of IT General Control Effectiveness

## PURPOSE

This form has been designed to

- Help you plan the scope of the tests of operating effectiveness of IT general controls
- Review the report of the IT specialist to determine that the scope of tests was sufficient

## INSTRUCTIONS

Determining an appropriate scope of tests for IT general controls involves two considerations

1. The IT systems that are to be tested

2. The control objectives for which controls should be tested

This form is divided into those two parts.

This form serves a dual purpose. First, you should complete the "Planning" columns of the form. This procedure will allow you to determine and document your assessment of the required scope of the work. You may wish to share this documentation with the IT specialist to avoid confusion.

Once the IT specialist has submitted his or her report, you should complete the "Review" columns of the form to indicate whether the item was included in the scope of the specialist's testwork. Items that you had planned to be included in the scope but that were not are a testing deficiency that may preclude you from reaching a supportable conclusion on IT general control operating effectiveness.

*Notations in italics are additional instructions to the preparer of the form and should be removed before the form is considered final.*

## PLANNING AND REVIEWING SCOPE OF TESTS: IT GENERAL CONTROL OPERATING EFFECTIVENESS

Company: _____          Reporting Date: _____

Prepared by: _____          Date Prepared: _____

This form summarizes our determination of which IT systems and control objectives should be included within the scope of testwork for IT general controls operating effectiveness as well as our review of the adequacy of the scope of the work actually performed.

## IT SYSTEMS

| Name of System | Description | Planning Included in Scope? Yes | No | Review of Report Included in Tests? Yes | No |
|---|---|---|---|---|---|
| *Financial Accounting* | | | | | |
| Hardware | | ❏ ❏ ❏ | ❏ ❏ ❏ | ❏ ❏ ❏ | ❏ ❏ ❏ |
| OS software | | ❏ ❏ ❏ | ❏ ❏ ❏ | ❏ ❏ ❏ | ❏ ❏ ❏ |
| Application software | | ❏ ❏ ❏ | ❏ ❏ ❏ | ❏ ❏ ❏ | ❏ ❏ ❏ |
| Other software (e.g., network, telecommunications) | | ❏ ❏ ❏ ❏ | ❏ ❏ ❏ ❏ | ❏ ❏ ❏ ❏ | ❏ ❏ ❏ ❏ |
| Data | | ❏ ❏ ❏ | ❏ ❏ ❏ | ❏ ❏ ❏ | ❏ ❏ ❏ |
| Facilities | | ❏ ❏ ❏ | ❏ ❏ ❏ | ❏ ❏ ❏ | ❏ ❏ ❏ |

| Name of System | Description | Planning | | Review of Report | |
|---|---|---|---|---|---|
| | | Included in Scope? | | Included in Tests? | |
| | | Yes | No | Yes | No |
| *Order Processing and Tracking* | | | | | |
| Hardware | | ❑ ❑ ❑ | ❑ ❑ ❑ | ❑ ❑ ❑ | ❑ ❑ ❑ |
| OS software | | ❑ ❑ ❑ | ❑ ❑ ❑ | ❑ ❑ ❑ | ❑ ❑ ❑ |
| Application software | | ❑ ❑ ❑ | ❑ ❑ ❑ | ❑ ❑ ❑ | ❑ ❑ ❑ |
| Other software (e.g., network, telecommunications) | | ❑ ❑ ❑ ❑ | ❑ ❑ ❑ ❑ | ❑ ❑ ❑ ❑ | ❑ ❑ ❑ ❑ |
| Data | | ❑ ❑ ❑ | ❑ ❑ ❑ | ❑ ❑ ❑ | ❑ ❑ ❑ |
| Facilities | | ❑ ❑ ❑ | ❑ ❑ ❑ | ❑ ❑ ❑ | ❑ ❑ ❑ |
| *Inventory Management* | | | | | |
| Hardware | | ❑ ❑ ❑ | ❑ ❑ ❑ | ❑ ❑ ❑ | ❑ ❑ ❑ |
| OS software | | ❑ ❑ ❑ | ❑ ❑ ❑ | ❑ ❑ ❑ | ❑ ❑ ❑ |
| Application software | | ❑ ❑ ❑ | ❑ ❑ ❑ | ❑ ❑ ❑ | ❑ ❑ ❑ |

| Name of System | Description | Planning Included in Scope? | | Review of Report Included in Tests? | |
|---|---|---|---|---|---|
| | | Yes | No | Yes | No |
| Other software (e.g., network, telecommunications) | | ❏ ❏ ❏ ❏ | ❏ ❏ ❏ ❏ | ❏ ❏ ❏ ❏ | ❏ ❏ ❏ ❏ |
| Data | | ❏ ❏ ❏ | ❏ ❏ ❏ | ❏ ❏ ❏ | ❏ ❏ ❏ |
| Facilities | | ❏ ❏ ❏ | ❏ ❏ ❏ | ❏ ❏ ❏ | ❏ ❏ ❏ |

## IT CONTROL OBJECTIVES

| IT Control Objective | Planning Included in Scope? | | Review of Report Included in Tests? | |
|---|---|---|---|---|
| | Yes | No | Yes | No |
| *Plan and Organize* | | | | |
| Define a strategic IT plan. | ❏ | ❏ | ❏ | ❏ |
| Define the information architecture. | ❏ | ❏ | ❏ | ❏ |
| Determine technological direction. | ❏ | ❏ | ❏ | ❏ |
| Define the IT organization and relationships. | ❏ | ❏ | ❏ | ❏ |
| Manage the IT investment. | ❏ | ❏ | ❏ | ❏ |
| Communicate management aims and direction. | ❏ | ❏ | ❏ | ❏ |
| Manage human resources. | ❏ | ❏ | ❏ | ❏ |

| IT Control Objective | Planning | | Review of Report | |
|---|---|---|---|---|
| | Included in Scope? | | Included in Tests? | |
| | Yes | No | Yes | No |
| Ensure compliance with external requirements. | ❏ | ❏ | ❏ | ❏ |
| Assess risks. | ❏ | ❏ | ❏ | ❏ |
| Manage projects. | ❏ | ❏ | ❏ | ❏ |
| Manage quality. | ❏ | ❏ | ❏ | ❏ |
| *Acquire and Implement* | | | | |
| Identify automated solutions. | ❏ | ❏ | ❏ | ❏ |
| Acquire and maintain application software. | ❏ | ❏ | ❏ | ❏ |
| Acquire and maintain technology infrastructure. | ❏ | ❏ | ❏ | ❏ |
| Develop and maintain procedures. | ❏ | ❏ | ❏ | ❏ |
| Install and accredit systems. | ❏ | ❏ | ❏ | ❏ |
| Manage change. | ❏ | ❏ | ❏ | ❏ |
| *Deliver and Support* | | | | |
| Define and manage service levels. | ❏ | ❏ | ❏ | ❏ |
| Manage third-party services. | ❏ | ❏ | ❏ | ❏ |
| Manage performance and capacity. | ❏ | ❏ | ❏ | ❏ |
| Ensure continuous service. | ❏ | ❏ | ❏ | ❏ |
| Ensure systems security. | ❏ | ❏ | ❏ | ❏ |
| Identify and allocate costs. | ❏ | ❏ | ❏ | ❏ |

| IT Control Objective | Planning | | Review of Report | |
| | Included in Scope? | | Included in Tests? | |
| | Yes | No | Yes | No |
|---|---|---|---|---|
| Educate and train users. | ❏ | ❏ | ❏ | ❏ |
| Assist and advise customers. | ❏ | ❏ | ❏ | ❏ |
| Manage the configuration. | ❏ | ❏ | ❏ | ❏ |
| Manage problems and incidents. | ❏ | ❏ | ❏ | ❏ |
| Manage data. | ❏ | ❏ | ❏ | ❏ |
| Manage facilities. | ❏ | ❏ | ❏ | ❏ |
| Manage operations. | ❏ | ❏ | ❏ | ❏ |
| *Monitor and Evaluate* | | | | |
| Monitor the processes. | ❏ | ❏ | ❏ | ❏ |
| Assess internal control adequacy. | ❏ | ❏ | ❏ | ❏ |
| Obtain independent assurance. | ❏ | ❏ | ❏ | ❏ |
| Provide for independent audit. | ❏ | ❏ | ❏ | ❏ |

# Work Program for Performing an IT General Controls Review

## PURPOSE

This form has been designed to—

- Facilitate the effective organization of an efficient process for performing a review of IT general controls
- Document the work performed to evaluate IT general controls

## INSTRUCTIONS

Use this form to guide the design and performance of the review of IT general controls. As the steps in program are completed, the person responsible for performing the step should initial and date in the indicated column on the worksheet. If the step is not applicable, indicate that by noting "N/A." Use the "Notes" column to cross reference to where the performance of the procedure is documented, or to make other notations.

*Notations in italics are additional instructions to the preparer of the form and should be removed before the form is considered final.*

## IT RISK INDICATORS

Step 6 of the work program asks you to identify IT risks for each significant financial reporting application. Indicators of a higher level of risk in IT processes include the following.

- Controls that failed during previous IT testing, for example, prior years' SOX 404 evaluations
- Older applications or applications that have been modified or customized frequently
- Known problems with the application or its data
- Frequent processing problems
- Staff turnover in key positions
- Inexperienced or poorly trained staff
- High number of user "workarounds" to modify or correct data produced by the application

## EVALUATING THE SIGNIFICANCE OF IT RISKS

The application of the top-down, risk-based approach to testing controls requires you to consider the relative magnitude of a risk and the likelihood that the failure of a control would result in a material error in the financial statements.

The significance of a risk may be affected by many factors, including the following.

- The design and approval of any changes to an existing application
- Controls related to the change of database schema and operating systems
- The nature and extent of the testing of any new and modified applications
- User acceptance of new and modified applications
- The prevention of unauthorized changes to applications
- The timely resolution of processing errors and exceptions
- Physical security
- Logical access to data and applications

## IT GENERAL CONTROLS REVIEW WORK PROGRAM

Company _____          Reporting Date: _____

Prepared by: _____          Date Prepared: _____

This form summarizes the procedures we performed to document, test, and report on the effectiveness of the company's internal control over financial reporting.

| Procedure Performed | N/A Performed by | Date | Notes |
|---|---|---|---|
| **Identify Key IT Controls** | | | |
| 1. Identify significant IT applications within the company's financial reporting process. | | | |
| 2. For each significant application, identify key controls and determine which are manual and which are automated. | | | |
| *Consider reviewing the key reports and other functionalities in the financial reporting process. When reviewing reports relating to prior years' evaluations of IT controls, be sure to consider manual controls that may have been automated since they originally were tested.* | | | |

| Procedure Performed | N/A Performed by | Date | Notes |
|---|---|---|---|
| 3. Identify manual controls that rely on the functionality of related IT controls. (For example, controls relating to an estimate of a bad debt reserve may rely on an automatically generated accounts receivable aging.) These IT controls should be included within the scope of the IT controls review. | | | |
| 4. Review list of controls included within the project scope and determine that if the control failed, there is at least a reasonable likelihood that a material error in the financial statements would not be detected. Controls that do not meet this threshold need not be included within the scope of the review. | | | |
| 5. Identify any other IT functionality within the significant financial reporting applications. For example, the application may include automated calculations or other functionality. Though these are processes not controls, risks related to these processes will need to be considered when setting the overall project scope. | | | |
| **Identify Process Risks and Describe Control Objectives** | | | |
| 6. For each financial significant application identify specific risks related to each of the following. <br> a. Change management <br> b. IT operations <br> c. Logical and physical access/security | | | |
| *When identifying specific risks be sure to include—in addition to the application— all related: databases, operating systems, and networks.* | | | |
| 7. For each identified risk, describe a related control objective. | | | |

| Procedure Performed | N/A Performed by | Date | Notes |
|---|---|---|---|
| **Identify Key IT Controls for Testing** | | | |
| 8. Identify those IT controls that are pervasive to the multiple financial reporting applications. When identifying pervasive controls, consider controls related to:<br>a. Databases<br>b. Operating systems<br>c. Network infrastructure<br>d. The overall IT operating environment. | | | |
| 9. Select those controls to test. When making your final selection, consider:<br>a. Manual compensating controls that would detect any material errors caused by a failure of an IT general control. For example, the periodic physical inventory may detect certain errors that may result from a failure of an IT control.<br>b. Whether the application has changed from the previous year.<br>c. Whether testing application level controls may be more efficient than relying on and testing the IT general control. For example, if there are only a few application level controls that are easy to test, it may be more efficient to test those controls periodically throughout the period rather than the related IT general control. | | | |

# Guidelines for Testing Activity-Level Control Effectiveness[1]

## TEST DESIGN CONSIDERATIONS

Your tests of activity-level controls should allow you to gather sufficient evidential matter to support your conclusion about the effectiveness of internal control. To be "sufficient," the evidence should be persuasive or convincing. A preponderance of the evidence gathered should support your conclusion about control effectiveness. The evidence does not have to be incontrovertible to support your conclusion. You do not have to prove your point beyond a shadow of a doubt.

Your tests of operating effectiveness should be designed to determine

- How the control procedure was performed
- The consistency with which it was applied
- By whom it was applied

### *Nature, Timing, and Extent of Tests*

#### NATURE

You will need to decide on the types of tests you will perform. For example, will you conduct inquiries, observe controls being performed, or reperform certain control procedures? The nature of the tests you perform depends on the type of control procedure being tested and whether its performance is documented.

Typically, you will perform a combination of one or more tests in order to gather evidence about control effectiveness. It would be unlikely that one test will give you all the evidence needed to support your conclusion. For example, suppose you observe the operation of a control procedure such as an edit check on the electronic input of information. You observe the control to be functioning properly, but how do you know that the control was in place and operating effectively throughout the reporting period? Your observation will have to be supplemented with other procedures, such as inquiry.

When determining the nature of the tests you will perform to support your conclusion,

[1]*This material was originally published in a slightly different format in* How to Comply with Sarbanes-Oxley Section 404: Assessing the Effectiveness of Internal Control, *by Michael Ramos, published by John Wiley & Sons, 2004, pages 209–221.*

consider that your opinion most likely will be formed by the congruence and consistency of the evidence you gather from several sources and types of tests.

## TIMING

The Sarbanes-Oxley Act requires management to report on the effectiveness of internal control as of a point in time, namely, year-end. As a practical matter, you most likely will perform many of your tests in advance of the reporting date. When you do, you must consider the need to perform additional tests to establish the effectiveness of the control procedure from the time the tests were performed until year-end. For example, if you tested the effectiveness of bank reconciliations as of June 30 and the reporting date was December 31, you will need to consider performing tests to cover the period from July 1 through December 31. These tests may not require you to repeat the detailed tests performed at June 30 for the subsequent six-month period. If you establish the effectiveness of the control procedure at June 30 you may be able to support a conclusion about the effectiveness of the control at the reporting date indirectly through the consideration of entity-level controls and other procedures such as

- The effectiveness of personnel-related controls such as the training and supervision of personnel who perform control procedures. For example, are the people performing the bank reconciliations adequately supervised, and was their work reviewed during the second half of the year?
- The effectiveness of risk identification and management controls, including change management. For example, would management be able to identify changes in the entity's business or its circumstances that would affect the continued effectiveness of bank reconciliations as a control procedure?
- The effectiveness of the monitoring component of the entity's internal control.
- Inquiries of personnel to determine what changes, if any, occurred during the period that would affect the performance of controls.
- Repeating the procedures performed earlier in the year, focusing primarily on elements of the control procedure that have changed during the period. For example, if the entity adding new bank accounts or new personnel were performing certain bank reconciliations, you would focus your tests on those accounts and individuals.

### Computer Application Controls

The COSO report describes two different levels of computer controls: general and application-specific. Application controls are the structure, policies, and procedures that apply to separate, individual business process application systems. They include both the automated control procedures (i.e., those routines contained within the computer program) and the policies and procedures associated with user activities, such as the manual follow-up required to investigate potential errors identified during processing.

As with all other control procedures, computer application controls should be designed to achieve specified control objectives, which in turn are driven by the risks to achieving certain business objectives. In general, the objectives of a computer application are to ensure that

- Data remain complete, accurate, and valid during their input, update, and storage
- Output files and reports are distributed and made available only to authorized users

Specific application-level controls should address the risks to achieving these objectives. The following exhibit provides examples of computer application control objectives and related controls.

| Example Computer Application Control Objectives and Controls | |
| --- | --- |
| **Control Objective** | **Control Activity** |
| *Authorization* | |
| All application users are appropriately identified and authenticated. | • Passwords and personal identification numbers<br>• "Nonrepudiation" that prevents senders and receivers of information from denying that they sent or received the information<br>• Emerging technologies such as digital certificates or smart cards |
| Access to the application and related data files is restricted to authorized users for authorized purposes. | • Logical access control system restricts access to the application and data to authorized users.<br>• Firewalls protect application and data from unauthorized use.<br>• Terminals automatically disconnect from the system when not used after a specified period of time.<br>• Computer equipment is located in physically secure locations. |
| All data are authorized before entering the application. | • Critical input information is tested against predefined criteria. All exceptions are reviewed by an individual with the proper authority to approve them.<br>• Paper-based information is reviewed and approved prior to input. |
| *Completeness* | |
| All authorized data enter and are processed by the application. | • Transactions are numbered prior to entry; sequence is checked periodically.<br>• Control totals, hash totals, and record counts ensure that all data are processed. |

| | • Transaction data are matched with data in a master or suspense file. Unmatched items from both the transaction data and master or suspense files are reported for investigation. |
|---|---|
| *Accuracy* | |
| Date entry design features contribute to data accuracy. | • Preformatted screens and menu-driven input<br>• Electronic input of information |
| Data validation and editing are performed to identify erroneous data. | • Automated validation and edit checks |
| Erroneous data are captured, reported, investigated, and corrected. | • Suspense files capture and control errors.<br>• Suspense files are regularly reviewed and items are appropriately resolved. |
| *Confidentiality* | |
| Access to application output is restricted to authorized users. | • Access to confidential information is limited to authorized individuals consistent with the entity's confidentiality policies.<br>• Data encryption technologies protect the transmission of user authentication, verification, and confidential information. |

The way in which computer control objectives are met will depend on the types of technologies used by the entity. For example, the specific control procedures used to control access to an online, real-time database will be different from those procedures related to access of a "flat file" stored on a disk.

An IT controls specialist most likely will be needed to understand the risks involved in various technologies and the related activity-level controls.

## Considering the Results of Entity-Level Tests

Entity-level controls affect the operational effectiveness of activity-level controls. For example, the entity may have thorough, well-designed controls to ensure a proper sales cutoff at year-end (activity-level control), but if they do a poor job of communicating and monitoring the performance of the people responsible for performing the procedure (an entity-level control), then ultimately the control will lack full effectiveness. When designing your activity-level tests, your conclusions about the effectiveness of entity-level controls should be used in two ways. First, plan your activity-level tests to gather firsthand information about the effectiveness of entity-level controls. Use this information to (hopefully) corroborate your earlier assessment of entity-level control effectiveness.

For example, when making inquiries of an individual about the control procedures he or she performs, consider expanding your inquiries to include questions about entity-level controls. Examples of inquiries that go beyond understanding activity-level control procedures include the following:

- If changes to your procedures were required, how would they be communicated?
- What kind of on-the-job or formal classroom training do you receive? Do you find it helpful?
- How closely is your work supervised?
- If any problems or errors that you can't fix are identified, do you ever get the impression that they are either ignored or "made to go away" without being adequately addressed?

The second way in which entity-level controls affect the design of activity-level controls is in the scope of your testwork. Weaknesses in entity-level controls should lead you to expand the scope of your activity-level testing. Conversely, strengths in entity-level controls may allow you to reduce the scope of activity-level tests.

For example, consider two companies, both in the same industry. Revenue is a significant activity, and the 10-Ks for both entities identify revenue recognition as a critical accounting policy. However, their entity-level controls have significant differences, as indicated in the following table.

### Example Entity-Level Controls

| Company A | Company B |
|---|---|
| • Management and employee incentives are based exclusively on profitability.<br>• The company has a highly competitive "up-or-out" culture.<br>• Communication and training of employees generally are poor.<br>• Oversight and supervision are lax. | • Incentives are based on profitability plus "balanced scorecard" financial and nonfinancial metrics such as customer satisfaction and product quality.<br>• The culture is built on product innovation and customer service.<br>• There are formal training methods for communicating policies and acceptable behavior.<br>• There is effective oversight and supervision. |

In the case of company A, you would want to expand the scope of your activity-level testwork for processing revenue transactions. For example, if your tests included transaction testing, you would increase your sample size. Inquiries might be made of more individuals or people you otherwise would not consider interviewing. You may even expand your procedures to include divisions or locations you otherwise would not consider. For company B, the opposite is true.

Additionally, the relative strength of entity-level controls should be considered when you plan the timing of your procedures. With company B, where entity-level controls are strong, you may be able to test the activity-level controls well in advance of the reporting date and place reliance on entity-level controls to draw a conclusion about operating effectiveness at the reporting date. With company A, you probably will have to adopt a different strategy, for example, testing the controls closer to the reporting date or reperforming a limited number of activity-level tests near the reporting date.

# TYPES OF TESTS

## Walkthroughs and Inquiries

A walkthrough is a procedure in which you trace a transaction from its origination through the company's information processing system and all the way to its reporting in the financial statements. Although inquiries of company personnel are a major component, a walkthrough is more than just inquiry. Walkthroughs and formal inquiries of entity personnel—either individually or as part of a focus group—can be a reliable source of evidence about the operating effectiveness of activity-level controls. Walkthroughs can serve two main purposes:

1. To confirm your understanding of the design of the control (what should happen)

2. To identify exceptions to the entity's stated control procedures (what really happens)

It is best to perform walkthroughs of major transactions first, before performing other tests of operating effectiveness.

Form TST-ACT-1 provides guidance and suggestions for performing walkthroughs and inquiries.

## Tests of Transactions

Some control procedures allow you to select a sample of transactions that were recorded during the period and

- Examine the documentation indicating that the control procedure was performed
- Reperform the procedure to determine that the control was performed properly

For example, the process for recording inventory purchases may require

- Physically matching a paper-based warehouse receiving report with an approved purchase order
- Determining that the purchase order was properly approved, as indicated by a signature
- Determining that the vendor is an approved vendor
- Observing evidence (e.g., checkmarks, initials) that warehouse personnel counted the goods received

To test the effectiveness of this control procedure you could

- Examine documentation that the control was performed, including that
  - Documents were matched
  - Purchase order was signed
  - Receiving report was marked

- Determine that the control was performed properly, including that
  - Purchase order and receiving report are for the same transaction
  - Vendor is an approved vendor
  - Signer of the purchase order has the authority to approve the transaction

Computer application controls also may lend themselves to similar testing techniques. For example, suppose that purchased goods are accompanied with a bar code that identifies the goods received and their quantities. The bar code is scanned, and the information is matched electronically to purchase order files and approved vendor master files. Unmatched transactions are placed in a suspense file for subsequent follow-up. (As indicated previously, the computer application control consists of both the programmed elements of the control and the manual follow-up of identified errors.) To test the effectiveness of this control, you could

- Prepare a file of test transactions and run through the system to determine that all errors are identified
- Review the resolution of the suspense account items performed throughout the period to determine that they were resolved properly

When performing tests of transactions, you will have to address issues related to scope—how many items to test.

Before performing your tests of transactions you also should define what you will consider a control procedure error. In instances in which the evidence of performing the procedure is documented (e.g., an initial or signature), the lack of documentation (a missing signature) should be considered an error in the operation of the control. That is, in order for a documented control to be considered properly performed, both of the following must be true:

- The documentation indicates that the control procedure was properly performed.
- Your reperformance of the procedures indicates it was performed properly.

## Testing Reconciliations

Reconciliations are a common control procedure, for example, bank reconciliations or the reconciliation of the general ledger account total to a subsidiary ledger. In some instances, a well-designed reconciliation can provide an effective control over the majority of a processing stream. Testing the effectiveness of a reconciliation is similar to tests of transactions:

- Review documentation that the test was performed on a timely basis throughout the period.
- Reperform the test to determine that all reconciling items were identified properly.
- Investigate the resolution of significant reconciling items.

## Observation

You may be able to observe the application of some control procedures, such as computer input controls like edit checks. A physical inventory count also lends itself to observation as a means of assessing effectiveness. For a control performed only occasionally, such as a physical count, it may be possible to observe the control each time it is performed. For controls that are performed continuously for large volumes of transactions, you will need to supplement your observations with other tests such as

- Inquiry
- Tests of entity-level controls

# Guidelines and Example Inquiries for Performing Walkthroughs

## PURPOSE

This form has been designed to

- Provide suggestions and example inquiries to help you perform more effective walk-through procedures
- Document the procedures performed and information gathered as a result of walk-through procedures

## INSTRUCTIONS

### What's a Walkthrough?

A walkthrough is a procedure in which you trace a transaction from its origination through the company's information processing system, and all the way to its reporting in the financial statements. Although inquiries of company personnel are a major component, a walkthrough is more than just inquiry. Think of a walkthrough as

- *Corroborative* inquiry, in which you ask questions of client personnel and then obtain corroborating evidence to support their answers
- *A test of one,* in which you take a single transaction and perform detailed procedures to test the operating effectiveness of the controls for processing that transaction

The company is not required to perform walkthrough procedures; however, it is in management's best interests to do so.

Sometimes, the company's documentation of its information processing stream does not match the reality of what actually happens on a daily basis. Companies that perform tests of controls based only on what has been documented often run into testing exceptions when they discover that documentation of the information stream and related controls was not accurate.

The walkthrough procedure will allow you to confirm your understanding of key elements of the information processing stream and related controls *before* you begin detailed testwork. The walkthrough can help you evaluate the effectiveness of the design of internal control for each major transaction. While performing your walkthrough, you also may obtain evidence about the operating effectiveness of controls.

### Updating the Walkthrough

Walkthrough procedures should continue to be relevant as long as there are no significant changes to the information processing stream. When significant changes do occur, you should update your walkthrough to confirm your understanding of the new processing and control procedures.

### Special Considerations for External Auditors

PCAOB Auditing Standard No. 2 requires external auditors to perform at least one walkthrough for each major class of transaction. Further, the external auditor is prohibited from relying on the work of management or others to perform the walkthroughs. Paragraphs 79 through 82 of Auditing Standard No. 2 provide further directions to auditors on the objectives, scope, and procedures to be performed when conducting a walkthrough.

### Suggestions Included on This Form

This form includes three separate sections:

1. *Guidelines for performing effective walkthroughs.* Because management is not required to perform walkthroughs, these guidelines are suggestions only. You may use these suggestions to help you plan more effective walkthroughs. (For external auditors, some of these "guidelines" are required by the auditing standards.)

2. *Example inquiries.* Inquiries of business process owners and other company personnel are an important component of the walkthrough procedure. Use these example inquiries to help you gain a better understanding of transaction processing and the related controls.

3. *Walkthrough documentation.* This form may be used to document the procedures performed, information gathered, and conclusions reached as a result of your walkthroughs. The form has been designed for you to fill out for each person interviewed during your walkthroughs.

---

# GUIDELINES FOR PERFORMING EFFECTIVE WALKTHROUGHS

# PLANNING THE WALKTHROUGH

- Plan on performing one walkthrough for each of the company's major transactions.
- Your walkthrough should encompass the entire scope of the transaction, including the processing and control of the transaction's
  - Initiation
  - Authorization

- Recording in the company's books and records
- Processing of accounting information
- Reporting in the financial statements

- It is typical to start your walkthrough at the initiation of the transaction and work forward.
- Plan on identifying the authorization control at the point where the transaction is initiated.
- Plan your procedures to identify and confirm other controls at each major processing step.
- As part of your walkthrough, you should evaluate whether there is adequate segregation of duties.

## MAKING INQUIRIES

- Make inquiries of the people who actually perform control procedures and process information as part of their daily job requirements. Don't limit your inquiries to those who supervise or review the process or are otherwise a step or two removed from actually performing the work. Talk to people in operations, outside of management, and outside of the accounting department.
- Design your inquiries to obtain information about the person's understanding of
  - What is required by the company's prescribed procedures and controls
  - Whether the procedures are performed as described and on a timely basis
- Ask questions to identify specific situations (which may occur regularly) in which personnel do not perform the control procedures as described in the company's internal control documentation.
- Consider conducting inquiries with a focus group, rather than one-on-one interviews.

## OBTAINING SUPPORTING, CORROBORATING INFORMATION

- Corroborate answers received to your inquiries by
  - Asking the individual to demonstrate the performance of the procedure they are describing
  - Using the same documents and information technology ("live data") that company personnel use to perform the procedures
  - Asking other individuals to describe their understanding of the previous and succeeding processing or control activities

## EVALUATE RESULTS OF WALKTHROUGH

- Use the results of your walkthrough to plan detailed tests of operating effectiveness. If necessary, make changes to the company's documentation of internal controls to reflect actual practice, as identified in your walkthrough.

# EXAMPLE INQUIRIES

## INQUIRY OBJECTIVES

To perform an effective walkthrough procedure, you should make inquiries of company personnel who are directly involved with each point in the processing of a transaction where important processing or controls occur. Your inquiries should be designed to obtain information about the person's understanding of

- What is required by the company's prescribed procedures and controls
- Whether the procedures are performed as described and on a timely basis

## EXAMPLE QUESTIONS

To perform more effective walkthroughs, consider asking the following questions.

### Nature of Procedures Performed

- Describe the procedures you perform related to the [initiation/authorization/recording/processing] of the transaction.
- How often are the procedures performed?
- When are the procedures required to be completed?
- From whom or from what electronic files do you receive the information to perform your procedures?
- To whom do you pass the results of the procedures?

### Nature of Controls and Performance of Control Procedures

- During the performance of your procedures, what controls exist to ensure that the procedures were performed properly? For example, how do you know that
  - All data were processed
  - The data were processed accurately
  - No unauthorized transactions or data entered into the processing
- What do you look for to determine if there has been a processing error?
- What do you do when you find an error?

### Deviations from Procedures and Processing Errors

- Under what circumstances are you required to deviate from the documented procedures?
- How often do these circumstances arise? How often have they arisen during the past year?

- What kind of errors have you found in the past year?
- What happened as a result of finding the errors? How were they resolved?

### Confirm Understanding of Other Processing Steps

- What procedures are performed on the data prior to your receiving it?
- What procedures are performed on the data after you are done with it?

---

## DOCUMENTATION OF WALKTHROUGH PROCEDURES

Company: _____     Reporting Date: _____

Prepared by: _____     Date Prepared: _____

The following documents the procedures performed, information gathered, and conclusions reached relating to walkthroughs of major transactions.

## PLANNING

Person we interviewed _____

Date of interview _____

Description of transaction discussed _____

_____

Processing step(s) we discussed:

❏ Initiation of transaction

❏ Authorization of transaction

❏ Transaction recording

❏ Transaction processing steps

Brief description of the company's prescribed processes and controls for the preceding step(s)

_____

_____

_____

_____

_____

_____

Assess the adequacy of the segregation of duties for the prescribed processes and controls, as described. If segregation of duties is not adequate, describe compensating controls.

_____

_____

_____

_____

_____

## PROCEDURES PERFORMED AND RESULTS

### *Nature of Controls and Performance of Control Procedures*

We made inquiries of the individual identified in part I of this form to obtain his or her understanding of processing procedures and controls. We determined that the individual's understanding was consistent with the company's prescribed policies and procedures for each of the following items.

|  | Individual's understanding is consistent with prescribed procedures and controls | |
|---|:---:|:---:|
|  | Yes | No |
| Processing procedures to be performed | ❏ | ❏ |
| Control activities | ❏ | ❏ |
| Definition of a processing error | ❏ | ❏ |
| Procedures for reporting or correcting errors | ❏ | ❏ |

### *Deviations from Prescribed Procedures*

We identified the following circumstances under which the individual deviates from the company's prescribed procedures.

_____

_____

_____

_____

_____

## *Identification and Resolution of Processing Errors*

The individual we interviewed described the following types of processing errors that were discovered during the past year and how these errors were resolved.

_____

_____

_____

_____

_____

## *Corroborating Support*

We performed the following procedures, as indicated, to corroborate the responses to our inquiries.

| Procedure | Procedure Performed? | | Comments |
|---|---|---|---|
| | Yes | N/A | |
| Reviewed original documents | ❑ | ❑ | |
| Made observations | ❑ | ❑ | |
| Received responses to inquiries made of others | ❑ | ❑ | |
| Performed other procedures | ❑ | ❑ | |

## *Assessment of Results of Walkthrough Procedures*

We have considered the results of the walkthrough procedures in designing the tests of operating effectiveness and, if necessary, evaluating the adequacy of the company's documentation of internal control, as described below.

_____

_____

_____

_____

_____

_____

# Example Testing Program for Activity-Level Tests of Controls

## PURPOSE

These forms have been designed to provide examples of

- The links between financial reporting objectives, risks to those objectives, and control activities
- Tests of the operating effectiveness of activity-level controls

## INSTRUCTIONS

The example testing programs in this section cover the following business activities that are common for many entities, including

- Revenue
- Purchases and expenditures
- Cash receipts and disbursements
- Payroll

These example programs are, by necessity, relatively generic and should be modified to fit the particular controls at your company.

To make this modification easier, the example testing procedures are linked not only to the example controls, but also to the overriding control objectives and risks to achieving those objectives. Control activities will vary greatly between companies, but it is anticipated that many entities will share common control objectives and related risks to achieving those objectives. Thus, in modifying these example programs, look first to control objectives that are comparable to the control objectives at your company. You then should be able to modify the example test procedures so that they are relevant and applicable to the way in which individual control activities are administered and documented at your company.

> **Note:** Prior to modifying the example testing program, you should consider performing walkthrough procedures to confirm your understanding of the processing steps and related controls. Walkthrough procedures also include

- Inquiries of relevant personnel to determine if they have knowledge of any known departures from prescribed procedures and controls
- The assessment of the adequacy of the segregation of duties

Form TST-ACT-1 provides guidelines and examples for performing walkthrough procedures.

# Example Testing Program for Control Operating Effectiveness: Revenue

## PURPOSE

This form provides an example testing program that links the tests of operating effectiveness of activity-level controls to related controls, control objectives, and risks to achieving those objectives. Use this form to help you design tests of activity-level controls at your organization.

## INSTRUCTIONS

To modify these example testing programs to fit the particular circumstances of your company, you should first identify the control objectives that are comparable to the control objectives at your company. Identify the control procedures in place to satisfy those objectives and which of those control procedures are most important in the prevention or detection of material misstatements. Using the example tests as a guide, design your own tests of operating effectiveness that are appropriate for the controls in place at the company.

You also should identify control objectives relevant to your company that are not included in the example testing program. Identify the control procedures related to these objectives, determine which of these procedures should be tested, and design the appropriate test.

| Objective and Risk | Example Controls | Example Tests of Operating Effectiveness |
|---|---|---|
| **Control Objective:** Process only valid customer orders. | | |
| **Risk to Achieving Objective** | | |
| • Customer orders may not be authorized. | • Verify appropriate marketing/sales personnel–approved customer order. | • Obtain a file of sales made during the period. Select a sample of transactions and examine customer order to determine that the transaction was authorized properly. |
| **Control Objective:** All goods shipped are accurately billed in the proper period. | | |
| **Risks to Achieving Objective** | | |
| • Missing documents or incorrect information | • Use standard shipping or contract terms.<br>• Communicate nonstandard shipping or contract terms to accounts receivable.<br>• Verify shipping or contract terms before invoice processing. | • Inspect standard contracts with customers and shippers.<br>• Inspect evidence documenting the communication of nonstandard sales or shipping terms to accounting department personnel.<br>• Obtain a file of invoices processed during the period. Select a sample of transactions and examine the executed sales contract and shipping documents supporting the sale. |

| Objective and Risk | Example Controls | Example Tests of Operating Effectiveness |
|---|---|---|
| • Improper cutoff of shipments at the end of a period | • Identify shipments as being before or after period-end by means of a shipping log and prenumbered shipping documents.<br>• Reconcile goods shipped to goods billed. | • Obtain the shipping log and select a sample of shipments. Ensure information reported on the shipping log agrees with the supporting shipping documents.<br>• Obtain the company's periodic reconciliations of goods shipped to goods billed. For a sample of reconciliations, reperform the procedures or otherwise determine that the procedures were performed properly. |

**Control Objective:** Accurately record invoices for all authorized shipments and only for such shipments.

| Risk to Achieving Objective | | |
|---|---|---|
| • Missing documents or incorrect information | • Prenumber and account for shipping documents and sales invoices.<br>• Match orders, shipping documents, invoices, and customer information, and follow through on missing or inconsistent information.<br>• Mail customer statements periodically and investigate and resolve disputes or inquiries, by individuals independent of the invoicing function.<br>• Monitor number of customer complaints regarding improper invoices or statements (performance indicator). | • Obtain files of shipping documents and sales invoices processed during the period. Identify and account for all gaps in sequencing.<br>• Select a sample of invoices processed during the period and examine the underlying shipping documents or shipping log to determine that shipping date information is correct.<br>• Obtain a file of all unmatched orders, shipping documents, and invoices that were identified during the period. Select a sample of items and determine that they were resolved appropriately.<br>• Review communications received from customers and identify indicators of possible control deficiencies. |

| Objective and Risk | Example Controls | Example Tests of Operating Effectiveness |
|---|---|---|

**Control Objective:** Accurately record all authorized sales returns and allowances and only such returns and allowances.

| Objective and Risk | Example Controls | Example Tests of Operating Effectiveness |
|---|---|---|
| **Risks to Achieving Objective**<br>• Missing documents or incorrect information | • Authorize credit memos by individuals independent of accounts receivable function.<br>• Prenumber and account for credit memos and receiving documents.<br>• Match credit memos and receiving documents and resolve unmatched items by individuals independent of the accounts receivable function. | • Obtain a file of credit memos processed during the period and<br>  - Select a sample and determine that<br>    -- The credit memo was authorized properly<br>    -- Key information on the credit memo agrees with the related receiving report<br>  - Identify and account for gaps in sequencing |
| • Inaccurate input of data | • Mail customer statements periodically and investigate and resolve disputes or inquiries, by individuals independent of the invoicing function. | • Review communications received from customers and identify indicators of possible control deficiencies.<br>• Observe operation of data input controls, such as edit checks. |

**Control Objective:** Ensure continued completeness and accuracy of accounts receivable.

| Objective and Risk | Example Controls | Example Tests of Operating Effectiveness |
|---|---|---|
| **Risk to Achieving Objective**<br>• Unauthorized input for nonexistent returns, allowances, and write-offs | • Review correspondence authorizing returns and allowances.<br>• Reconcile accounts receivable subsidiary ledger with the sale and cash receipts transactions. | • Obtain a file of returns, allowances, and other credits to accounts receivable that were posted during the period. Select a sample of entries and determine that the transaction was authorized properly. |

265

| Objective and Risk | Example Controls | Example Tests of Operating Effectiveness |
|---|---|---|
| | • Resolve differences between the accounts receivable subsidiary ledger with the accounts receivable subsidiary ledger and the accounts receivable control account. | • Obtain the company's periodic reconciliation of the accounts receivable general ledger control account. For a sample of reconciliations, reperform the procedures or otherwise determine that the procedures were performed properly. |

**Control Objective:** Safeguard accounts receivable records.

**Risk to Achieving Objective**

| Objective and Risk | Example Controls | Example Tests of Operating Effectiveness |
|---|---|---|
| • Unauthorized access to accounts receivable records and stored data | • Restrict access to accounts receivable files and data used in processing receivables. | • Test logical access to accounts receivable and data files used in processing receivables as part of the tests of IT general controls. |

# Example Testing Program for Control Operating Effectiveness: Purchases and Expenditures

## PURPOSE

This form provides an example testing program that links the tests of operating effectiveness of activity-level controls to related controls, control objectives, and risks to achieving those objectives. Use this form to help you design tests of activity-level controls at your organization.

## INSTRUCTIONS

To modify these example testing programs to fit the particular circumstances of your company, you should first identify the control objectives that are comparable to the control objectives at your company. Identify the control procedures in place to satisfy those objectives and which of those control procedures are most important in the prevention or detection of material misstatements. Using the example tests as a guide, design your own tests of operating effectiveness that are appropriate for the controls in place at the company.

You also should identify control objectives relevant to your company that are not included in the example testing program. Identify the control procedures related to these objectives, determine which of these procedures should be tested, and design the appropriate test.

| Objective and Risk | Example Controls | Example Tests of Operating Effectiveness |
|---|---|---|
| **Control Objective:** Accurately record invoices on a timely basis for accepted purchases that have been authorized and only for such purchases. | | |
| **Risks to Achieving Objective** | | |
| • Missing documents or incorrect information | • Prenumber and account for purchase orders and receiving reports.<br>• Match invoice, receiving, and purchase order information and follow up on missing or inconsistent information.<br>• Follow up on unmatched open purchase orders, receiving reports and invoices and resolve missing, duplicate, or unmatched items, by individuals independent of purchasing and receiving functions. | • Obtain a file of purchase orders and receiving reports. Identify and account for all gaps in sequencing.<br>• Obtain a file of all purchases processed during the period. Select a sample and determine that key information on the vendor invoice, receiving report, and company purchase order are in agreement.<br>• Obtain a file of all unmatched purchase orders, receiving reports and vendor invoices that were identified during the period. Select a sample of items and determine that they were resolved appropriately. |
| • Inaccurate input of data | • Use control totals or one-for-one checking. | • Observe operation of data input controls, such as data checks. |
| • Invalid accounts payable fraudulently created for unauthorized or nonexistent purchases | • Restrict ability to modify data.<br>• Reconcile vendor statements to accounts payable items.<br>• Maintain physical security of purchase orders. | • Obtain a file of approved vendors. Select a sample of vendors and examine supporting documentation indicating that vendor was properly approved.<br>• Test logical access to accounts payable files and related data as part of the tests of IT general controls.<br>• Select a sample of vendor statements received during the period. Determine that statements were reconciled properly to the company's accounts payable records.<br>• Observe operation of controls to restrict physical access to unused purchase orders. |

**Control Objective:** Accurately record returns and allowances for all authorized credits, and only for such credits.

## Risks to Achieving Objective

| | |
|---|---|
| • Missing documents or information | • Prenumber and account for shipping orders for returned goods.<br>• Match shipping orders for returned goods with vendors' credit memos.<br>• Follow up on unmatched shipping orders for returned goods and related receiving reports and invoices and resolve missing, duplicate, or unmatched items, by individuals independent of accounts payable function.<br>• Review vendor correspondence authorizing returns and allowances. | • Obtain a file of shipping orders for returned goods. Identify and account for all gaps in sequencing.<br>• Obtain a file of all purchase returns processed during the period. Select a sample and determine that key information on the vendor credit memo and company shipping order are in agreement.<br>• Obtain a file of all unmatched shipping orders for returned goods. Select a sample of items and determine that they were resolved appropriately.<br>• Review vendor correspondence for indications of possible control deficiencies. |
| • Inaccurate input of data | • Reconcile accounts payable records with vendor statements.<br>• Use control totals or one-for-one checking. | • Select a sample of vendor statements received during the period. Determine that statements were reconciled properly to the company's accounts payable records.<br>• Observe operation of data input controls, such as data checks. |

**Control Objective:** Ensure completeness and accuracy of accounts payable.

## Risks to Achieving Objective

| | |
|---|---|
| • Unauthorized input for nonexistent returns | • Reconcile accounts payable subsidiary ledger with purchase and cash disbursement transactions. | • Obtain the files of the company's accounts payable subsidiary ledger and the cash disbursements register. Reconcile all payments recorded in the accounts payable subsidiary ledger to the vendor payments recorded in the cash disbursements journal. Determine that the company identified and resolved properly all reconciling items identified in your test. |

| Objective and Risk | Example Controls | Example Tests of Operating Effectiveness |
|---|---|---|
| **Control Objective:** Ensure completeness and accuracy of accounts payable. | | |
| **Risks to Achieving Objective** | | |
| • Unauthorized additions to accounts payable | • Resolve differences between the accounts payable subsidiary ledger and the accounts payable control account. | • Obtain the company's periodic reconciliation of the accounts payable subsidiary ledger to the accounts payable general ledger control account. For a sample of reconciliations, reperform the procedures or otherwise determine that the reconciliation was performed properly. |
| **Control Objective:** Safeguard accounts payable records. | | |
| **Risks to Achieving Objective** | | |
| • Unauthorized access to accounts payable records and stored data | • Restrict access to accounts payable and files used in processing payables.<br>• Restrict access to mechanical check signers and signature plates. | • Test logical access to accounts payable and data files used in processing payables as part of the tests of IT general controls.<br>• Observe the controls in place to restrict physical access to mechanical check signers and signature plates. |

# Example Testing Program for Control Operating Effectiveness: Cash Receipts and Disbursements

## PURPOSE

This form provides an example testing program that links the tests of operating effectiveness of activity-level controls to related controls, control objectives, and risks to achieving those objectives. Use this form to help you design tests of activity-level controls at your organization.

## INSTRUCTIONS

To modify these example testing programs to fit the particular circumstances of your company, you should first identify the control objectives that are comparable to the control objectives at your company. Identify the control procedures in place to satisfy those objectives and which of those control procedures are most important in the prevention or detection of material misstatements. Using the example tests as a guide, design your own tests of operating effectiveness that are appropriate for the controls in place at the company.

You also should identify control objectives relevant to your company that are not included in the example testing program. Identify the control procedures related to these objectives, determine which of these procedures should be tested, and design the appropriate test.

| Objective and Risk | Example Controls | Example Tests of Operating Effectiveness |
|---|---|---|
| **Control Objective:** Record cash receipts on accounts receivable completely and accurately. | | |
| **Risks to Achieving Objective** | | |
| • Cash received is diverted, lost, or otherwise not reported accurately to accounts receivable. | • Assign opening of mail to an individual with no responsibility for or access to files or documents pertaining to accounts receivable or cash accounts; compare listed receipts to credits to accounts receivable and bank deposits. | • Obtain the files of the company's cash receipts and accounts receivable subsidiary ledger. Reconcile all payments received recorded in the accounts receivable ledger to vendor cash receipts recorded in the cash accounts. Determine that company personnel identified and resolved properly all reconciling items identified in your test. |
| • Receipts are for amounts different from invoiced amounts, or are not identifiable. | • Send periodic statements to customers and investigate customer noted differences (performance indicator). | • Read correspondence from customers and identify indications of potential control deficiencies. Assess whether company personnel follow-up on these potential deficiencies was appropriate. |
| | • Reconcile general ledger with accounts receivable subsidiary records; investigate differences. | • Obtain the company's periodic reconciliation of the accounts receivable subsidiary ledger to the accounts receivable general ledger control account. For a sample of reconciliations, reperform the procedures or otherwise determine that the reconciliation was performed properly. |
| | • Contact payor to determine reasons for payment or payment different from amounts invoiced. | |
| **Control Objective:** Disburse cash only for authorized purchases. | | |
| **Risks to Achieving Objective** | | |
| • Fictitious documentation is created. | • Examine supporting documents, payments approved by individuals independent of procurement, receiving, and accounts payable. | • Obtain a file of all cash disbursement processed during the period. Select a sample and examine the underlying supporting documents to determine that purchase was properly authorized. |

| Risk to Achieving Objective | | |
|---|---|---|
| • Reuse of supporting documents | • Cancel supporting documents to prevent resubmission for payment. | • Observe operation of control to prevent reuse of supporting purchase documents. |

**Control Objective:** Remit disbursements to vendors and others, such as for dividends, debt service, and tax or other payments, in a timely and accurate manner.

### Risk to Achieving Objective

| | | |
|---|---|---|
| • Inaccurate, untimely, or unavailable information regarding amounts or due dates of payments | • Compare payment amounts and recipients with source documents; verify accuracy of supporting documents. | • Obtain a file of cash disbursements recorded during the period. Select a sample of disbursements and examine supporting documentation to determine that key information is in agreement. |

**Control Objective:** Record cash disbursements completely and accurately.

### Risk to Achieving Objective

| | | |
|---|---|---|
| • Missing documents or information | • Match disbursement records against accounts payable/open invoice files.<br>• Prenumber and account for checks.<br>• Reconcile bank statements to cash accounts and investigate long-outstanding checks by individuals independent of accounts payable and cash disbursement functions. | • Obtain a file of checks used during the period and identify and account for all gaps in sequencing.<br>• Obtain the company's bank reconciliations for all open bank accounts. For a sample of reconciliations, reperform the procedures or otherwise determine that the reconciliation was performed properly. |

| Objective and Risk | Example Controls | Example Tests of Operating Effectiveness |
|---|---|---|
| **Control Objective:** Safeguard cash and the related accounting records. | | |
| **Risk to Achieving Objective** | | |
| • Inadequate physical security over cash and documents that can be used to transfer cash | • Segregate custodial and record-keeping functions.<br>• Reconcile bank accounts by individuals without responsibility for cash receipts, disbursements, or custody.<br>• Receive and prelist cash by individuals independent of recording cash receipts.<br>• Restrictively endorse checks on receipt.<br>• Deposit receipts intact daily.<br>• Restrict access to accounts receivable files and files used in processing cash receipts.<br>• Mail checks by individuals independent of recording accounts payable.<br>• Authorized check signers are independent of cash receipts functions.<br>• Physically protect mechanical check signers and signature plates.<br>• Restrict access to accounts payable files and files used in processing cash disbursements. | • Obtain the company's bank reconciliations for all open bank accounts. For a sample of reconciliations, reperform the procedures or otherwise determine that the reconciliation was performed properly.<br>• Make inquiries relating to and observe the operation of the company's controls over the endorsement of checks on receipt.<br>• Test logical access to accounts receivable files and other files used in processing cash receipts and disbursements as part of the tests of IT general controls.<br>• Make inquiries of and observe the controls that restrict physical access to mechanical check signers and signature plates. |

# Example Testing Program for Control Operating Effectiveness: Payroll

## PURPOSE

This form provides an example testing program that links the tests of operating effectiveness of activity-level controls to related controls, control objectives, and risks to achieving those objectives. Use this form to help you design tests of activity-level controls at your organization.

## INSTRUCTIONS

To modify these example testing programs to fit the particular circumstances of your company, you should first identify the control objectives that are comparable to the control objectives at your company. Identify the control procedures in place to satisfy those objectives and which of those control procedures are most important in the prevention or detection of material misstatements. Using the example tests as a guide, design your own tests of operating effectiveness that are appropriate for the controls in place at the company.

You also should identify control objectives relevant to your company that are not included in the example testing program. Identify the control procedures related to these objectives, determine which of these procedures should be tested, and design the appropriate test.

| Objective and Risk | Example Controls | Example Tests of Operating Effectiveness |
|---|---|---|
| **Control Objective:** Calculate and record payroll accurately and completely for all services actually performed and approved, and only for such services. | | |
| **Risk to Achieving Objective** | | |
| • Pay rates or deductions are not properly authorized or are inaccurate. | • Review and approve initial pay and any subsequent additions or changes.<br>• Periodically verify payroll database information.<br>• Review and approve initial deductions/benefit elections.<br>• Use standard forms for making changes to payroll information.<br>• Review and approve all nonstandard items such as sick, vacation, and bonus pay.<br>• Review payroll register and checks for reasonableness.<br>• Establish security controls that limit access to payroll database. | • Obtain payroll database. Select a sample of data and compare it to supporting information. Data selected for testing should include employee name and<br>- Pay rate<br>- Deductions and benefit elections<br>Make inquiries and observe operation of payroll data input controls.<br>• Obtain a file of nonstandard payroll items such as sick, vacation, or bonus pay. Select a sample of items and ensure key information agrees with relevant supporting documents.<br>• Test logical access controls over payroll database as part of IT general controls review. |
| • Hours are not authorized or are inaccurate. | • Review and approve time records for unusual or nonstandard hours and for overtime. | • Obtain a file of overtime pay or other pay related to unusual or nonstandard hours. Select a sample of transactions and compare key data to supporting documentation and determine that circumstances requiring the overtime or other hours were authorized properly. |

| | | |
|---|---|---|
| • Time cards or other source information is submitted for nonexistent employees. | • Use standardized policies and procedures when hiring employees.<br>• Establish security procedures relating to additions and deletions of employees to or from the database.<br>• Maintain logs or other documentation supporting or tracking changes to the payroll database.<br>• Where practical, require valid identification and employee signature to receive paycheck.<br>• Prohibit payment of wages in cash, except in prescribed circumstances.<br>• Use direct-deposit systems. | • Make inquiries and observe the operation of controls related to the addition or deletion of employees to or from the payroll database.<br>• Test logical access controls over the payroll database as part of IT general controls review.<br>• Obtain a file of changes made to the payroll database during the period. Select a sample of transactions and examine supporting documentation to determine that the change was authorized properly. |
| • Lack or loss of information or documents | • Verify that source documents such as time cards are received for all employees.<br>• Maintain backup records of employees' time in case source documents are lost.<br>• Reconcile the employee subsidiary ledger to the general ledger control accounts; investigate any differences.<br>• Compare total hours and number of employees input with the totals in the payroll register. | • Obtain reconciliations of payroll subsidiary ledger to general ledger payroll accounts. Select a sample of reconciliations and determine that the reconciliations were performed properly. |

| Objective and Risk | Example Controls | Example Tests of Operating Effectiveness |
|---|---|---|
| **Control Objective:** Restrict access to payroll data information to only those individuals who need such information to discharge duties. | | |
| **Risk to Achieving Objective** | | |
| • Unauthorized personnel may gain access to payroll information. | • Access to information stored on electronic media is restricted by frequently changed passwords.<br>• Payroll processing systems and written information are subject to physical security. | • Test logical access controls over payroll database as part of IT general controls review.<br>• Make inquiries and observe the performance of controls that restrict the physical access to payroll processing systems and documents. |

# Work Program for the Review of a Type 2 SAS No. 70 Report

## PURPOSE

This form has been designed to

- Facilitate the effective review of a Type 2 SAS No. 70 report on service organization controls
- Help ensure that the company's assessment of internal control at a service organization is complete and thorough

## INSTRUCTIONS

Use this form to guide the review of a Type 2 SAS No. 70 report received from the company's service organization. As each step in the program is completed, the person responsible for performing the step should write his or her initials and the date in the indicated column on the worksheet. If the step is not applicable, indicate that by noting "N/A."

Issues related to the planning of the receipt of such reports (e.g., identifying the business processes, accounts, and relevant assertions affected by service organization processing) are covered in ADM-1, General Work Program.

*Notations in italics are additional instructions to the preparer of the form and should be removed before the form is considered final.*

### WORK PROGRAM FOR THE REVIEW OF A TYPE 2 SAS NO. 70 REPORT

Company: _____     Reporting Date: _____

Prepared by: _____     Date Prepared: _____

This form summarizes the procedures we performed to review and assess the effectiveness of internal controls maintained by a service organization, as described in a service auditor's Type 2 SAS No. 70 Report.

| Procedure Performed | N/A Performed by | Date |
|---|---|---|
| **Read and Assess the Implications of the Type 2 SAS No. 70 Report** | | |
| 1. Read the service auditor's report and assess its implications for the company's assessment of internal control effectiveness. Consider<br>a. Whether the service auditor prepared a Type 2 report<br>b. The nature of the opinions rendered and whether these included any modifications to the standard reporting language<br>c. The timing of the SAS No. 70 engagement, that is,<br>    i. The date as of which the description of controls applies<br>    ii. The period of time covered by the tests of operating effectiveness of controls<br>2. Read the description of the service organization's controls and evaluate the effect of the following on the company's assessment of internal control effectiveness.<br>a. Whether the description includes all significant transactions, processes, computer applications, or business units that are within the scope of the company's assessment of internal control effectiveness<br>b. Whether the description includes all five components of internal control<br>c. Whether the description is sufficiently detailed to understand how the service organization's processing affects the company's internal control over financial reporting<br>d. Changes to service organization controls<br>e. Instances of noncompliance with service organization controls<br>f. Whether the description of controls is adequate to provide an understanding of those elements of the company's accounting information system maintained by the service organization | | |

| Procedure Performed | N/A<br>Performed<br>by | Date |
|---|---|---|
| 3. List all complementary user organization controls identified in the SAS No. 70 report that the service auditor assumed were maintained by the company ("user controls"). Cross-reference this list to the work performed to<br>  a. Assess the design effectiveness of these user controls<br>  b. Test the operating effectiveness of these user controls<br><br>**Tests of Operating Effectiveness**<br><br>4. Review the service auditor's description of the tests of controls and assess their adequacy for your purposes. Consider<br>  a. The link between the financial statement assertion and the control objective<br>  b. The link between the control objective and the controls tested<br>  c. The nature, timing, and extent of the tests performed<br>5. Evaluate the results of the tests of controls.<br>  a. Identify control testing exceptions and determine whether they indicate a control deficiency.<br>  b. Summarize all control deficiencies and assess their significance, both individually and in combination. | | |

# Type 2 SAS No. 70 Report
# Review Checklist

## PURPOSE

This form has been designed to

- Document the procedures performed and conclusions reached on the effectiveness of internal controls maintained at a service organization, as documented in a service auditor's Type 2 SAS No. 70 report.

## INSTRUCTIONS

Use this form to document the review of a Type 2 SAS No. 70 report.

*Notations in italics are additional instructions to the preparer of the form and should be removed before the form is considered final.*

## TYPE 2 SAS NO. 70 REPORT REVIEW CHECKLIST

Company: _____         Reporting Date: _____

Prepared by: _____       Date Prepared: _____

This form summarizes the procedures we performed and conclusions reached on the effectiveness of internal controls maintained at service organization, as documented in a service auditor's Type 2 SAS No. 70 report.

## PART I: GENERAL INFORMATION

Name of Service Organization _____

As of date for description of service organization controls _____

Period covered by service auditor's tests of control operating effectiveness _____

Types of transactions processed by the service organization that affect the company's financial statements

---

---

---

---

---

The significant financial statement accounts and disclosures and relevant assertions affected by transactions processed by the service organization

---

---

---

---

## PART II: REVIEW OF SERVICE AUDITOR'S REPORT

The following summarizes the opinions provided in the service auditor's report.

| Required Opinion | Service Auditor Opinion | |
|---|---|---|
| | Standard | Modified |
| Whether the service organization's description of its controls presents fairly, in all material respects, the relevant aspects of the service organization's controls that had been placed in operation as of a specific date | ❏ | ❏ |
| Whether the controls were suitably designed to achieve specified control objectives | ❏ | ❏ |
| Whether the controls that were tested were operating with sufficient effectiveness to provide reasonable, but not absolute, assurance that the control objectives were achieved during the period specified | ❏ | ❏ |

Describe any modifications to the service auditor's standard opinion and the effect these modifications have on the company's assessment of internal control effectiveness.

_____

_____

_____

_____

# PART III: REVIEW OF THE SERVICE ORGANIZATION'S DESCRIPTION OF CONTROLS

| | Internal Control Component | | | | | | | | | |
|---|---|---|---|---|---|---|---|---|---|---|
| | Control Environment | | Risk Assessment | | Information and Communication | | Monitoring | |
| | Yes | No | Yes | No | Yes | No | Yes | No |
| 1. All transactions, processes, computer applications, or business units that affect the company's assessment of internal control effectiveness are described in the SAS 70 report. | ☐ | ☐ | ☐ | ☐ | ☐ | ☐ | ☐ | ☐ |
| 2. The level of detail provided is sufficient to allow us to understand how the service organization's processing affects the company's internal control. | ☐ | ☐ | ☐ | ☐ | ☐ | ☐ | ☐ | ☐ |
| 3. The SAS 70 report identified *no* changes to controls since the later of the date of the last service auditor's report or within the last 12 months. | ☐ | ☐ | ☐ | ☐ | ☐ | ☐ | ☐ | ☐ |
| 4. The SAS 70 report identified *no* instances of noncompliance with the service organization's controls identified in the service organization's description of controls. | ☐ | ☐ | ☐ | ☐ | ☐ | ☐ | ☐ | ☐ |

## Additional Questions for the Information Component of Internal Control

These questions apply only to those elements of the information system that are maintained by the service organization. To the extent that the company is responsible for performing certain accounting information functions (e.g., the preparation of significant estimates or disclosures), you should mark the question "N/A."

|  | Yes | No | N/A |
|---|---|---|---|
| 5. The service auditor's report is adequate to allow us to obtain sufficient knowledge of the information relevant to the company's financial reporting to understand those elements of the information system maintained by the service organization related to |  |  |  |
| a. The classes of transactions in the company's operations that are significant to the financial statements | ❏ | ❏ | ❏ |
| b. The procedures, both automated and manual, by which transactions are initiated, recorded, processed, and reported from their occurrence to their inclusion in the financial statements | ❏ | ❏ | ❏ |
| c. The related accounting records, whether electronic or manual; supporting information; and specific accounts in the financial statements involved in initiating, recording, processing, and reporting transactions | ❏ | ❏ | ❏ |
| d. How the information system captures other events and conditions that are significant to the financial statements | ❏ | ❏ | ❏ |

## Tests of Controls

*Identify the relevant financial statement assertions affected by service organization services. Summarize these assertions across the horizontal axis. For each assertion, answer the questions listed in the first column, and document your answers by checking the appropriate box.*

| | Assertions for Which Control Risk to Be Assessed below Maximum | | | | | | | | | |
|---|---|---|---|---|---|---|---|---|---|---|
| | A | | B | | C | | D | | E | |
| | Y | N | Y | N | Y | N | Y | N | Y | N |
| 1. Is the assertion linked to a service organization control objective? | ❏ | ❏ | ❏ | ❏ | ❏ | ❏ | ❏ | ❏ | ❏ | ❏ |
| 2. Is the control objective linked to related control activities? | ❏ | ❏ | ❏ | ❏ | ❏ | ❏ | ❏ | ❏ | ❏ | ❏ |
| 3. Is the description of the nature, timing, and extent of the tests applied in sufficient detail to enable you to determine the effect of the tests on your assessment of internal control effectiveness? | ❏ | ❏ | ❏ | ❏ | ❏ | ❏ | ❏ | ❏ | ❏ | ❏ |
| 4. Do the results of the service auditor's tests support an assessment that internal control is effective? | ❏ | ❏ | ❏ | ❏ | ❏ | ❏ | ❏ | ❏ | ❏ | ❏ |

## Response

The following describes how any "No" responses to the preceding questions were considered in our internal control assessment.

*Describe any "No" responses to the preceding questions by documenting*

* *The conditions cited in the SAS 70 report that gave rise to the "no" response*
* *How the conditions were considered in the overall assessment of internal control effectiveness*

_____

_____

_____

_____

## PART III: COMPLEMENTARY USER ORGANIZATION CONTROLS

The following describes significant user organization controls and the procedures we performed to test their effectiveness.

*List the controls identified in the SAS 70 report that the service organization assumed were placed in operation at the user organization ("user controls"). Describe (or indicate where the relevant information can be found regarding) the procedures performed, information gathered, and conclusions reached regarding the design and operating effectiveness of these user controls.*

_____

_____

_____

_____

_____

_____

# Process Owners' Monitoring of Control Effectiveness

## PURPOSE

This form has been designed to

- Obtain the business process owner's perspective on the most significant transactions and related controls in his or her area of operations
- Gather information about the monitoring component of internal control at the activity level
- Identify possible control deficiencies related to activity-level controls

## INSTRUCTIONS

The questionnaire on the following pages is designed to gather information from business process owners about the procedures they perform to monitor the ongoing effectiveness of control activities in their process area. The questionnaire should be completed by the process owner and should serve as a basis for follow-up questions.

### *Monitoring*

Monitoring is a process that assesses the quality of internal control performance over time. It involves assessing the design and operation of controls on a timely basis and taking necessary corrective actions. Monitoring may be done at both the entity and the activity level. Examples of ongoing monitoring activities at the activity level include

- The regular management and supervisory activities carried out in the normal course of business
- The provision that employees may be required to "sign off" to evidence the performance of critical control functions, which allows management to monitor the performance of these control functions

### REPORTING CONTROL DEFICIENCIES

Providing information regarding internal control deficiencies to the right people is critical if the internal control system is to continue to function effectively. For this reason, the monitoring component of internal controls should include a mechanism for reporting internal control deficiencies and taking appropriate action. COSO uses the term "deficiency" broadly to mean any condition of an internal control system "worthy of attention." Certainly all deficiencies that can affect the entity's ability to produce reliable financial information should be identified and reported. However, the COSO report also makes the point that even seemingly simple problems with a relatively simple, obvious solution should be carefully considered because they might have far-reaching implications. Reinforcing a concept introduced in its discussion of information and communication, when errors and deficiencies are identified, their underlying causes should be investigated.

Findings of internal control deficiencies should be reported to the individuals who are in the best position to take action. This includes not only the person responsible for the activity involved, but also to at least one level of management above the directly responsible person.

---

# PROCESS OWNERS MONITORING
# OF CONTROL EFFECTIVENESS

*This questionnaire should be distributed to the business process owners from whom you want to gather information.*

## INTRODUCTION

One of the key components of your company's internal control is the way in which management monitors the continued effectiveness of the control policies and procedures it has put into place. As a process owner, you play an important role in identifying conditions that indicate that controls are *not* operating effectively and in taking appropriate corrective actions. This questionnaire is designed to help us better understand how you perform this function.

## BACKGROUND INFORMATION

Your Name _____

1. Briefly describe the business process for which you are responsible (e.g., sales, purchasing, inventory management).

_____

_____

_____

2. Within your business process, what are the most significant business transactions for which you are responsible? Consider those transactions that either
   - Generate revenue for the company
   - Create or acquire company assets

- Incur company obligations or liabilities
- Result in company expenses
- Involve the receipt or disbursement of cash

---

---

---

---

---

---

---

---

3. For each of the transactions described in question 2, briefly summarize the control procedures that you rely on most to ensure that the information related to these transactions is properly captured and processed. In preparing your summary, please describe the controls in place to ensure that

- Transactions are properly authorized
- *All* authorized transactions are captured and processed
- *Only* authorized transactions are captured and processed
- Data are captured and processed at their proper amounts

---

---

---

---

---

---

---

---

---

## MONITORING ONGOING CONTROL EFFECTIVENESS

4. Suppose that one or more of the control procedures described in question 3 were *not* functioning effectively.

a. What activities do you regularly perform that would alert you to the possibility that controls in your process area were not functioning effectively?

_____

_____

_____

_____

_____

b. What information do you receive from parties outside the company that would alert you to the possibility that controls in your process area were not functioning effectively (e.g., customer complaints about the accuracy of their billing statements)? Consider outside parties such as

- Customers
- Vendors
- Regulators
- Others with whom the company does business

_____

_____

_____

_____

_____

5. Describe the procedures in place to ensure that you receive feedback from both internal and external auditors about control deficiencies or suggestions for ways to improve internal control.

_____

_____

_____

6. If you have responsibility for tangible assets (e.g., inventory), describe the procedures followed to compare the information recorded in the company's books and records to the physical assets.

_____

_____

_____

## IDENTIFICATION AND FOLLOW-UP ON IDENTIFIED DEFICIENCIES

7. Describe any indications that currently exist that may indicate that the controls described in question 3 are not functioning effectively. Consider those indications that arose from
   - The performance of your regular activities
   - Information received from third parties
   - Feedback from internal or external auditors

_____

_____

_____

_____

_____

8. With regard to the items identified in question 7, what actions did you take? (If no items were identified in question 7, please describe the actions that you would take if you became aware of control deficiencies.)

_____

_____

_____

_____

_____

# PART IV
# Example Letters and Other Communications

# Example Engagement Letter for Outside Consultants to Management

## PURPOSE

Outside consultants who have been engaged to assist management in their assessment of internal control effectiveness should reach an understanding with management regarding key elements of their engagement, including

- The services to be performed, including their
  - Objectives
  - Nature
  - Timing
  - Limitations
- Deliverables or work product
- The responsibilities of the parties
- Fees

The following is an example of a letter that can be used to confirm such an understanding between management and the outside consultant. Typically, this letter is sent from the consultant to company management.

## EXAMPLE LETTER

[Consulting Firm's Letterhead]

[Date]

[Client's Name and Address]

It was a pleasure to discuss with you how [consulting firm's name] can help [client's name] in its assessment of the effectiveness of internal control over financial reporting, as required by Section 404 of the Sarbanes-Oxley Act of 2002, for the year ended [year-end]. We are writing to confirm our understanding of the services we are to provide, including the limitations of those services.

The objective of our services is to assist [client's name] management in [provide general description].[a]

We will work with you and the selected project team from [client's name] to:

- [List nature of services to be performed]
- 
- 
- 

Upon completion of the work described in the preceding paragraph, we will work with you and the selected project team from [client's name] to complete the following:

- [List key deliverables]
- 
- 
- 

During the performance of our engagement we may become aware of testing exceptions or other conditions that indicate a control deficiency may exist. We will inform you of all such exceptions or conditions as they become known to us.

The management of [client's name] is responsible for

- Establishing and maintaining adequate internal control over financial reporting for the company
- Assessing the effectiveness of the company's internal control over financial reporting as of the end
- Identifying and disclosing material weaknesses in internal control[b]

Throughout our engagement we may provide advice, research materials, as appropriate, and recommendations to assist [client's name] management in performing its functions and making decisions. However, we will not perform management functions or make management decisions, which are the responsibility of [client's name] management and which include but are not limited to the following.

- The general oversight of [client's name] management's assessment of the effectiveness of internal control over financial reporting
- The evaluation of whether the nature, timing, scope, and deliverables of the services performed are sufficient for your purposes
- The determination of whether identified control testing exceptions constitute a control deficiency
- The evaluation of the relative significance of identified control deficiencies, including whether such deficiencies constitute a "significant deficiency" or "material weakness," as defined in PCAOB Auditing Standard No. 2

- The formation of an assessment of the effectiveness of internal control over financial reporting

*Disclaimer.* Given the subjective nature of assessing the effectiveness of internal control over financial reporting, as well as the heavy reliance on active participation of [client name] personnel in achieving the objectives of this project, we cannot warrant or guarantee the objectives will be met to the satisfaction of [client name] external auditors.

The senior members of the project team from [consulting firm] will consist of [list senior members of project team]. Other resources will be added to the project team as needed to meet the needs of [client's name] management. As team members are added, we will notify [client's name] management of each team member and their role on the project team.

[Client name] management will provide the majority of the resources for the project team. The timeline and fee estimates in this agreement assume the focused attention of this team on the project. We also assume that [client individual] will be the senior member of [client's name] management's project team and in that capacity will have primary oversight responsibilities for the team. We will communicate directly with [him or her] in regard to project issues as needed.

We expect to begin our engagement on approximately [date].[c]

We estimate our fees for these services will range from \$_____ to \$_____, plus a reimbursement of reasonable and ordinary expenses including, but not limited to, travel, meals, supplies, and communication costs. If unexpected circumstances arise that may result in the incurrence of significant additional time, we will inform you immediately and, if necessary, discuss any adjustments to our fees. These fees will be billed as the work progresses and are payable [describe payment terms].

If the above terms and conditions meet with your approval, please sign and return the enclosed copy of this letter. We are enthusiastic about the opportunity to provide services to [client name]. Of course, should you have any questions or comments, please do not hesitate to call me.[d]

---

[a] *The objective of the consultant's services is to assist management in the fulfillment of its responsibilities. In this paragraph you should provide a general description of the phase of management's assessment of internal control that you will be helping them with. For example, ". . . to assist management in the documentation of entity-level controls," or "to assist management in testing the operating effectiveness of certain activity-level controls."*

[b] *This list of responsibilities was adapted from the SEC rules. See Items 308(a) and (c) of Regulation S-B and S-K, 17 C.F.R. 228.308 (a) and (c) and 229.309 (a) and (c), respectively.*

[c] *You may wish to attach a timeline of the expected start and completion dates of significant phases of the engagement.*

[d] *You may wish to include other clauses in your engagement letter, such as those relating to*
- *Ownership of work product*
- *Alternative dispute resolution*
- *Compensation for firm employees hired by client or client employees hired by firm*
- *Circumstances under which agreement may be terminated*

Very truly yours,


ACCEPTANCE:

This letter correctly sets forth the understanding of the engagement.

Signature: _____

Title: _____

Date: _____

# Example Management Representation Letter

## PURPOSE

Paragraph 142 of PCAOB Auditing Standard No. 2 requires the external auditor to obtain certain written representations from management in connection with their audit of the company's internal control over financial reporting. The following is an example of a letter that can be used for this purpose.

## EXAMPLE LETTER

[Company Letterhead]

[Date][1]

To [Independent Auditor]

We are providing this letter in connection with your audit of internal control over financial reporting of [name of entity] as of [date]. This audit was performed for the purpose of expressing an opinion on management's assessment of the effectiveness of the company's internal control over financial reporting. We confirm that we are responsible for establishing and maintaining effective internal control over financial reporting.

Certain representations in this letter are described as being limited to matters that are material. Items are considered material, regardless of size, if they involve an omission or misstatement of accounting information that, in light of surrounding circumstances, makes it probable that the judgment of a reasonable person relying on the information would be changed or influenced by the omission or misstatement.

We confirm, to the best of our knowledge and belief, as of [date of auditor's report], the following representations made to you during your audit.

1. We have performed an assessment of the effectiveness of the company's internal control over financial reporting using the criteria set forth by [identify criteria].[2]

2. We did not use the procedures performed during your audits of internal control over financial reporting or the financial statements as part of the basis for our assessment of the effectiveness of internal control over financial reporting.

3. Based on our assessment, we believe that, as of [year-end], the company's internal control over financial reporting [is/is not] effective based on the criteria identified in 1 above.

4. We have disclosed to you all deficiencies in the design or operation of internal control over financial reporting identified as part of our assessment, including separately disclosing all such deficiencies that we believe to be significant deficiencies or material weaknesses in internal control over financial reporting.

5. We have no knowledge of any material fraud involving our employees.

6. We have no knowledge of any fraud that involves[3]
   a. Senior management or
   b. Management or
   c. Other employees who have a significant role in the company's internal control over financial reporting

7. All control deficiencies identified and communicated to the audit committee during previous audit engagements have been resolved, except for [list those control deficiencies that have not been resolved, if applicable].

Subsequent to [year-end], there have been no changes in internal control over financial reporting or other factors that might significantly affect internal control over financial reporting, including any corrective actions we have taken with regard to significant deficiencies and material weaknesses.

_____

[Name of Chief Executive Officer and Title]

_____

[Name of Chief Financial Officer and Title]

---

[1] *The letter should be dated no earlier than the date of the auditor's report on internal control over financial reporting.*

[2] *For example, "the Committee of Sponsoring Organizations of the Treadway Commission (COSO) in* Internal Control Integrated Framework.*"*

[3] *If you have knowledge of any material fraud or any other fraud that, although not material, involves senior management or management or other employees who have a significant role in the company's internal control over financial reporting, these should be described in the letter.*

# Example Management Reports on Effectiveness of Internal Control over Financial Reporting[1]

## PURPOSE

Guidance on the preparation of management's reports on the effectiveness of internal control over financial reporting is provided by the following.

- Item 308(a) of Regulation S-B and S-K, 17 C.F.R 228.308(a) and 17 C.F.R. 229.308(a)
- Questions 1, 2, 3, and 19 of Internal Control over Financial Reporting and Certification of Disclosure in Exchange Act Periodic Reports: Frequently Asked Questions, published by the staff of the SEC Office of the Chief Accountant and the Division of Corporation Finance

The following are examples of such reports.

## EXAMPLE 1: MANAGEMENT REPORT WHEN INTERNAL CONTROL OVER FINANCIAL REPORTING IS EFFECTIVE

The management of [company name] is responsible for establishing and maintaining adequate internal control over financial reporting. This internal control system was designed to provide reasonable assurance to the company's management and board of directors regarding the preparation and fair presentation of published financial statements.

All internal control systems, no matter how well designed, have inherent limitations. Therefore, even those systems determined to be effective can provide only reasonable assurance with respect to financial statement preparation and presentation. *(Author's note: This statement regarding the inherent limitation of internal control is not required by SEC rules. It is included in this example report solely for illustrative purposes.)*

---

[1] *These example reports originally appeared, in slightly different form, in the article "Section 404 Compliance in the Annual Report," by Michael Ramos, published by the* Journal of Accountancy, *October 2004, page 43. Reprinted with the permission of the* Journal of Accountancy. *Opinions of the author are his own and do not necessarily reflect policies of the AICPA. The author wishes to thank Chuck Landes and Laura Phillips for their input during the development of these examples.*

[Company name] management assessed the effectiveness of the company's internal control over financial reporting as of [year-end]. In making this assessment, it used the criteria set forth by the Committee of Sponsoring Organizations of the Treadway Commission (COSO) in *Internal Control—Integrated Framework*. Based on our assessment, we believe that, as of [year-end], the company's internal control over financial reporting is effective based on those criteria.

[Company name]'s independent auditors have issued an audit report on our assessment of the company's internal control over financial reporting. This report appears on page XX.

## EXAMPLE 2: MANAGEMENT REPORT ON INTERNAL CONTROL OVER FINANCIAL REPORTING WHEN MATERIAL WEAKNESSES HAVE BEEN IDENTIFIED

[Introductory paragraph—same as in example 1.]

[Optional, inherent limitations paragraph—see example 1.]

An internal control material weakness is a significant deficiency, or combination of them, that results in more than a remote likelihood that a material misstatement of the annual or interim financial statements will not be prevented or detected.

The management of [company name] assessed the effectiveness of the company's internal control over financial reporting as of [year-end], and this assessment identified the following material weakness in the company's internal control over financial reporting.

[Describe the material weakness.]

[Company name] management assessed the effectiveness of the company's internal control over financial reporting as of [year-end]. In making this assessment, management used the criteria set forth by the Committee of Sponsoring Organizations of the Treadway Commission (COSO) in *Internal Control—Integrated Framework*. Because of the material weakness described in the preceding paragraph, management believes that, as of [year-end], the company's internal control over financial reporting was not effective based on those criteria.

[Company name]'s independent auditors have issued an attestation report on management's assessment of the company's internal control over financial reporting. It appears on page XX.

# Example Subcertification

## PURPOSE

A great deal of the information included in financial statements and other reports filed with the SEC originates in areas of the company that are outside the direct control of the chief executive officer (CEO) and chief financial officer (CFO). Because of the significance of information processed and related controls that are the responsibility of others, the CEO and CFO may request those individuals to provide certain representations. This process is known as *subcertification,* and it usually requires the individuals to provide a written affidavit to the CEO and CFO that will allow them to sign their report on internal control effectiveness in good faith.

The following is an example of a subcertification letter.

## EXAMPLE LETTER

[Company Letterhead]

[Date][1]

To [CEO and CFO]

I am providing this letter in connection with your assessment of the effectiveness of internal control over financial reporting of [name of entity] as of [date].[2] As the [title of individual signing the letter], I am responsible for establishing and maintaining effective internal control over financial reporting for [name of business unit, location, division, etc.].[3]

Certain representations in this letter are described as being limited to matters that are material. Items are considered material, regardless of size, if they involve an omission or misstatement of accounting information that, in the light of surrounding circumstances, makes it probable that the judgment of a reasonable person relying on the information would be changed or influenced by the omission or misstatement.

I confirm, to the best of my knowledge and belief, as of [date of management's representation letter to the external auditors], the following representations made to you.

1. I have performed an assessment of the effectiveness of [name of business unit, location, division, etc.] internal control over financial reporting using the criteria set forth by [identify criteria].[4]

2. I did not use the procedures performed during the external auditor's audits of internal control over financial reporting or the financial statements as part of the basis

for my assessment of the effectiveness of internal control over financial reporting for [name of business unit, location, division, etc.].

3. Based on my assessment, I believe that, as of [year-end], the [name of business unit, location, division, etc.] internal control over financial reporting [is/is not] effective based on the criteria identified in 1 above.

4. I have disclosed to you all deficiencies in the design or operation of internal control over financial reporting identified as part of my assessment, including separately disclosing all such deficiencies that I believe to be significant deficiencies or material weaknesses in internal control over financial reporting.

5. I have no knowledge of any material fraud involving the employees of [name of business unit, location, division, etc.].

6. I have no knowledge of any fraud that involves[5]

   a. Senior management of [name of business unit, location, division, etc.] or

   b. Management of [name of business unit, location, division, etc.] or

   c. Other employees of [name of business unit, location, division, etc.] who have a significant role in internal control over financial reporting

7. All control deficiencies relating to [name of business unit, location, division, etc.] that were identified and communicated to the audit committee during previous audit engagements have been resolved, except for [list those control deficiencies that have not been resolved, if applicable].

Subsequent to [year-end], there have been no changes in internal control over financial reporting or other factors that might significantly affect internal control over financial reporting, including any corrective actions we have taken with regard to significant deficiencies and material weaknesses.

---

[Name]

---

[Title]

[1] *The letter should be dated the same as the CEO's and CFO's representation letter to the external auditors.*

[2] *This example letter is limited to representations required as a result of the external auditor's audit of internal control. Additional letters may be required for representations relating to the audit of the financial statements. Alternatively, the representations related to internal control and those related to the audit of the financial statements may be combined into one comprehensive letter.*

[3] *The signer of the letter should clearly indicate the scope of the representations being made, for example, that they are limited to the business unit or location for which the signer has direct responsibility.*

[4] *For example, "the Committee of Sponsoring Organizations of the Treadway Commission (COSO) in Internal Control Integrated Framework."*

[5] *If you have knowledge of any material fraud or any other fraud that, although not material, involves senior management or management or other employees who have a significant role in the company's internal control over financial reporting, these should be described in the letter.*

# Appendix A

## INTRODUCTION

In June 2007, the SEC provided interpretative guidance to help management comply with its requirements for reporting on internal control. In general, that guidance described a top-down, risk-based approach to evaluating internal control. The methodology described in this book (summarized in the General Work Program, ADM-1) incorporates this overall approach. Other practice aids reflect the more specific guidance included in the SEC release.

This appendix is the complete text of the SEC interpretation, and it has been included as an additional reference source to help you use the practice aids included in this toolkit.

SECURITIES AND EXCHANGE COMMISSION

17 CFR PART 241

[RELEASE NOS. 33-8810; 34-55929; FR-77; File No. S7-24-06]

Commission Guidance Regarding Management's Report on Internal Control Over Financial Reporting Under Section 13(a) or 15(d) of the Securities Exchange Act of 1934

AGENCY: Securities and Exchange Commission.

ACTION: Interpretation.

SUMMARY: The SEC is publishing this interpretive release to provide guidance for management regarding its evaluation and assessment of internal control over financial reporting. The guidance sets forth an approach by which management can conduct a top-down, risk-based evaluation of internal control over financial reporting. An evaluation that complies with this interpretive guidance is one way to satisfy the evaluation requirements of Rules 13a-15(c) and 15d-15(c) under the Securities Exchange Act of 1934.

EFFECTIVE DATE: June 27, 2007.

FOR FURTHER INFORMATION CONTACT: Josh K. Jones, Professional Accounting Fellow, Office of the Chief Accountant, at (202) 551-5300, or N. Sean Harrison, Special Counsel, Division of Corporation Finance, at (202) 551-3430, U.S. Securities and Exchange Commission, 100 F Street, NE, Washington, DC 20549.

SUPPLEMENTARY INFORMATION: The amendments to Rules 13a-15(c)[1] and 15d-15(c)[2] under the Securities Exchange Act of 1934[3] (the "Exchange Act"), which

---

[1] 17 CFR 240.13a-15(c).

[2] 17 CFR 240.15d-15(c).

[3] 15 U.S.C. 78a et seq.

clarify that an evaluation of internal control over financial reporting that complies with

this interpretive guidance is one way to satisfy those rules, are being made in a separate

release.[4]

## I. Introduction

Management is responsible for maintaining a system of internal control over

financial reporting ("ICFR") that provides reasonable assurance regarding the reliability

of financial reporting and the preparation of financial statements for external purposes in

accordance with generally accepted accounting principles. The rules we adopted in June

2003 to implement Section 404 of the Sarbanes-Oxley Act of 2002[5] ("Sarbanes-Oxley")

require management to annually evaluate whether ICFR is effective at providing

reasonable assurance and to disclose its assessment to investors.[6] Management is

responsible for maintaining evidential matter, including documentation, to provide

reasonable support for its assessment. This evidence will also allow a third party, such as

the company's external auditor, to consider the work performed by management.

ICFR cannot provide absolute assurance due to its inherent limitations; it is a

process that involves human diligence and compliance and is subject to lapses in

judgment and breakdowns resulting from human failures. ICFR also can be

circumvented by collusion or improper management override. Because of such

limitations, ICFR cannot prevent or detect all misstatements, whether unintentional errors

or fraud. However, these inherent limitations are known features of the financial

---

[4] Release No. 34-55928 (Jun. 20, 2007).

[5] 15 U.S.C. 7262.

[6] Release No. 33-8238 (Jun. 5, 2003) [68 FR 36636] (hereinafter "Adopting Release").

reporting process, therefore, it is possible to design into the process safeguards to reduce, though not eliminate, this risk.

The "reasonable assurance" referred to in the Commission's implementing rules relates to similar language in the Foreign Corrupt Practices Act of 1977 ("FCPA").[7] Exchange Act Section 13(b)(7) defines "reasonable assurance" and "reasonable detail" as "such level of detail and degree of assurance as would satisfy prudent officials in the conduct of their own affairs."[8] The Commission has long held that "reasonableness" is not an "absolute standard of exactitude for corporate records."[9] In addition, the Commission recognizes that while "reasonableness" is an objective standard, there is a range of judgments that an issuer might make as to what is "reasonable" in implementing Section 404 and the Commission's rules. Thus, the terms "reasonable," "reasonably," and "reasonableness" in the context of Section 404 implementation do not imply a single conclusion or methodology, but encompass the full range of appropriate potential conduct, conclusions or methodologies upon which an issuer may reasonably base its decisions.

Since companies first began complying in 2004, the Commission has received significant feedback on our rules implementing Section 404.[10] This feedback included requests for further guidance to assist company management in complying with our ICFR

---

[7] Title 1 of Pub. L. 95-213 (1977).

[8] 15 U.S.C. 78m(b)(7). The conference committee report on the 1988 amendments to the FCPA also noted that the standard "does not connote an unrealistic degree of exactitude or precision. The concept of reasonableness of necessity contemplates the weighing of a number of relevant factors, including the costs of compliance." Cong. Rec. H2116 (daily ed. Apr. 20, 1988).

[9] Release No. 34-17500 (Jan. 29, 1981) [46 FR 11544].

[10] Release Nos. 33-8762; 34-54976 (Dec. 20, 2006) [71 FR 77635] (hereinafter "Proposing Release"). For a detailed history of the implementation of Section 404 of Sarbanes-Oxley, see Section I., Background, of the Proposing Release. An analysis of the comments we received on the Proposing Release is included in Section III of this release.

evaluation and disclosure requirements. This guidance is in response to those requests and reflects the significant feedback we have received, including comments on the interpretive guidance we proposed on December 20, 2006. In addressing a number of the commonly identified areas of concerns, the interpretive guidance:

- Explains how to vary evaluation approaches for gathering evidence based on risk assessments;

- Explains the use of "daily interaction," self-assessment, and other on-going monitoring activities as evidence in the evaluation;

- Explains the purpose of documentation and how management has flexibility in approaches to documenting support for its assessment;

- Provides management significant flexibility in making judgments regarding what constitutes adequate evidence in low-risk areas; and

- Allows for management and the auditor to have different testing approaches.

The Interpretive Guidance is organized around two broad principles. The first principle is that management should evaluate whether it has implemented controls that adequately address the risk that a material misstatement of the financial statements would not be prevented or detected in a timely manner. The guidance describes a top-down, risk-based approach to this principle, including the role of entity-level controls in assessing financial reporting risks and the adequacy of controls. The guidance promotes efficiency by allowing management to focus on those controls that are needed to adequately address the risk of a material misstatement of its financial statements. The guidance does not require management to identify every control in a process or document the business processes impacting ICFR. Rather, management can focus its evaluation process and the documentation supporting the assessment on those controls that it determines adequately address the risk of a material misstatement of the financial statements. For example, if management determines that a risk of a material misstatement is adequately addressed by an entity-level control, no further evaluation of other controls is required.

The second principle is that management's evaluation of evidence about the operation of its controls should be based on its assessment of risk. The guidance provides an approach for making risk-based judgments about the evidence needed for the evaluation. This allows management to align the nature and extent of its evaluation procedures with those areas of financial reporting that pose the highest risks to reliable financial reporting (that is, whether the financial statements are materially accurate). As a result, management may be able to use more efficient approaches to gathering evidence, such as self-assessments, in low-risk areas and perform more extensive testing in high-risk areas. By following these two principles, we believe companies of all sizes and complexities will be able to implement our rules effectively and efficiently.

The Interpretive Guidance reiterates the Commission's position that management should bring its own experience and informed judgment to bear in order to design an evaluation process that meets the needs of its company and that provides a reasonable basis for its annual assessment of whether ICFR is effective. This allows management sufficient and appropriate flexibility to design such an evaluation process.[11]

---

[11] Exchange Act Rules 13a-15 and 15d-15 [17 CFR 240.13a-15 and 15d-15] require management to evaluate the effectiveness of ICFR as of the end of the fiscal year. For purposes of this document, the term "evaluation" or "evaluation process" refers to the methods and procedures that management implements to comply with these rules. The term "assessment" is used in this document to describe the disclosure required by Item 308 of Regulations S-B and S-K [17 CFR 228.308 and 229.308]. This disclosure must include discussion of any material weaknesses

Smaller public companies, which generally have less complex internal control systems

than larger public companies, can use this guidance to scale and tailor their evaluation

methods and procedures to fit their own facts and circumstances. We encourage smaller

public companies[12] to take advantage of the flexibility and scalability to conduct an

evaluation of ICFR that is both efficient and effective at identifying material weaknesses.

The effort necessary to conduct an initial evaluation of ICFR will vary among

companies, partly because this effort will depend on management's existing financial

reporting risk assessment and control monitoring activities. After the first year of

compliance, management's effort to identify financial reporting risks and controls should

ordinarily be less, because subsequent evaluations should be more focused on changes in

risks and controls rather than identification of all financial reporting risks and the related

controls. Further, in each subsequent year, the documentation of risks and controls will

only need to be updated from the prior year(s), not recreated anew. Through the risk and

control identification process, management will have identified for testing only those

controls that are needed to meet the objective of ICFR (that is, to provide reasonable

assurance regarding the reliability of financial reporting) and for which evidence about

their operation can be obtained most efficiently. The nature and extent of procedures

---

which exist as of the end of the most recent fiscal year and management's assessment of the effectiveness of ICFR, including a statement as to whether or not ICFR is effective. Management is not permitted to conclude that ICFR is effective if there are one or more material weaknesses in ICFR.

[12] While a company's individual facts and circumstances should be considered in determining whether a company is a smaller public company and the resulting implications to management's evaluation, a company's public market capitalization and annual revenues are useful indicators of its size and complexity. The Final Report of the Advisory Committee on Smaller Public Companies to the United States Securities and Exchange Commission (Apr. 23, 2006), available at http://www.sec.gov/info/smallbus/acspc/acspc-finalreport.pdf, defined smaller companies, which included microcap companies, and the SEC's rules include size characteristics for "accelerated filers" and "non-accelerated filers" which approximately fit the same definitions.

implemented to evaluate whether those controls continue to operate effectively can be tailored to the company's unique circumstances, thereby avoiding unnecessary compliance costs.

The guidance assumes management has established and maintains a system of internal accounting controls as required by the FCPA. Further, it is not intended to explain how management should design its ICFR to comply with the control framework management has chosen. To allow appropriate flexibility, the guidance does not provide a checklist of steps management should perform in completing its evaluation.

The guidance in this release shall be effective immediately upon its publication in the Federal Register.[13]

As a companion[14] to this interpretive release, we are adopting amendments to Exchange Act Rules 13a-15(c) and 15d-15(c) and revisions to Regulation S-X.[15] The amendments to Rules 13a-15(c) and 15d-15(c) will make it clear that an evaluation that is conducted in accordance with this interpretive guidance is one way to satisfy the annual management evaluation requirement in those rules. We are also amending our rules to define the term "material weakness" and to revise the requirements regarding the auditor's attestation report on ICFR. Additionally, we are seeking additional comment on the definition of the term "significant deficiency."[16]

---

[13] The Commission finds good cause under 5 U.S.C. 808(2) for this interpretation to take effect on the date of Federal Register publication. Further delay would be unnecessary and contrary to the public interest because following the guidance is voluntary. Additionally, delay may deter companies from realizing all the efficiencies intended by this guidance, and immediate effectiveness will assist in preparing for 2007 evaluations and assessments of internal control over financial reporting.

[14] Release No. 34-55928.

[15] 17 CFR 210.1-01 et seq.

[16] Release No. 34-55930 (Jun. 20, 2007).

**II. Interpretive Guidance – Evaluation and Assessment of Internal Control Over Financial Reporting**

The interpretive guidance addresses the following topics:

A. The Evaluation Process

    1. Identifying Financial Reporting Risks and Controls

        a.  Identifying Financial Reporting Risks

        b.  Identifying Controls that Adequately Address Financial Reporting Risks

        c.  Consideration of Entity-Level Controls

        d.  Role of Information Technology General Controls

        e.  Evidential Matter to Support the Assessment

    2. Evaluating Evidence of the Operating Effectiveness of ICFR

        a.  Determining the Evidence Needed to Support the Assessment

        b.  Implementing Procedures to Evaluate Evidence of the Operation of ICFR

        c.  Evidential Matter to Support the Assessment

    3. Multiple Location Considerations

B. Reporting Considerations

    1. Evaluation of Control Deficiencies

    2. Expression of Assessment of Effectiveness of ICFR by Management

    3. Disclosures about Material Weaknesses

    4. Impact of a Restatement of Previously Issued Financial Statements on Management's Report on ICFR

    5. Inability to Assess Certain Aspects of ICFR

## A. The Evaluation Process

The objective of internal control over financial reporting[17] ("ICFR") is to provide

reasonable assurance regarding the reliability of financial reporting and the preparation of

financial statements for external purposes in accordance with generally accepted

accounting principles ("GAAP"). The purpose of the evaluation of ICFR is to provide

management with a reasonable basis for its annual assessment as to whether any material

weaknesses[18] in ICFR exist as of the end of the fiscal year.[19] To accomplish this,

management identifies the risks to reliable financial reporting, evaluates whether controls

exist to address those risks, and evaluates evidence about the operation of the controls

---

[17] Exchange Act Rules 13a-15(f) and 15d-15(f) [17 CFR 240.13a-15(f) and 15d-15(b)] define
internal control over financial reporting as:

> A process designed by, or under the supervision of, the issuer's principal executive and
> principal financial officers, or persons performing similar functions, and effected by the
> issuer's board of directors, management and other personnel, to provide reasonable
> assurance regarding the reliability of financial reporting and the preparation of financial
> statements for external purposes in accordance with generally accepted accounting
> principles and includes those policies and procedures that:
>
> (1) Pertain to the maintenance of records that in reasonable detail accurately and
>     fairly reflect the transactions and dispositions of the assets of the issuer;
>
> (2) Provide reasonable assurance that transactions are recorded as necessary to
>     permit preparation of financial statements in accordance with generally accepted
>     accounting principles, and that receipts and expenditures of the issuer are being
>     made only in accordance with authorizations of management and directors of the
>     registrant; and
>
> (3) Provide reasonable assurance regarding prevention or timely detection of
>     unauthorized acquisition, use or disposition of the issuer's assets that could have a
>     material effect on the financial statements.

[18] As defined in Exchange Act Rule 12b-2 [17 CFR 240.12b-2] and Rule 1-02 of Regulation S-X
[17 CFR 210.1-02], a material weakness is a deficiency, or a combination of deficiencies, in
ICFR such that there is a reasonable possibility that a material misstatement of the registrant's
annual or interim financial statements will not be prevented or detected on a timely basis. See
Release No. 34-55928.

[19] This focus on material weaknesses will lead to a better understanding by investors about the
company's ICFR, as well as its inherent limitations. Further, the Commission's rules
implementing Section 404, by providing for public disclosure of material weaknesses,
concentrate attention on the most important internal control issues.

included in the evaluation based on its assessment of risk.[20]  The evaluation process will

vary from company to company; however, the top-down, risk-based approach which is

described in this guidance will typically be the most efficient and effective way to

conduct the evaluation.

The evaluation process guidance is described in two sections.  The first section

explains the identification of financial reporting risks and the evaluation of whether the

controls management has implemented adequately address those risks.  The second

section explains an approach for making judgments about the methods and procedures for

evaluating whether the operation of ICFR is effective.  Both sections explain how entity-

level controls[21] impact the evaluation process, as well as how management should focus

its evaluation efforts on the highest risks to reliable financial reporting. [22]

---

[20] If management's evaluation process identifies material weaknesses, but all material weaknesses
are remediated by the end of the fiscal year, management may conclude that ICFR is effective as
of the end of the fiscal year.  However, management should consider whether disclosure of such
remediated material weaknesses is appropriate or required under Item 307 or Item 308 of
Regulations S-K or S-B or other Commission disclosure rules.

[21] The term "entity-level controls" as used in this document describes aspects of a system of
internal control that have a pervasive effect on the entity's system of internal control such as
controls related to the control environment (for example, management's philosophy and operating
style, integrity and ethical values; board or audit committee oversight; and assignment of
authority and responsibility); controls over management override; the company's risk assessment
process; centralized processing and controls, including shared service environments; controls to
monitor results of operations; controls to monitor other controls, including activities of the
internal audit function, the audit committee, and self-assessment programs; controls over the
period-end financial reporting process; and policies that address significant business control and
risk management practices.  The terms "company-level" and "entity-wide" are also commonly
used to describe these controls.

[22] Because management is responsible for maintaining effective ICFR, this interpretive guidance
does not specifically address the role of the board of directors or audit committee in a company's
evaluation and assessment of ICFR.  However, we would ordinarily expect a board of directors or
audit committee, as part of its oversight responsibilities for the company's financial reporting, to
be reasonably knowledgeable and informed about the evaluation process and management's
assessment, as necessary in the circumstances.

Under the Commission's rules, management's annual assessment of the effectiveness of ICFR must be made in accordance with a suitable control framework's[23] definition of effective internal control.[24] These control frameworks define elements of internal control that are expected to be present and functioning in an effective internal control system. In assessing effectiveness, management evaluates whether its ICFR includes policies, procedures and activities that address the elements of internal control that the applicable control framework describes as necessary for an internal control system to be effective. The framework elements describe the characteristics of an internal control system that may be relevant to individual areas of the company's ICFR, pervasive to many areas, or entity-wide. Therefore, management's evaluation process includes not only controls involving particular areas of financial reporting, but also the entity-wide and other pervasive elements of internal control defined by its selected control framework. This guidance is not intended to replace the elements of an effective system of internal control as defined within a control framework.

---

[23] In the Adopting Release, the Commission specified characteristics of a suitable control framework and identified the <u>Internal Control—Integrated Framework (1992)</u> created by the Committee of Sponsoring Organizations of the Treadway Commission ("COSO") as an example of a suitable framework. We also cited the <u>Guidance on Assessing Control</u> published by the Canadian Institute of Chartered Accountants ("CoCo") and the report published by the Institute of Chartered Accountants in England & Wales <u>Internal Control: Guidance for Directors on the Combined Code</u> (known as the Turnbull Report) as examples of other suitable frameworks that issuers could choose in evaluating the effectiveness of their ICFR. We encourage companies to examine and select a framework that may be useful in their own circumstances; we also encourage the further development of existing and alternative frameworks.

[24] For example, both the COSO framework and the Turnbull Report state that determining whether a system of internal control is effective is a subjective judgment resulting from an assessment of whether the five components (that is, control environment, risk assessment, control activities, monitoring, and information and communication) are present and functioning effectively. Although CoCo states that an assessment of effectiveness should be made against twenty specific criteria, it acknowledges that the criteria can be regrouped into different structures, and includes a table showing how the criteria can be regrouped into the five-component structure of COSO.

**1. Identifying Financial Reporting Risks and Controls**

Management should evaluate whether it has implemented controls that will achieve the objective of ICFR (that is, to provide reasonable assurance regarding the reliability of financial reporting). The evaluation begins with the identification and assessment of the risks to reliable financial reporting (that is, materially accurate financial statements), including changes in those risks. Management then evaluates whether it has controls placed in operation (that is, in use) that are designed to adequately address those risks. Management ordinarily would consider the company's entity-level controls in both its assessment of risks and in identifying which controls adequately address the risks.

The evaluation approach described herein allows management to identify controls and maintain supporting evidential matter for its controls in a manner that is tailored to the company's financial reporting risks (as defined below). Thus, the controls that management identifies and documents are those that are important to achieving the objective of ICFR. These controls are then subject to procedures to evaluate evidence of their operating effectiveness, as determined pursuant to Section II.A.2.

**a. Identifying Financial Reporting Risks**

Management should identify those risks of misstatement that could, individually or in combination with others, result in a material misstatement of the financial statements ("financial reporting risks"). Ordinarily, the identification of financial reporting risks begins with evaluating how the requirements of GAAP apply to the company's business, operations and transactions. Management must provide investors with financial statements that fairly present the company's financial position, results of operations and cash flows in accordance with GAAP. A lack of fair presentation arises when one or more financial statement amounts or disclosures ("financial reporting elements") contain misstatements (including omissions) that are material.

Management uses its knowledge and understanding of the business, and its organization, operations, and processes, to consider the sources and potential likelihood of misstatements in financial reporting elements. Internal and external risk factors that impact the business, including the nature and extent of any changes in those risks, may give rise to a risk of misstatement. Risks of misstatement may also arise from sources such as the initiation, authorization, processing and recording of transactions and other adjustments that are reflected in financial reporting elements. Management may find it useful to consider "what could go wrong" within a financial reporting element in order to identify the sources and the potential likelihood of misstatements and identify those that could result in a material misstatement of the financial statements.

The methods and procedures for identifying financial reporting risks will vary based on the characteristics of the company. These characteristics include, among others, the size, complexity, and organizational structure of the company and its processes and financial reporting environment, as well as the control framework used by management. For example, to identify financial reporting risks in a larger business or a complex business process, management's methods and procedures may involve a variety of company personnel, including those with specialized knowledge. These individuals, collectively, may be necessary to have a sufficient understanding of GAAP, the underlying business transactions and the process activities, including the role of computer technology, that are required to initiate, authorize, record and process transactions. In contrast, in a small company that operates on a centralized basis with less complex business processes and with little change in the risks or processes, management's daily involvement with the business may provide it with adequate knowledge to appropriately identify financial reporting risks.

Management's evaluation of the risk of misstatement should include consideration of the vulnerability of the entity to fraudulent activity (for example, fraudulent financial reporting, misappropriation of assets and corruption), and whether any such exposure could result in a material misstatement of the financial statements.[25] The extent of activities required for the evaluation of fraud risks is commensurate with the size and complexity of the company's operations and financial reporting environment.[26]

Management should recognize that the risk of material misstatement due to fraud ordinarily exists in any organization, regardless of size or type, and it may vary by specific location or segment and by individual financial reporting element. For example, one type of fraud risk that has resulted in fraudulent financial reporting in companies of all sizes and types is the risk of improper override of internal controls in the financial reporting process. While the identification of a fraud risk is not necessarily an indication that a fraud has occurred, the absence of an identified fraud is not an indication that no

---

[25] For example, COSO's <u>Internal Control Over Financial Reporting – Guidance for Smaller Public Companies</u> (2006), Volume 1: Executive Summary, Principle 10: Fraud Risk (page 10) states, "The potential for material misstatement due to fraud is explicitly considered in assessing risks to the achievement of financial reporting objectives."

[26] Management may find resources such as "Management Antifraud Programs and Controls – Guidance to Help Prevent, Deter, and Detect Fraud," which was issued jointly by seven professional organizations and is included as an exhibit to AU Sec. 316, <u>Consideration of Fraud in a Financial Statement Audit</u> (as adopted on an interim basis by the PCAOB in PCAOB Rule 3200T) helpful in assessing fraud risks. Other resources also exist (for example, the American Institute of Certified Public Accountants' (AICPA) <u>Management Override of Internal Controls: The Achilles' Heel of Fraud Prevention</u> (2005)), and more may be developed in the future.

fraud risks exist. Rather, these risk assessments are used in evaluating whether adequate

controls have been implemented.

### b. Identifying Controls that Adequately Address Financial Reporting Risks

Management should evaluate whether it has controls[27] placed in operation (that is,

in use) that adequately address the company's financial reporting risks. The

determination of whether an individual control, or a combination of controls, adequately

addresses a financial reporting risk involves judgments about whether the controls, if

operating properly, can effectively prevent or detect misstatements that could result in

material misstatements in the financial statements.[28] If management determines that a

deficiency in ICFR exists, it must be evaluated to determine whether a material

weakness exists.[29] The guidance in Section II.B.1. is designed to assist management

with that evaluation.

Management may identify preventive controls, detective controls, or a

combination of both, as adequately addressing financial reporting risks.[30] There might

---

[27] A control consists of a specific set of policies, procedures, and activities designed to meet an objective. A control may exist within a designated function or activity in a process. A control's impact on ICFR may be entity-wide or specific to an account balance, class of transactions or application. Controls have unique characteristics – for example, they can be: automated or manual; reconciliations; segregation of duties; review and approval authorizations; safeguarding and accountability of assets; preventing or detecting error or fraud. Controls within a process may consist of financial reporting controls and operational controls (that is, those designed to achieve operational objectives).

[28] Companies may use "control objectives," which provide specific criteria against which to evaluate the effectiveness of controls, to assist in evaluating whether controls can prevent or detect misstatements.

[29] A deficiency in the design of ICFR exists when (a) necessary controls are missing or (b) existing controls are not properly designed so that, even if the control operates as designed, the financial reporting risks would not be addressed.

[30] Preventive controls have the objective of preventing the occurrence of errors or fraud that could result in a misstatement of the financial statements. Detective controls have the objective of detecting errors or fraud that has already occurred that could result in a misstatement of the

be more than one control that addresses the financial reporting risks for a financial reporting element; conversely, one control might address the risks of more than one financial reporting element. It is not necessary to identify all controls that may exist or identify redundant controls, unless redundancy itself is required to address the financial reporting risks. To illustrate, management may determine that the risk of a misstatement in interest expense, which could result in a material misstatement of the financial statements, is adequately addressed by a control within the company's period-end financial reporting process (that is, an entity-level control). In such a case, management may not need to identify, for purposes of the ICFR evaluation, any additional controls related to the risk of misstatement in interest expense.

Management may also consider the efficiency with which evidence of the operation of a control can be evaluated when identifying the controls that adequately address the financial reporting risks. When more than one control exists and each adequately addresses a financial reporting risk, management may decide to select the control for which evidence of operating effectiveness can be obtained more efficiently. Moreover, when adequate information technology ("IT") general controls exist and management has determined that the operation of such controls is effective, management may determine that automated controls are more efficient to evaluate than manual controls. Considering the efficiency with which the operation of a control can be evaluated will often enhance the overall efficiency of the evaluation process.

In addition to identifying controls that address the financial reporting risks of individual financial reporting elements, management also evaluates whether it has

---

financial statements. Preventive and detective controls may be completely manual, involve some degree of computer automation, or be completely automated.

controls in place to address the entity-level and other pervasive elements of ICFR that its

chosen control framework prescribes as necessary for an effective system of internal

control. This would ordinarily include, for example, considering how and whether

controls related to the control environment, controls over management override, the

entity-level risk assessment process and monitoring activities,[31] controls over the period-

end financial reporting process,[32] and the policies that address significant business

control and risk management practices are adequate for purposes of an effective system

of internal control. The control frameworks and related guidance may be useful tools for

evaluating the adequacy of these elements of ICFR.

When identifying the controls that address financial reporting risks, management

learns information about the characteristics of the controls that should inform its

judgments about the risk that a control will fail to operate as designed. This includes, for

example, information about the judgment required in its operation and information about

the complexity of the controls. Section II.A.2. discusses how these characteristics are

considered in determining the nature and extent of evidence of the operation of the

controls that management evaluates.

At the end of this identification process, management has identified for evaluation

those controls that are needed to meet the objective of ICFR (that is, to provide

---

[31] Monitoring activities may include controls to monitor results of operations and controls to monitor other controls, including activities of the internal audit function, the audit committee, and self-assessment programs.

[32] The nature of controls within the period-end financial reporting process will vary based on a company's facts and circumstances. The period-end financial reporting process may include matters such as: procedures to enter transaction totals into the general ledger; the initiation, authorization, recording and processing of journal entries in the general ledger; procedures for the selection and application of accounting policies; procedures used to record recurring and non-recurring adjustments to the annual and quarterly financial statements; and procedures for preparing annual and quarterly financial statements and related disclosures.

reasonable assurance regarding the reliability of financial reporting) and for which evidence about their operation can be obtained most efficiently.

## c. Consideration of Entity-Level Controls

Management considers entity-level controls when identifying financial reporting risks and related controls for a financial reporting element. In doing so, it is important for management to consider the nature of the entity-level controls and how those controls relate to the financial reporting element. The more indirect the relationship to a financial reporting element, the less effective a control may be in preventing or detecting a misstatement. [33]

Some entity-level controls, such as certain control environment controls, have an important, but indirect, effect on the likelihood that a misstatement will be prevented or detected on a timely basis. These controls might affect the other controls management determines are necessary to adequately address financial reporting risks for a financial reporting element. However, it is unlikely that management will identify only this type of entity-level control as adequately addressing a financial reporting risk identified for a financial reporting element.

Other entity-level controls may be designed to identify possible breakdowns in lower-level controls, but not in a manner that would, by themselves, adequately address financial reporting risks. For example, an entity-level control that monitors the results of operations may be designed to detect potential misstatements and investigate whether a breakdown in lower-level controls occurred. However, if the amount of potential

---

[33] Controls can be either directly or indirectly related to a financial reporting element. Controls that are designed to have a specific effect on a financial reporting element are considered directly related. For example, controls established to ensure that personnel are properly counting and recording the annual physical inventory relate directly to the existence of the inventory.

misstatement that could exist before being detected by the monitoring control is too high, then the control may not adequately address the financial reporting risks of a financial reporting element.

Entity-level controls may be designed to operate at the process, application, transaction or account-level and at a level of precision that would adequately prevent or detect on a timely basis misstatements in one or more financial reporting elements that could result in a material misstatement of the financial statements. In these cases, management may not need to identify or evaluate additional controls relating to that financial reporting risk.

## d. Role of Information Technology General Controls

Controls that management identifies as addressing financial reporting risks may be automated,[34] dependent upon IT functionality,[35] or a combination of both manual and automated procedures.[36] In these situations, management's evaluation process generally considers the design and operation of the automated or IT dependent application controls and the relevant IT general controls over the applications providing the IT functionality. While IT general controls alone ordinarily do not adequately address financial reporting risks, the proper and consistent operation of automated controls or IT functionality often depends upon effective IT general controls. The identification of risks and controls within IT should not be a separate evaluation. Instead, it should be an integral part of

---

[34] For example, application controls that perform automated matching, error checking or edit checking functions.

[35] For example, consistent application of a formula or performance of a calculation and posting correct balances to appropriate accounts or ledgers.

[36] For example, a control that manually investigates items contained in a computer generated exception report.

management's top-down, risk-based approach to identifying risks and controls and in
determining evidential matter necessary to support the assessment.

Aspects of IT general controls that may be relevant to the evaluation of ICFR will
vary depending upon a company's facts and circumstances. For purposes of the
evaluation of ICFR, management only needs to evaluate those IT general controls that are
necessary for the proper and consistent operation of other controls designed to adequately
address financial reporting risks. For example, management might consider whether
certain aspects of IT general control areas, such as program development, program
changes, computer operations, and access to programs and data, apply to its facts and
circumstances.[37] Specifically, it is unnecessary to evaluate IT general controls that
primarily pertain to efficiency or effectiveness of a company's operations, but which are
not relevant to addressing financial reporting risks.

### e. Evidential Matter to Support the Assessment

As part of its evaluation of ICFR, management must maintain reasonable support
for its assessment.[38] Documentation of the design of the controls management has
placed in operation to adequately address the financial reporting risks, including the
entity-level and other pervasive elements necessary for effective ICFR, is an integral part
of the reasonable support. The form and extent of the documentation will vary
depending on the size, nature, and complexity of the company. It can take many forms
(for example, paper documents, electronic, or other media). Also, the documentation

---

[37] However, the reference to these specific IT general control areas as examples within this
guidance does not imply that these areas, either partially or in their entirety, are applicable to all
facts and circumstances. As indicated, companies need to take their particular facts and
circumstances into consideration in determining which aspects of IT general controls are relevant.

[38] See instructions to Item 308 of Regulations S-K and S-B.

can be presented in a number of ways (for example, policy manuals, process models, flowcharts, job descriptions, documents, internal memorandums, forms, etc). The documentation does not need to include all controls that exist within a process that impacts financial reporting. Rather, the documentation should be focused on those controls that management concludes are adequate to address the financial reporting risks.[39]

In addition to providing support for the assessment of ICFR, documentation of the design of controls also supports other objectives of an effective system of internal control. For example, it serves as evidence that controls within ICFR, including changes to those controls, have been identified, are capable of being communicated to those responsible for their performance, and are capable of being monitored by the company.

## 2. Evaluating Evidence of the Operating Effectiveness of ICFR

Management should evaluate evidence of the operating effectiveness of ICFR. The evaluation of the operating effectiveness of a control considers whether the control is operating as designed and whether the person performing the control possesses the necessary authority and competence to perform the control effectively. The evaluation procedures that management uses to gather evidence about the operation of the controls it identifies as adequately addressing the financial reporting risks for financial reporting elements (pursuant to Section II.A.1.b) should be tailored to management's assessment of the risk characteristics of both the individual financial reporting elements and the related controls (collectively, ICFR risk). Management should ordinarily focus its evaluation of the operation of controls on areas posing the highest ICFR risk. Management's

---

[39] Section II.A.2.c also provides guidance with regard to the documentation required to support management's evaluation of operating effectiveness.

assessment of ICFR risk also considers the impact of entity-level controls, such as the

relative strengths and weaknesses of the control environment, which may influence

management's judgments about the risks of failure for particular controls.

Evidence about the effective operation of controls may be obtained from direct

testing of controls and on-going monitoring activities. The nature, timing and extent of

evaluation procedures necessary for management to obtain sufficient evidence of the

effective operation of a control depend on the assessed ICFR risk. In determining

whether the evidence obtained is sufficient to provide a reasonable basis for its evaluation

of the operation of ICFR, management should consider not only the quantity of evidence

(for example, sample size), but also the qualitative characteristics of the evidence. The

qualitative characteristics of the evidence include the nature of the evaluation procedures

performed, the period of time to which the evidence relates, the objectivity[40] of those

evaluating the controls, and, in the case of on-going monitoring activities, the extent of

validation through direct testing of underlying controls. For any individual control,

different combinations of the nature, timing, and extent of evaluation procedures may

provide sufficient evidence. The sufficiency of evidence is not necessarily determined by

any of these attributes individually.

---

[40] In determining the objectivity of those evaluating controls, management is not required to make an absolute conclusion regarding objectivity, but rather should recognize that personnel will have varying degrees of objectivity based on, among other things, their job function, their relationship to the control being evaluated, and their level of authority and responsibility within the organization. Personnel whose core function involves permanently serving as a testing or compliance authority at the company, such as internal auditors, normally are expected to be the most objective. However, the degree of objectivity of other company personnel may be such that the evaluation of controls performed by them would provide sufficient evidence. Management's judgments about whether the degree of objectivity is adequate to provide sufficient evidence should take into account the ICFR risk.

a. **Determining the Evidence Needed to Support the Assessment**

Management should evaluate the ICFR risk of the controls identified Section

II.A.1.b as adequately addressing the financial reporting risks for financial reporting

elements to determine the evidence needed to support the assessment. This evaluation

should consider the characteristics of the financial reporting elements to which the

controls relate and the characteristics of the controls themselves. This concept is

illustrated in the following diagram.

Determining the Sufficiency of Evidence Based on ICFR Risk

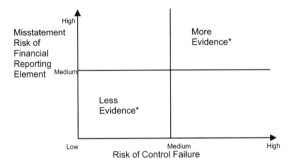

\* The references to "more" or "less" include both the quantitative and qualitative characteristics of the evidence (that is, its sufficiency).

Management's consideration of the misstatement risk of a financial reporting element includes both the materiality of the financial reporting element and the susceptibility of the underlying account balances, transactions or other supporting information to a misstatement that could be material to the financial statements. As the materiality of a financial reporting element increases in relation to the amount of misstatement that would be considered material to the financial statements, management's assessment of misstatement risk for the financial reporting element generally would correspondingly increase. In addition, management considers the extent to which the financial reporting elements include transactions, account balances or other supporting information that are prone to material misstatement. For example, the extent to which a financial reporting element: (1) involves judgment in determining the recorded amounts; (2) is susceptible to fraud; (3) has complex accounting requirements; (4) experiences change in the nature or volume of the underlying transactions; or (5) is sensitive to changes in environmental factors, such as technological and/or economic developments, would generally affect management's judgment of whether a misstatement risk is higher or lower.

Management's consideration of the likelihood that a control might fail to operate effectively includes, among other things:

- The type of control (that is, manual or automated) and the frequency with which it operates;

- The complexity of the control;

- The risk of management override;

- The judgment required to operate the control;

- The competence of the personnel who perform the control or monitor its performance;

- Whether there have been changes in key personnel who either perform the control or monitor its performance;

- The nature and materiality of misstatements that the control is intended to prevent or detect;

- The degree to which the control relies on the effectiveness of other controls (for example, IT general controls); and

- The evidence of the operation of the control from prior year(s).

For example, management's judgment of the risk of control failure would be higher for controls whose operation requires significant judgment than for non-complex controls requiring less judgment.

Financial reporting elements that involve related party transactions, critical accounting policies,[41] and related critical accounting estimates[42] generally would be assessed as having a higher misstatement risk. Further, when the controls related to these financial reporting elements are subject to the risk of management override, involve

---

[41] "Critical accounting policies" are defined as those policies that are most important to the financial statement presentation, and require management's most difficult, subjective, or complex judgments, often as the result of a need to make estimates about the effect of matters that are inherently uncertain. See Release No. 33-8040 (Dec. 12, 2001) [66 FR 65013].

[42] "Critical accounting estimates" relate to estimates or assumptions involved in the application of generally accepted accounting principles where the nature of the estimates or assumptions is material due to the levels of subjectivity and judgment necessary to account for highly uncertain matters or the susceptibility of such matters to change and the impact of the estimates and assumptions on financial condition or operating performance is material. See Release No. 33-8350 (Dec. 19, 2003) [68 FR 75056]. For additional information, see, for example, Release No. 33-8098 (May 10, 2002) [67 FR 35620].

significant judgment, or are complex, they should generally be assessed as having higher ICFR risk.

When a combination of controls is required to adequately address the risks related to a financial reporting element, management should analyze the risk characteristics of the controls. This is because the controls associated with a given financial reporting element may not necessarily share the same risk characteristics. For example, a financial reporting element involving significant estimation may require a combination of automated controls that accumulate source data and manual controls that require highly judgmental determinations of assumptions. In this case, the automated controls may be subject to a system that is stable (that is, has not undergone significant change) and is supported by effective IT general controls and are therefore assessed as lower risk, whereas the manual controls would be assessed as higher risk.

The consideration of entity-level controls (for example, controls within the control environment) may influence management's determination of the evidence needed to sufficiently support its assessment of ICFR. For example, management's judgment about the likelihood that a control fails to operate effectively may be influenced by a highly effective control environment and thereby impact the evidence evaluated for that control. However, a strong control environment would not eliminate the need to evaluate the operation of the control in some manner.

### b. Implementing Procedures to Evaluate Evidence of the Operation of ICFR

Management should evaluate evidence that provides a reasonable basis for its assessment of the operating effectiveness of the controls identified in Section II.A.1. Management uses its assessment of ICFR risk, as determined in Section II.A.2 to determine the evaluation methods and procedures necessary to obtain sufficient evidence. The evaluation methods and procedures may be integrated with the daily responsibilities of its employees or implemented specifically for purposes of the ICFR evaluation. Activities that are performed for other reasons (for example, day-to-day activities to manage the operations of the business) may also provide relevant evidence. Further, activities performed to meet the monitoring objectives of the control framework may provide evidence to support the assessment of the operating effectiveness of ICFR.

The evidence management evaluates comes from direct tests of controls, on-going monitoring, or a combination of both. Direct tests of controls are tests ordinarily performed on a periodic basis by individuals with a high degree of objectivity relative to the controls being tested. Direct tests provide evidence as of a point in time and may provide information about the reliability of on-going monitoring activities. On-going monitoring includes management's normal, recurring activities that provide information about the operation of controls. These activities include, for example, self-assessment[43] procedures and procedures to analyze performance measures designed to track the operation of controls.[44] Self-assessment is a broad term that can refer to different types of procedures performed by individuals with varying degrees of objectivity. It includes assessments made by the personnel who operate the control as well as members of management who are not responsible for operating the control. The evidence provided

---

[43] For example, COSO's 1992 framework defines self-assessments as "evaluations where persons responsible for a particular unit or function will determine the effectiveness of controls for their activities."

[44] Management's evaluation process may also consider the results of key performance indicators ("KPIs") in which management reconciles operating and financial information with its knowledge of the business. The procedures that management implements pursuant to this section should evaluate the effective operation of these KPI-type controls when they are identified pursuant to Section II.A.1.b. as addressing financial reporting risk.

by self-assessment activities depends on the personnel involved and the manner in which the activities are conducted. For example, evidence from self-assessments performed by personnel responsible for operating the control generally provides less evidence due to the evaluator's lower degree of objectivity.

As the ICFR risk increases, management will ordinarily adjust the nature of the evidence that is obtained. For example, management can increase the evidence from on-going monitoring activities by utilizing personnel who are more objective and/or increasing the extent of validation through periodic direct testing of the underlying controls. Management can also vary the evidence obtained by adjusting the period of time covered by direct testing. When ICFR risk is assessed as high, the evidence management obtains would ordinarily consist of direct testing or on-going monitoring activities performed by individuals who have a higher degree of objectivity. In situations where a company's on-going monitoring activities utilize personnel who are not adequately objective, the evidence obtained would normally be supplemented with direct testing by those who are independent from the operation of the control. In these situations, direct testing of controls corroborates evidence from on-going monitoring activities as well as evaluates the operation of the underlying controls and whether they continue to adequately address financial reporting risks. When ICFR risk is assessed as low, management may conclude that evidence from on-going monitoring is sufficient and that no direct testing is required. Further, management's evaluation would ordinarily consider evidence from a reasonable period of time during the year, including the fiscal year-end.

In smaller companies, management's daily interaction with its controls may provide it with sufficient knowledge about their operation to evaluate the operation of ICFR. Knowledge from daily interaction includes information obtained by on-going direct involvement with and direct supervision of the execution of the control by those responsible for the assessment of the effectiveness of ICFR. Management should consider its particular facts and circumstances when determining whether its daily interaction with controls provides sufficient evidence to evaluate the operating effectiveness of ICFR. For example, daily interaction may be sufficient when the operation of controls is centralized and the number of personnel involved is limited. Conversely, daily interaction in companies with multiple management reporting layers or operating segments would generally not provide sufficient evidence because those responsible for assessing the effectiveness of ICFR would not ordinarily be sufficiently knowledgeable about the operation of the controls. In these situations, management would ordinarily utilize direct testing or on-going monitoring-type evaluation procedures to obtain reasonable support for the assessment.

Management evaluates the evidence it gathers to determine whether the operation of a control is effective. This evaluation considers whether the control operated as designed. It also considers matters such as how the control was applied, the consistency with which it was applied, and whether the person performing the control possesses the necessary authority and competence to perform the control effectively. If management determines that the operation of the control is not effective, a deficiency exists that must be evaluated to determine whether it is a material weakness.

### c. Evidential Matter to Support the Assessment

Management's assessment must be supported by evidential matter that provides reasonable support for its assessment. The nature of the evidential matter may vary based on the assessed level of ICFR risk of the underlying controls and other circumstances. Reasonable support for an assessment would include the basis for management's assessment, including documentation of the methods and procedures it utilizes to gather and evaluate evidence.

The evidential matter may take many forms and will vary depending on the assessed level of ICFR risk for controls over each of its financial reporting elements. For example, management may document its overall strategy in a comprehensive memorandum that establishes the evaluation approach, the evaluation procedures, the basis for management's conclusion about the effectiveness of controls related to the financial reporting elements and the entity-level and other pervasive elements that are important to management's assessment of ICFR.

If management determines that the evidential matter within the company's books and records is sufficient to provide reasonable support for its assessment, it may determine that it is not necessary to separately maintain copies of the evidence it evaluates. For example, in smaller companies, where management's daily interaction with its controls provides the basis for its assessment, management may have limited documentation created specifically for the evaluation of ICFR. However, in these instances, management should consider whether reasonable support for its assessment would include documentation of how its interaction provided it with sufficient evidence.

This documentation might include memoranda, e-mails, and instructions or directions to and from management to company employees.

Further, in determining the nature of supporting evidential matter, management should also consider the degree of complexity of the control, the level of judgment required to operate the control, and the risk of misstatement in the financial reporting element that could result in a material misstatement of the financial statements. As these factors increase, management may determine that evidential matter supporting the assessment should be separately maintained. For example, management may decide that separately maintained documentation in certain areas will assist the audit committee in exercising its oversight of the company's financial reporting.

The evidential matter constituting reasonable support for management's assessment would ordinarily include documentation of how management formed its conclusion about the effectiveness of the company's entity-level and other pervasive elements of ICFR that its applicable framework describes as necessary for an effective system of internal control.

### 3. Multiple Location Considerations

Management's consideration of financial reporting risks generally includes all of its locations or business units.[45] Management may determine that financial reporting risks are adequately addressed by controls which operate centrally, in which case the evaluation approach is similar to that of a business with a single location or business unit. When the controls necessary to address financial reporting risks operate at more than one

---

[45] Consistent with the guidance in Section II.A.1., management may determine when identifying financial reporting risks that some locations are so insignificant that no further evaluation procedures are needed.

location or business unit, management would generally evaluate evidence of the
operation of the controls at the individual locations or business units.

Management may determine that the ICFR risk of the controls (as determined
through Section II.A.2.a) that operate at individual locations or business units is low. In
such situations, management may determine that evidence gathered through self-
assessment routines or other on-going monitoring activities, when combined with the
evidence derived from a centralized control that monitors the results of operations at
individual locations, constitutes sufficient evidence for the evaluation. In other
situations, management may determine that, because of the complexity or judgment in the
operation of the controls at the individual location, the risk that controls will fail to
operate is high, and therefore more evidence is needed about the effective operation of
the controls at the location.

Management should generally consider the risk characteristics of the controls for
each financial reporting element, rather than making a single judgment for all controls at
that location when deciding whether the nature and extent of evidence is sufficient.
When performing its evaluation of the risk characteristics of the controls identified,
management should consider whether there are location-specific risks that might impact
the risk that a control might fail to operate effectively. Additionally, there may be
pervasive risk factors that exist at a location that cause all controls, or a majority of
controls, at that location to be considered higher risk.

## B. Reporting Considerations

## 1. Evaluation of Control Deficiencies

In order to determine whether a control deficiency, or combination of control deficiencies, is a material weakness, management evaluates the severity of each control deficiency that comes to its attention.  Control deficiencies that are determined to be a material weakness must be disclosed in management's annual report on its assessment of the effectiveness of ICFR.  Control deficiencies that are considered to be significant deficiencies are reported to the company's audit committee and the external auditor pursuant to management's compliance with the certification requirements in Exchange Act Rule 13a-14. [46]

Management may not disclose that it has assessed ICFR as effective if one or more deficiencies in ICFR are determined to be a material weakness.  As part of the evaluation of ICFR, management considers whether each deficiency, individually or in combination, is a material weakness as of the end of the fiscal year.  Multiple control deficiencies that affect the same financial statement amount or disclosure increase the likelihood of misstatement and may, in combination, constitute a material weakness if there is a reasonable possibility[47] that a material misstatement of the financial statements

---

[46] Pursuant to Exchange Act Rules 13a-14 and 15d-14 [17 CFR 240.13a-14 and 240.15d-14], management discloses to the auditors and to the audit committee of the board of directors (or persons fulfilling the equivalent function) all material weaknesses and significant deficiencies in the design or operation of internal controls which could adversely affect the issuer's ability to record, process, summarize and report financial data.  The term "material weakness" is defined in the Commission's rules in Exchange Act Rule 12b-2 and Rule 1-02 of Regulation S-X.  See Release No. 34-55928.  The Commission is seeking additional comment on the definition of the term "significant deficiency" in the Commission's rules in Exchange Act Rule 12b-2 and Rule 1-02 of Regulation S-X.  See Release No. 34-55930.

[47] There is a reasonable possibility of an event when the likelihood of the event is either "reasonably possible" or "probable" as those terms are used in Financial Accounting Standards Board Statement No. 5, Accounting for Contingencies.  The use of the phrase "reasonable

would not be prevented or detected in a timely manner, even though such deficiencies may be individually less severe than a material weakness. Therefore, management should evaluate individual control deficiencies that affect the same financial statement amount or disclosure, or component of internal control, to determine whether they collectively result in a material weakness.

The evaluation of the severity of a control deficiency should include both quantitative and qualitative factors. Management evaluates the severity of a deficiency in ICFR by considering whether there is a reasonable possibility that the company's ICFR will fail to prevent or detect a misstatement of a financial statement amount or disclosure; and the magnitude of the potential misstatement resulting from the deficiency or deficiencies. The severity of a deficiency in ICFR does not depend on whether a misstatement actually has occurred but rather on whether there is a reasonable possibility that the company's ICFR will fail to prevent or detect a misstatement on a timely basis.

Risk factors affect whether there is a reasonable possibility[48] that a deficiency, or a combination of deficiencies, will result in a misstatement of a financial statement amount or disclosure. These factors include, but are not limited to, the following:

- The nature of the financial reporting elements involved (for example, suspense accounts and related party transactions involve greater risk);

---

possibility that a material misstatement of the financial statements would not be prevented or detected in a timely manner" is intended solely to assist management in identifying matters for disclosure under Item 308 of Regulation S-K. It is not intended to interpret or describe management's responsibility under the FCPA or modify a control framework's definition of what constitutes an effective system of internal control.

[48] The evaluation of whether a deficiency in ICFR presents a reasonable possibility of misstatement can be made without quantifying the probability of occurrence as a specific percentage or range.

- The susceptibility of the related asset or liability to loss or fraud (that is, greater susceptibility increases risk);

- The subjectivity, complexity, or extent of judgment required to determine the amount involved (that is, greater subjectivity, complexity, or judgment, like that related to an accounting estimate, increases risk);

- The interaction or relationship of the control with other controls, including whether they are interdependent or redundant;

- The interaction of the deficiencies (that is, when evaluating a combination of two or more deficiencies, whether the deficiencies could affect the same financial statement amounts or disclosures); and

- The possible future consequences of the deficiency.

Factors that affect the magnitude of the misstatement that might result from a deficiency or deficiencies in ICFR include, but are not limited to, the following:

- The financial statement amounts or total of transactions exposed to the deficiency; and

- The volume of activity in the account balance or class of transactions exposed to the deficiency that has occurred in the current period or that is expected in future periods.

In evaluating the magnitude of the potential misstatement, the maximum amount that an account balance or total of transactions can be overstated is generally the recorded amount, while understatements could be larger. Also, in many cases, the probability of a small misstatement will be greater than the probability of a large misstatement.

Management should evaluate the effect of compensating controls[49] when determining whether a control deficiency or combination of deficiencies is a material weakness. To have a mitigating effect, the compensating control should operate at a level of precision that would prevent or detect a misstatement that could be material.

In determining whether a deficiency or a combination of deficiencies represents a material weakness, management considers all relevant information. Management should evaluate whether the following situations indicate a deficiency in ICFR exists and, if so, whether it represents a material weakness:

- Identification of fraud, whether or not material, on the part of senior management;[50]

- Restatement of previously issued financial statements to reflect the correction of a material misstatement;[51]

- Identification of a material misstatement of the financial statements in the current period in circumstances that indicate the misstatement would not have been detected by the company's ICFR; and

- Ineffective oversight of the company's external financial reporting and internal control over financial reporting by the company's audit committee.

When evaluating the severity of a deficiency, or combination of deficiencies, in ICFR, management also should determine the level of detail and degree of assurance that

[49] Compensating controls are controls that serve to accomplish the objective of another control that did not function properly, helping to reduce risk to an acceptable level.

[50] For purposes of this indicator, the term "senior management" includes the principal executive and financial officers signing the company's certifications as required under Section 302 of Sarbanes Oxley as well as any other members of senior management who play a significant role in the company's financial reporting process.

[51] See FAS 154, Accounting Changes and Error Corrections, regarding correction of a misstatement.

would satisfy prudent officials in the conduct of their own affairs that they have

reasonable assurance that transactions are recorded as necessary to permit the preparation

of financial statements in conformity with GAAP. If management determines that the

deficiency, or combination of deficiencies, might prevent prudent officials in the conduct

of their own affairs from concluding that they have reasonable assurance that transactions

are recorded as necessary to permit the preparation of financial statements in conformity

with GAAP, then management should treat the deficiency, or combination of

deficiencies, as an indicator of a material weakness.

## 2. Expression of Assessment of Effectiveness of ICFR by Management

Management should clearly disclose its assessment of the effectiveness of ICFR

and, therefore, should not qualify its assessment by stating that the company's ICFR is

effective subject to certain qualifications or exceptions. For example, management

should not state that the company's controls and procedures are effective except to the

extent that certain material weakness(es) have been identified. In addition, if a material

weakness exists, management may not state that the company's ICFR is effective.

However, management may state that controls are ineffective for specific reasons.

## 3. Disclosures about Material Weaknesses

The Commission's rule implementing Section 404 was intended to bring

information about material weaknesses in ICFR into public view. Because of the

significance of the disclosure requirements surrounding material weaknesses beyond

specifically stating that the material weaknesses exist, companies should also consider

including the following in their disclosures:[52]

---

[52] Significant deficiencies in ICFR are not required to be disclosed in management's annual report on its evaluation of ICFR required by Item 308(a).

- The nature of any material weakness,

- Its impact on the company's financial reporting and its ICFR, and

- Management's current plans, if any, or actions already undertaken, for
  remediating the material weakness.

Disclosure of the existence of a material weakness is important, but there is other information that also may be material and necessary to form an overall picture that is not misleading.[53] The goal underlying all disclosure in this area is to provide an investor with disclosure and analysis that goes beyond describing the mere existence of a material weakness. There are many different types of material weaknesses and many different factors that may be important to the assessment of the potential effect of any particular material weakness. While management is required to conclude and state in its report that ICFR is ineffective when there are one or more material weaknesses, companies should also consider providing disclosure that allows investors to understand the cause of the control deficiency and to assess the potential impact of each particular material weakness. This disclosure will be more useful to investors if management differentiates the potential impact and importance to the financial statements of the identified material weaknesses, including distinguishing those material weaknesses that may have a pervasive impact on ICFR from those material weaknesses that do not.

### 4. Impact of a Restatement of Previously Issued Financial Statements on Management's Report on ICFR

Item 308 of Regulation S-K requires disclosure of management's assessment of the effectiveness of the company's ICFR as of the end of the company's most recent fiscal year. When a material misstatement of previously issued financial statements is

---

[53] See Exchange Act Rule 12b-20 [17 CFR 240.12b-20].

discovered, a company is required to restate those financial statements. However, the restatement of financial statements does not, by itself, necessitate that management consider the effect of the restatement on the company's prior conclusion related to the effectiveness of ICFR.

While there is no requirement for management to reassess or revise its conclusion related to the effectiveness of ICFR, management should consider whether its original disclosures are still appropriate and should modify or supplement its original disclosure to include any other material information that is necessary for such disclosures not to be misleading in light of the restatement. The company should also disclose any material changes to ICFR, as required by Item 308(c) of Regulation S-K.

Similarly, while there is no requirement that management reassess or revise its conclusion related to the effectiveness of its disclosure controls and procedures, management should consider whether its original disclosures regarding effectiveness of disclosure controls and procedures need to be modified or supplemented to include any other material information that is necessary for such disclosures not to be misleading. With respect to the disclosures concerning ICFR and disclosure controls and procedures, the company may need to disclose in this context what impact, if any, the restatement has on its original conclusions regarding effectiveness of ICFR and disclosure controls and procedures.

5.    **Inability to Assess Certain Aspects of ICFR**

In certain circumstances, management may encounter difficulty in assessing certain aspects of its ICFR. For example, management may outsource a significant process to a service organization and determine that evidence of the operating effectiveness of the controls over that process is necessary. However, the service organization may be unwilling to provide either a Type 2 SAS 70 report or to provide management access to the controls in place at the service organization so that management could assess effectiveness.[54] Finally, management may not have compensating controls in place that allow a determination of the effectiveness of the controls over the process in an alternative manner. The Commission's disclosure requirements state that management's annual report on ICFR must include a statement as to whether or not ICFR is effective and do not permit management to issue a report on ICFR with a scope limitation.[55] Therefore, management must determine whether the inability to assess controls over a particular process is significant enough to conclude in its report that ICFR is not effective.

---

[54] AU Sec. 324, Service Organizations (as adopted on an interim basis by the Public Company Accounting Oversight Board ("PCAOB") in PCAOB Rule 3200T), defines a report on controls placed in operation and test of operating effectiveness, commonly referred to as a "Type 2 SAS 70 report." This report is a service auditor's report on a service organization's description of the controls that may be relevant to a user organization's internal control as it relates to an audit of financial statements, on whether such controls were suitably designed to achieve specified control objectives, on whether they had been placed in operation as of a specific date, and on whether the controls that were tested were operating with sufficient effectiveness to provide reasonable, but not absolute, assurance that the related control objectives were achieved during the period specified.

[55] See Item 308(a)(3) of Regulations S-K and S-B [17 CFR 229.308(a)(3) and 228.308(a)(3)].

## III. Discussion of Comments on the Proposing Release

The Proposing Release proposed for public comment interpretive guidance for management regarding the annual evaluation of ICFR required by Rules 13a-15(c) and 15d-15(c) under the Exchange Act. We received letters from 211 commenters in response to the Proposing Release.[56] The majority of commenters were supportive of the Commission's efforts in developing this Interpretive Guidance. We have reviewed and considered all of the comments received on the proposal, and we discuss our conclusions with respect to the comments in more detail in the following sections.

### A. Alignment between Management's Evaluation and Assessment and the External Audit

Commenters expressed concern that confusion and inefficiencies may arise from differences between the proposed guidance for management's evaluation of ICFR and the PCAOB's proposed auditing standard for ICFR.[57] Commenters cited a lack of alignment between the two with regard to the terminology and definitions used[58] as well as

---

[56] Of the 211 commenters, 43 were issuers, 33 professional associations and business groups, 19 foreign private issuers and foreign professional associations, 10 investor advocacy and other similar groups, 8 major accounting firms, 11 smaller accounting firms and Section 404 service providers, 8 banks and banking associations, 4 law firms and law associations, and 75 other interested parties including students, academics, and other individuals. The comment letters are available for inspection in the Commission's Public Reference Room at 100 F Street, NE, Washington DC 20549 in File No. S7-24-06, or may be viewed at http://www.sec.gov/comments/s7-24-06/s72406.shtml.

[57] In PCAOB Release No. 2006-007 the PCAOB proposed for public comment An Audit of Internal Control Over Financial Reporting That Is Integrated With An Audit of Financial Statements and Considering and Using the Work of Others in an Audit. See http://www.pcaobus.org/Rules/Docket_021/2006-12-19_Release_No._2006-007.pdf (hereinafter "Proposed Auditing Standard").

[58] See, for example, letters from American Bar Association's Committees on Federal Regulation of Securities and Law and Accounting of the Section of Business Law (ABA), Association of Chartered Certified Accountants (ACCA), Edison Electric Institute (EEI), European Federation of Accountants (FEE), Financial Executives International Committee on Corporate Reporting (FEI CCR), Frank Gorrell (F. Gorrell), Society of Corporate Secretaries and Governance Professionals, and The Institute of Chartered Accountants in England and Wales (ICAEW).

differences in the overall approach. Some commenters that were supportive of the

principles-based approach to the proposed interpretive guidance expressed concern that

improvements in the efficiency of management's evaluation of ICFR would be limited by

what they viewed as comparatively more prescriptive guidance for external auditors in

the Proposed Auditing Standard.[59] Other commenters suggested that maximizing their

auditor's ability to rely on the work performed in management's evaluation would require

aligning the evaluation approach for management with the Proposed Auditing Standard.[60]

Even so, some of these commenters still viewed the interpretive guidance as an

improvement because it provides management the ability to choose whether, and to what

extent, it should align its evaluation with the auditing standard; whereas commenters said

that management feels compelled to align with the auditing standard under the current

rules. Other commenters suggested that the proposed interpretive guidance was

compatible with the Proposed Auditing Standard and that improvements in

implementation could be attained with close coordination between management and

auditors.[61]

In response to the comment letters, we have revised our proposal to more closely

align it with how we anticipate the PCAOB will revise its proposed auditing standard.

For example, the definition of a material weakness and the related guidance for

---

[59] See, for example, letters from Eli Lilly and Company (Eli Lilly), FEI CCR, Hutchinson Technology Inc. (Hutchinson), Independent Community Bankers of America (ICBA), MetLife Inc. (MetLife), Procter & Gamble Company (P&G), and Supervalu Inc. (Supervalu).

[60] See, for example, letters from Heritage Financial Corporation and Southern Company.

[61] See, for example, letters from BDO Seidman LLP (BDO), McGladrey & Pullen LLP (M&P), and PricewaterhouseCoopers LLP (PwC).

evaluating deficiencies, including indicators of a material weakness, have been revised.[62]

In addition, alignment revisions were made to the guidance for evaluating whether

controls adequately address financial reporting risks, including entity-level controls, the

factors to consider when identifying financial reporting risks and the factors for assessing

the risk associated with individual financial reporting elements and controls.

However, some differences between our final interpretive guidance for

management and the PCAOB's audit standard remain. These differences are not

necessarily contradictions or misalignment; rather they reflect the fact that management

and the auditor have different roles and responsibilities with respect to evaluating and

auditing ICFR. Management is responsible for designing and maintaining ICFR and

performing an evaluation annually that provides it with a reasonable basis for its

assessment as to whether ICFR is effective as of fiscal year-end. Management's daily

involvement with its internal control system provides it with knowledge and information

that may influence its judgments about how best to conduct the evaluation and the

sufficiency of evidence it needs to assess the effectiveness of ICFR. In contrast, the

auditor is responsible for conducting an independent audit that includes appropriate

professional skepticism. Moreover, the audit of ICFR is integrated with the audit of the

company's financial statements. While there is a close relationship between the work

performed by management and its auditor, the ICFR audit will not necessarily be limited

to the nature and extent of procedures management has already performed as part of its

evaluation of ICFR. There will be differences in the approaches used by management

and the auditor because the auditor does not have the same information and

---

[62] The revisions made to the proposed definition of material weakness and the related guidance, including the strong indicators, are discussed in Section III.F. of this document.

understanding as management and because the auditor will need to integrate its tests of ICFR with the financial statement audit. We agree with those commenters that suggested coordination between management and auditors on their respective efforts will ensure that both the evaluation by management and the independent audit are completed in an efficient and effective manner.

## B. Principles-based Nature of Guidance for Conducting the Evaluation

The guidance is intended to assist management in complying with two broad principles: (1) evaluate whether controls have been implemented to adequately address the risk that a material misstatement of the financial statements would not be prevented or detected in a timely manner and (2) evaluate evidence about the operation of controls based on an assessment of risk. We believe the guidance will enable companies of all sizes and complexities to comply with our rules effectively and efficiently.

Commenters expressed support for the proposed guidance's principles-based approach.[63] However, some requested that the proposal be revised to include additional guidance and illustrative examples in the following areas:[64]

- the identification of controls that address financial reporting risks;[65]

- the assessment of ICFR risk, including how evidence gained over prior periods should impact management's assessment of risks associated with

---

[63] See, for example, letters from ACE Limited (ACE), American Electric Power Company, Inc. (AEP), Business Roundtable (BR), Canadian Bankers Association, Center for Audit Quality (Center), Ernst & Young LLP (EY), Grant Thornton LLP (GT), ING Groep N.V. (ING), Manulife Financial (Manulife), PwC, P&G, and Reznick Group, P.C. (Reznick).

[64] See, for example, letters from Brown-Forman, Ford Motor Company, MasterCard Incorporated (MasterCard), Northrop Grumman Corporation, Supervalu, UFP Technologies (UFP), and UnumProvident Corporation (UnumProvident).

[65] See, for example, letter from Nina Stofberg (N. Stofberg).

controls identified and therefore, the evidence needed to support its assessment;[66]

- how varying levels of risk impact the nature of the evidence necessary to support its assessment;[67]

- when on-going monitoring activities, including self-assessments, could be used to support management's assessment and reduce direct testing;[68]

- sampling techniques, sample sizes, and testing methods;[69]

- the type and manner in which supporting evidence should be maintained;[70] including specific guidelines regarding the amount, form and medium of evidence;[71] and

- how management should document the effectiveness of monitoring activities utilized to support its assessment, as well as how management should support the evidence obtained from its daily interaction with controls as part of its assessment.[72]

---

[66] See, for example, letters from ISACA and IT Governance Institute (ISACA), Manulife, and Ohio Society of Certified Public Accountants (Ohio).

[67] See, for example, letters from Cardinal Health, Inc. (Cardinal), Cleary Gottlieb Steen & Hamilton LLP (Cleary), and ISACA.

[68] See, for example, letters from BASF Aktiengesellschaft (BASF), Cardinal, Computer Sciences Corporation (CSC), ING, ISACA, Ohio, PPL Corporation (PPL), R. Malcolm Schwartz, N. Stofberg, and UnumProvident.

[69] See, for example, letters from BDO, National Association of Real Estate Investment Trusts, Reznick, and UFP.

[70] See, for example, letters from AEP, BDO, Center, EEI, Frank Consulting, PLLP (Frank), The Hundred Group of Finance Directors (100 Group), Institut Der Wirtschaftsprufer [Institute of Public Auditors in Germany] (IDW), Managed Funds Association (MFA), Nasdaq Stock Market, Inc. (Nasdaq), Ohio, N. Stofberg, and UFP.

[71] See, for example, letter from Nasdaq.

[72] See, for example, letters from BDO and Center.

We have considered the requests for additional guidance and decided to retain the principles-based nature of the proposed guidance. We believe an evaluation of ICFR will be most effective and efficient when management makes use of all available facts and information to make reasonable judgments about the evaluation methods and procedures that are necessary to have a reasonable basis for the assessment of the effectiveness of ICFR and the evidential matter maintained in support of the assessment. Additional guidance and examples in the areas requested would likely have the negative consequence of establishing "bright line" or "one-size fits all" evaluation approaches. Such an outcome would be contrary to our view that the evaluations must be tailored to a company's individual facts and circumstances to be both effective and efficient. Moreover, an evaluation by management that is focused on compliance with detailed guidance, rather than the risks to the reliability of its financial reporting, would likely lead to evaluations that are inefficient, ineffective or both.

Detailed guidance and examples from the Commission may also limit or hinder the natural evolution and further development of control frameworks and evaluation methodologies as technology, control systems, and financial reporting evolve. As we have previously stated, the Commission supports and encourages the further development of control frameworks and related implementation guidance. For example, the July 2006 small business guidance issued by COSO addresses the identification of financial reporting risks and the related controls. Additionally, we note that COSO is currently working on a project to further define how the effectiveness of control systems can be monitored.[73]  As such, companies may find that there are other sources for the additional guidance in the areas they are seeking.

Commenters also expressed the view that companies may abuse the flexibility afforded by the proposed principles-based guidance to perform inadequate evaluations, thereby undermining the intended investor protection benefits.[74]  Other commenters have observed that material weakness disclosures to investors are too often simultaneous with, rather than in advance of, the restatement of financial statements, which undermines the usefulness of the disclosures.[75]  In response to these comments, we note that this principles-based guidance enables management to tailor its evaluation so that it focuses on those areas of financial reporting that pose the highest risk to reliable financial reporting.  We believe that a tailored evaluation approach that focuses resources on areas of highest risk will improve, rather than degrade, the effectiveness of many company's evaluations and improve the timeliness of material weakness disclosures to investors.

## C.  Scalability and Small Business Considerations

Commenters believed that the proposed interpretive guidance can be scaled to companies of all sizes and will benefit smaller public companies in completing their

---

[73] In a press release on January 8, 2007, COSO announced that Grant Thornton LLP had been commissioned to develop guidance to help organizations monitor the quality of their internal control systems.  According to that press release, the guidance will serve as a tool for effectively monitoring internal controls while complying with Sarbanes-Oxley.  The press release is available at http://www.coso.org/Publications/COSO%20Monitoring%20GT%20Final%20Release_1.8.07.pdf.

[74] See, for example, letters from Joseph V. Carcello, Consumer Federation of America, Consumer Action, U.S. Public Interest Research Group (CFA), and Moody's Investors Service (Moody's).

[75] See, for example, letters from CFA and Moody's.

assessments.[76] However, some commenters requested more guidance to enable them to conduct the evaluation in an effective and efficient manner. For example, commenters requested more guidance on how some of the unique characteristics of smaller companies, including a lack of segregation of duties, should be considered in the evaluation.[77]

Other commenters, mostly comprised of investor groups, requested that the guidance emphasize that scaled or tailored evaluation methods and procedures for smaller public companies should be based on both the size and complexity of the business and do not imply less rigorous evaluation methods and procedures.[78]

Some commenters indicated that smaller public companies should continue to be exempt at least until a thorough examination is conducted of both the Interpretive Guidance and the new Auditing Standard to ensure that smaller companies are not disproportionately burdened.[79] Some commenters requested that the SEC further delay

---

[76] See, for example, letters from American Bankers Association (American Bankers), Anthony S. Chan, Chandler (U.S.A.), Inc. (Chandler), CNB Corporation & Citizens National Bank of Cheboygan (CNB), Financial Services Forum, GT, Greater Boston Chamber of Commerce, Minn-Dak Farmers Cooperative (MDFC), RAM Energy Resources, Inc., and San Jose Water Company.

[77] See, for example, letters from American Electronics Association (AeA), EY, Financial Executives International Small Public Company Task Force (FEI SPCTF), Frank, Institute of Management Accountants (IMA), MFA, U.S. Chamber of Commerce (Chamber), and U.S. Small Business Administration's Office of Advocacy (SBA).

[78] See, for example, letters from California Public Employees' Retirement System (CalPERS), CFA, Council of Institutional Investors, Ethics Resource Center, International Brotherhood of Teamsters, and Pension Reserves Investment Management Board (PRIMB).

[79] See, for example, letters from AeA, Biotechnology Industry Organization, Committee on Capital Markets Regulation (CCMR), Financial Reporting Committee of the Association of the Bar of the City of New York (NYC Bar), International Association of Small Broker Dealers and Advisers, National Venture Capital Association, SBA, Silicon Valley Leadership Group (SVLG), Small Business Entrepreneurship Council, TechNet, and Telecommunications Industry Association.

the implementation for one additional year[80] or continued to call for a complete

exemption from Section 404 for smaller public companies.[81] Other commenters

requested that smaller public companies not be exempted.[82]

We believe the principles-based guidance permits flexible and scalable evaluation

approaches that will enable management of smaller public companies to evaluate and

assess the effectiveness of ICFR without undue cost burdens. The guidance recognizes

that internal control systems and the methods and procedures necessary to evaluate their

effectiveness may be different in smaller public companies than in larger companies.

However, the flexibility provided in the guidance is not meant to imply that evaluations

for smaller public companies be conducted with less rigor, or to provide anything less

than reasonable assurance as to the effectiveness of ICFR at such companies. Rather,

smaller public companies should utilize the flexibility provided in the guidance to cost-

effectively tailor and scale their methods and approaches for identifying and documenting

financial reporting risks and the related controls and for evaluating whether operation of

controls is effective (for example, by utilizing evidence gathered through management's

daily interaction with its controls), so that they provide the evidence needed to assess

whether ICFR is effective.

In addition, as previously mentioned, companies may find that there are other

sources for guidance, such as the July 2006 guidance for applying the COSO framework

to smaller public companies. We believe our guidance, when used in conjunction with

---

[80] See, for example, letters from American Bankers, America's Community Bankers, Chandler, CNB, FEI SPCTF, F. Gorrell, ICBA, MFA, and Washington Legal Foundation (WLF).

[81] See, for example, letters from American Stock Exchange, ICBA, UFP, and WLF.

[82] See, for example, letters from American Federation of Labor and Congress of Industrial Organizations (AFL-CIO), CalPERS, Frank, F. Gorrell, PRIMB, and WithumSmith+Brown Global Assurance, LLC.

other such guidance, will enable smaller public companies to have a better understanding of the requirements of a control framework, its role in effective internal control systems and the relationship to our evaluation and disclosure requirements. This should enable management to plan and conduct its evaluation in an effective and efficient manner.

The Commission believes that compliance with the ICFR evaluation and assessment requirements by smaller public companies will further the primary goal of Sarbanes-Oxley which is to enhance the quality of financial reporting and increase investor confidence in the fairness and integrity of the securities markets. We note that all financial statements filed with the Commission, even those by smaller public companies, result from a system of internal controls. Such systems are required by the FCPA to operate at a level that provides "reasonable assurance" about the reliability of financial reporting. Our rules implementing Section 404 direct management of all companies to evaluate and assess whether the company's system of internal controls is effective at achieving reasonable assurance. Our guidance is intended to help them do so in a cost-effective manner. Given the principles-based nature of our guidance and the flexibility it provides, we do not believe further postponement of the evaluation requirements are needed for smaller companies. We believe that the timing of the issuance of the Interpretive Guidance is adequate to allow for its effective implementation in 2007 evaluations.

## D. Identifying Financial Reporting Risks and Controls

### 1. Summary of the Proposal

The proposal directed management to consider the sources and potential likelihood of misstatements, including those arising from fraudulent activity, and identify those that could result in a material misstatement of the financial statements (that is, financial reporting risks). The proposal indicated that management's consideration of the risk of misstatement generally includes all of its locations or business units and that the methods and procedures for identifying financial reporting risks will vary based on the characteristics of the individual company. The proposal discussed factors for management to consider in selecting methods and procedures for evaluating financial reporting risks and in identifying the sources and potential likelihood of misstatement.

The proposal directed management to evaluate whether controls were placed in operation to adequately address the financial reporting risks it identifies. The proposal indicated that controls were not adequate when their design was such that there was a reasonable possibility that a misstatement in a financial reporting element that could result in a material misstatement of the financial statements would not be prevented or detected in a timely manner. The proposal discussed the fact that some controls may be automated or may depend upon IT functionality. In these situations, the proposal stated that management's evaluation should consider not only the design and operation of the automated or IT dependent controls, but also the aspects of IT general controls necessary to adequately address financial reporting risks.

The proposal also indicated that entity-level controls should be considered when identifying financial reporting risks and related controls for a financial reporting element. The proposal discussed the nature of entity-level controls, how they relate to a financial reporting element and the need to consider whether they would prevent or detect material misstatements. If a financial reporting risk for a financial reporting element is adequately addressed by an entity-level control, the proposal indicated that no further controls needed to be identified and tested by management for purposes of the evaluation of

ICFR.

## 2. Comments on the Proposal and Revisions Made

The Commission received a number of comments on the proposed guidance for

identifying financial reporting risks and controls. As discussed in Section III.B above,

many of these commenters requested more examples or more detailed guidance. Other

comments received related to the identification of fraud risks and related controls; entity-

level controls; and IT general controls.

### Identification of fraud risks and related controls

Commenters suggested the guidance be revised to more strongly emphasize

management's responsibility to identify and evaluate fraud risks and the related controls

that address those risks.[83] Commenters also discussed the nature of fraud risks that most

often lead to materially misstated financial statements and requested additional guidance

regarding which fraud related controls are within the scope of the evaluation;[84] whether

management can consider the risk of fraud through the overall risk assessment or if a

specific fraud threat analysis is required;[85] and examples of the types of fraud that should

be considered.[86] Other commenters noted that there is existing guidance for

management, beyond what was referenced in the proposal, for assessing fraud risks and

---

[83] See, for example, letters from ACE, ACCA, BDO, Center, CSC, Deloitte & Touche LLP (Deloitte), GT, IMA, KPMG LLP (KPMG), M&P, Moody's, and PwC.

[84] See, for example, letters from BASF, BDO, and GT.

[85] See, for example, letter from Tatum LLC (Tatum).

[86] See, for example, letters from FEI CCR, P&G, and N. Stofberg.

the related controls. These commenters suggested that the proposal be revised to directly incorporate the most relevant elements of such guidance.[87]

In response to the comments, the proposal was revised to clarify that fraud risks are expected to exist at every company and that the nature and extent of the fraud risk assessment activities should be commensurate with the size and complexity of the company. Additionally, we expanded the references to existing guidance to include the AICPA's 2005 Management Override of Internal Controls: The Achilles' Heel of Fraud Prevention and COSO's July 2006 Guidance for Smaller Public Companies. Given the availability of existing information and guidance on fraud and consistent with the principles-based nature of the interpretive guidance, we determined that it was unnecessary to provide a list of fraud risks expected to be present at every company or a list of the areas of financial reporting expected to have a risk of material misstatement due to fraud. Moreover, providing such a list may result in a "checklist" type approach to fraud risk assessments that would likely be ineffective as financial reporting changes over time, or given the wide variety of facts and circumstances that exist in different companies and industries. While management may find such checklists a useful starting point, effective fraud risk assessments will require sound and thoughtful judgments that reflect a company's individual facts and circumstances.

Entity-Level Controls

Commenters requested further clarification of how entity-level controls can address financial reporting risks in a top-down, risk based approach.[88] Commenters also

---

[87] See, for example, letters from Center, GT, KPMG, and M&P.

[88] See, for example, letters from EY, Frank, MetLife, and UnumProvident.

suggested that the guidance place more emphasis on entity-level controls given their pervasive impact on all other aspects of ICFR.[89]

In response to the comments received, we expanded the discussion of entity-level controls and how they relate to financial reporting elements. This discussion further clarifies that some entity-level controls, such as controls within the control environment, have an important, but indirect, effect on the likelihood that a misstatement will be prevented or detected on a timely basis. While these controls might affect the other controls management determines are necessary to address financial reporting risks for a financial reporting element, it is unlikely management will identify only this type of entity-level control as adequately addressing a financial reporting risk. Further, the guidance clarifies that some entity-level controls may be designed to identify possible breakdowns in lower-level controls, but not in a manner that would, by themselves, adequately address financial reporting risks. In these cases, management would identify the additional controls needed to adequately address financial reporting risks, which may include those that operate at the transaction or account balance level. Consistent with the proposal, management does not need to identify or evaluate additional controls relating to a financial reporting risk if it determines that the risk is being adequately addressed by an entity-level control.

We have also revised the proposed guidance to further clarify that the controls management identifies in Section II.A.1 should include the entity-level and pervasive elements of its ICFR that are necessary to have a system of internal control that provides reasonable assurance as to the reliability of financial reporting. Management can use the

---

[89] See, for example, letters from ACCA, ACE, Eli Lilly, European Association of Listed Companies (EALIC), and PwC.

existing control frameworks and related guidance to assist them in evaluating the adequacy of these aspects of their ICFR.

Information Technology General Controls

Commenters expressed concern that the proposal's guidance on IT general controls was too vague or that it lacked sufficient clarity[90] and requested further guidance and illustrative examples[91] to clarify the extent to which IT general controls are within the scope of the ICFR evaluation.[92] Commenters also suggested that the Commission directly incorporate the May 16, 2005 Staff Guidance[93] on IT general controls[94] and that we clarify that IT general controls alone, without consideration of application controls, will not sufficiently address the risk of material misstatement.[95] One commenter noted that providing such guidance could have the unintended consequence of setting a precedent for providing more detailed guidance in other areas of the evaluation.[96]

Commenters also suggested that we revise the proposal to clarify how a top-down approach considers IT general controls,[97] that we encourage a "benchmarking" approach for evaluating automated controls,[98] and that we permit companies who implement IT

---

[90] See, for example, letters from Aerospace Industries Association, MasterCard, and Nasdaq.

[91] See, for example, letter from Microsoft Corporation (MSFT).

[92] See, for example, letters from Faisal Danka, ISACA, MSFT, Rod Scott, and The Travelers Companies, Inc. (Travelers).

[93] Division of Corporation Finance and Office of the Chief Accountant: Staff Statement on Management's Report on Internal Control Financial Reporting (May 16, 2005), available at http://www.sec.gov/spotlight/soxcom/.htm.

[94] See, for example, letters from FEI CCR and P&G.

[95] See, for example, letter from IDW.

[96] See, for example, letter from ICAEW.

[97] See, for example, letters from Cardinal and ISACA.

[98] See, for example, letter from CSC.

systems late in the year to do so while still being able to satisfy their ICFR responsibilities.[99]

We made several revisions to the proposed guidance based on the comment letters. We revised the proposal to explain that the identification of risks and controls within IT should be integral to, and not separate from, management's top-down, risk-based approach to evaluating ICFR and in determining the necessary supporting evidential matter. We clarified that controls which address financial reporting risks may be automated, dependent upon IT functionality, or require a combination of both manual and automated procedures and that IT general controls alone, without consideration of application controls, ordinarily do not adequately address financial reporting risks. We also incorporated guidance from the May 16, 2005 Staff Statement which explains that it is unnecessary to evaluate IT general controls that primarily pertain to efficiency or effectiveness of operations, but which are not relevant to addressing financial reporting risks.

We have declined to further specify categories or areas of IT general controls that will be relevant to the ICFR evaluation for all companies. We continue to believe that such determinations require consideration of each company's individual facts and circumstances. Moreover, we have concluded it is not necessary to include a discussion of a "benchmarking" approach to evaluating automated controls. The lack of such discussion in our guidance does not preclude management from taking such an approach if they believe it to be both efficient and effective.

---

[99] See, for example, letter from Chamber.

Additionally, we did not revise the proposed guidance to discuss implementation

of IT systems, or changes thereto, late in the year because we do not believe such

decisions should be impacted by the requirement to evaluate and assess the effectiveness

of ICFR. Even without the evaluation and assessment requirements, the implementation

of an IT system late in the year does not change management's responsibility to maintain

a system of internal control that provides reasonable assurance regarding the reliability of

financial reporting. Allowing an exclusion from the evaluation for controls placed in

operation late in the year could have the unintended consequence of negatively impacting

the reliability of financial reporting. Management has the ability to mitigate the risk of

material misstatement that arises from ineffective controls in a new IT system. For

example, management may perform pre-implementation testing of the IT controls needed

to adequately address financial reporting risks. Additionally, management may

implement compensating controls, such as manual reconciliations and verification, until

such time that management has concluded that the IT controls within the system are

adequate. Accordingly, we do not believe it is necessary or appropriate to exclude new

IT systems or changes to existing systems from the scope of the evaluation of ICFR.

### E. Evaluating Evidence of the Operating Effectiveness of ICFR

#### 1. Summary of the Proposal

Our proposal indicated that management should consider both the risk

characteristics of the financial reporting elements to which the controls relate and the risk

characteristics of the controls themselves (collectively, ICFR risk) in making judgments

about the nature and extent of evidence necessary to provide a reasonable basis for the

assessment of whether the operation of controls is effective. The proposal identified

significant accounting estimates, related party transactions and critical accounting
policies as examples of financial reporting areas that generally would be assessed as
having a higher risk of misstatement and control failure. However, the proposed
guidance recognizes that since not all controls have the same risk characteristics, when a
combination of controls is required to adequately address the risks to a financial reporting
element, management should analyze the risk characteristics of each control separately.
Further, under the proposed guidance, when evaluating risks in multi-location
environments, management should generally consider the risk characteristics of the
controls related to each financial reporting element, rather than making a single judgment
for all controls at a particular location when determining the sufficiency of evidence to
support its assessment.

The proposal indicated that the evidence of the operation of controls that
management evaluates may come from a combination of on-going monitoring and direct
testing and that management should vary the nature, timing and extent of these based on
its assessment of the ICFR risk. Our proposal stated that this evidence would ordinarily
cover a reasonable period of time during the year and include the fiscal year-end. The
proposal also acknowledged that, in smaller companies, those responsible for assessing
the effectiveness of ICFR may, through their on-going direct knowledge and supervision
of the operation of controls (that is, daily interaction) have a reasonable basis to evaluate
the effectiveness of some controls without performing direct tests specifically for
purposes of the evaluation.

The proposal explained that the evidential matter constituting reasonable support
for the assessment would generally include the basis for management's assessment and

documentation of the evaluation methods and procedures for gathering and evaluating evidence. Additionally, the proposal indicated that the nature of the supporting evidential matter, including documentation, may take many forms and may vary based on management's assessment of ICFR risk. For example, management may determine that it is not necessary to maintain separate copies of the evidence evaluated if such evidence already exists in the company's books and records. The proposal also indicates that as the degree of complexity of the control, the level of judgment required to operate the control, and the risk of misstatement in the financial reporting element increase, management may determine that separate evidential matter supporting a control's operation should be maintained.

## 2. Comments on the Proposal and Revisions Made

The Commission received a number of comments on the proposed guidance for evaluating whether the operation of controls was effective. As discussed in Section III.B above, many of these commenters requested more examples or more detailed guidance. Other comments received related to the appropriateness of various "rotational" approaches to evaluating evidence of whether the operation of controls was effective; the nature of on-going monitoring activities, including self-assessments and daily interaction; the time period to be covered by evaluation procedures; and supporting evidential matter.

<u>Rotational Approaches to Evaluating Evidence</u>

Commenters requested that the guidance explicitly allow management to rotate its evaluation of evidence of the operation of controls and a variety of different approaches for doing so were suggested. These approaches included, for example, a rotational approach for lower risk controls,[100] a rotational approach in areas where management

determines there are no changes in the controls since the previous assessment,[101] or a

rotational approach where there is both lower risk and no changes in controls.[102]  In

addition, some suggested a "benchmarking" approach, similar to that used for IT

controls, be allowed for non-IT controls.[103]  Other commenters agreed with the

proposal's requirement that management consider evidence of the operation of controls

each year.[104]  Others noted that while they believed it is appropriate for management to

consider the results of its prior year assessments, the guidance should make it clear that

the evaluation of operating effectiveness is an annual requirement.[105]

Other commenters raised the issue of a rotational approach specific to multi-

location considerations.  For example, commenters suggested that the guidance allow for

rotation of locations based upon risk (for example, once every three years).[106]  However,

some commenters suggested that the risk-based approach provided in the proposed

guidance would appropriately allow companies to vary testing in locations based more on

risk than coverage, which would improve the efficiency of their assessment.[107]

After considering the comments, the Commission has retained the guidance

substantially as proposed.  We did not introduce a concept that allows management to

---

[100] See, for example, letters from CSC, EALIC, ING, MasterCard, and NYC Bar.

[101] See, for example, letters from P&G and Travelers.

[102] See, for example, letters from EEI and Supervalu.

[103] See, for example, letters from Eli Lilly and FEI CCR.

[104] See, for example, letters from CCMR, Deloitte, and KPMG.

[105] See, for example, letters from AFL-CIO, Center, CFA, Deloitte, and PwC.

[106] See, for example, letter from CSC.

[107] See, for example, letters from MSFT, New York State Society of Certified Public Accountants, and Plains Exploration & Production Company.

eliminate from its annual evaluation those controls that are necessary to adequately

address financial reporting risks.  For example, management cannot decide to include

controls for a particular location or process within the scope of its evaluation only once

every three years or exclude controls from the scope of its evaluation based on prior year

evaluation results.  To have a reasonable basis for its assessment of the effectiveness of

ICFR, management must have sufficient evidence supporting the operating effectiveness

of all aspects of its ICFR as of the date of its assessment.  The guidance provides a

framework to assist management in making judgments regarding the nature, timing and

extent of evidence needed to support its assessment.  Management can use this

framework to scale its evaluation methods and procedures in response to the risks

associated with both the financial reporting elements and related controls in its particular

facts and circumstances.

However, the guidance has been clarified to reflect that management's experience

with a control's operation both during the year and as part of its prior year assessment(s)

may influence its decisions regarding the risk that controls will fail to operate as

designed.  This, in turn, may have a corresponding impact on the evidence needed to

support management's conclusion that controls operated effectively as of the date of

management's assessment.

Nature of On-Going Monitoring Activities

Commenters expressed concern that, as defined in the proposal, some on-going

monitoring activities would not be deemed to provide sufficient evidence.[108]  Other

commenters were concerned that the guidance placed too much emphasis on the amount

---

[108] See, for example, letters from BASF and Cees Klumper & Matthew Shepherd (C. Klumper & M. Shepherd).

of evidence that could be obtained from on-going monitoring activities and called for

further examples of when they may provide sufficient evidence and when direct testing

would be required.[109]  With regard to self-assessments, commenters suggested that self-

assessments can be an integral source of evidence when their effective operation is

verified by direct testing over varying periods of time based on the manner in which the

self-assessments were conducted and on the level of risk associated with the controls.[110]

Other commenters requested the proposed guidance be revised to clarify how, based on

the definitions provided, self-assessments differed from direct testing.[111]

Some commenters questioned the sufficiency of evidence that would result from

management's daily interaction with controls and requested more specifics on when it

would be appropriate as a source of evidence[112] and how management should

demonstrate that its daily interaction with controls provided it with sufficient evidence to

have a reasonable basis to assess whether the operation of controls was effective.[113]

Based on the feedback received, we modified the discussion of on-going

monitoring activities, including self-assessments, and direct testing to clarify how the

evidence obtained from each of the activities can vary.  As commenters in this area noted,

on-going monitoring, including self-assessments, encompasses a wide array of activities

that can be performed by a variety of individuals within an organization.  These

individuals have varying degrees of objectivity, ranging from internal auditors to the

personnel involved in business processes, and can include both those responsible for

---

[109] See, for example, letters from Center and EY.

[110] See, for example, letters from GT and C. Klumper & M. Shepherd.

[111] See, for example, letter from Cardinal.

[112] See, for example, letters from BDO, EY, Ohio, and Tatum.

[113] See, for example, letter from Ohio.

executing a control as well as those responsible for overseeing its effective operation. Because of the varying degrees of objectivity, the sufficiency of the evidence management obtains from on-going monitoring activities is determined by the nature of the activities (that is, what they entail and how they are performed).

We clarified the proposed guidance to indicate that when evaluating the objectivity of personnel, management is not required to make an absolute conclusion regarding objectivity, but rather should recognize that personnel will have varying degrees of objectivity based on, among other things, their job function, their relationship to the control being evaluated, and their level of authority and responsibility within the organization. Management should consider the ICFR risk of the controls when determining whether the objectivity of the personnel involved in the monitoring activities results in sufficient evidence. For example, for areas of high ICFR risk, management's on-going monitoring activities may provide sufficient evidence when the monitoring activities are carried out by individuals with a high degree of objectivity. However, when management's support includes evidence obtained from activities performed by individuals who are not highly objective, management would ordinarily supplement the evidence with some degree of direct testing by individuals who are independent from the operation of the control to corroborate the information from the monitoring activity.

With regard to requests for more guidance related to management's daily interaction, we have adopted the guidance substantially as proposed. We believe that in smaller companies, management's daily interaction with the operation of controls may provide it with sufficient evidence to assess whether controls are operating effectively. The guidance is not intended to limit management's flexibility with regard to the areas of

ICFR where its interaction can provide it with sufficient evidence or the manner by which

management obtains knowledge of the operation of the controls. However, as noted in

the guidance, daily interaction as a source of evidence for the operation of controls

applies to management who are responsible for assessing the effectiveness of ICFR and

whose knowledge about the effective operation is gained from its on-going direct

knowledge and direct supervision of controls. In addition, the evidence management

maintains in support of its assessment should include the design of the controls that

adequately address the financial reporting risks as well as how its interaction provides an

adequate basis for its assessment of the effectiveness of ICFR.

<u>Time Period Covered by Evaluation Procedures</u>

Commenters requested that the guidance allow for, and encourage, management

to gather evidence throughout the year to support its assessment in lieu of having to

gather some evidence close to or as-of year-end.[114]  These commenters believed that such

guidance would encourage companies to better integrate their evaluation procedures into

the normal activities of their daily operations, spread the effort more evenly throughout

the year, and help reduce the strain on resources at year-end when company personnel are

preparing the annual financial statements and complying with other financial reporting

activities.

We agree with the comments received in this area with respect to allowing

management the flexibility to gather evidence in support of its assessment during the

year. Since management's assessment is performed as of the end of its fiscal year-end,

the evidence management utilizes to support its assessment would ordinarily include a

---

[114] See, for example, letters from Eli Lilly, The Financial Services Roundtable, and Neenah Paper, Inc.

reasonable period of time during the year, including some evidence as of the date of its assessment. However, the proposal was not intended to limit management's flexibility to conduct its evaluation activities during the year. Rather, the proposed guidance was intended to provide management with the ability to perform a variety of activities covering periods of time that vary based on its assessment of risk in order to provide it with a sufficient basis for its evaluation. This could include, for example, a strategy that employs direct testing over a control during the year (but prior to year-end), that is supplemented with a self-assessment activity at year-end. As a result, we have adopted the guidance related to the period of time for which management should obtain evidence of the operation of controls substantially as proposed.

<u>Supporting Evidential Matter</u>

Commenters expressed support for the guidance in the proposal related to the supporting evidential matter and believed it would allow management to make better judgments and allow for sufficient flexibility to vary the nature and extent of evidence based on the company's particular facts and circumstances.[115] Other commenters observed that a certain level of documentation was required in order to facilitate an efficient and effective audit and suggested the guidance explicitly state this fact and/or clarify how the guidance for management was intended to interact with the requirements provided to auditors.[116] One commenter requested that we clarify our intention related to

---

[115] See, for example, letters from BR, EY, Hudson Financial Solutions (HFS), and MSFT.

[116] See, for example, letters from Center, Deloitte, EY, GT, M&P, MetLife, MDFC, PwC, and N. Stofberg.

the audit committee's involvement in the review of evidential matter prepared by management in support of its assessment.[117]

After consideration of the comments, we are adopting the guidance substantially as proposed. We continue to believe that management should have considerable flexibility as to the nature and extent of the documentation it maintains to support its assessment, while at the same time maintaining sufficient evidence to provide reasonable support for its assessment. Providing specific guidelines and detailed examples of various types of documentation would potentially limit the flexibility we intended to afford management.

With respect to the concerns raised regarding the interaction of the proposed guidance and the audit requirements, we determined that no changes were necessary. Similar to an audit of the financial statements, the nature and extent of evidential matter maintained by management may impact how an auditor conducts the audit and the efficiency of the audit. We believe that the most efficient implementation by management and the auditor is achieved when flexibility exists to determine the appropriate manner by which to complete their respective tasks. However, we also believe that the Proposed Auditing Standard allows auditors sufficient flexibility to consider various types of evidence utilized by management. The audit standard allows auditors to adjust their approach in certain circumstances, if necessary, so that audit procedures should not place any undue burden or expense on management's evaluation process.

---

[117] See, for example, letter from ABA.

## F. Evaluation of Control Deficiencies

### 1. Summary of the Proposal

The proposal directed management to evaluate each control deficiency that comes to its attention in order to determine whether the deficiency, or combination of control deficiencies, is a material weakness. The proposal defined a material weakness as a deficiency, or combination of deficiencies, in ICFR such that there is a reasonable possibility that a material misstatement of the company's annual or interim financial statements will not be prevented or detected on a timely basis by the company's ICFR. The proposal contained guidance on the aggregation of deficiencies by indicating that multiple control deficiencies that affect the same financial reporting element increase the likelihood of misstatement and may, in combination, constitute a material weakness, even though such deficiencies may be individually insignificant. The proposal also highlighted four circumstances that were strong indicators that a material weakness in ICFR existed. In summary, the following four items were listed:

- An ineffective control environment, including identification of fraud of any magnitude on the part of senior management; significant deficiencies that remain unaddressed after some reasonable period of time; and ineffective oversight by the audit committee (or entire board of directors if no audit committee exists).

- Restatement of previously issued financial statements to reflect the correction of a material misstatement.

- Identification by the auditor of a material misstatement of financial statements in the current period under circumstances that indicate the misstatement would not have been discovered by the company's ICFR.

- For complex entities in highly regulated industries, an ineffective regulatory compliance function.

## 2. Comments on the Proposal and Revisions Made

Definition of Material Weakness

Commenters expressed concern about differences between our proposed definition of material weakness and that proposed by the PCAOB in its Proposed Auditing Standard and requested that the two definitions be aligned.[118] Commenters provided feedback on the reasonably possible threshold for determining the likelihood of a potential material misstatement as well as the reference to interim financial statements for determining whether a potential misstatement could be material. Commenters also suggested that a single definition of material weakness be established for use by both auditors and management and that definition be established by the SEC in its rules.[119] Based on comments on the proposal, we are amending Exchange Act Rule 12b-2 and Rule 1-02 of Regulation S-X to define the term material weakness. Further discussion and analysis of the definition of material weakness and commenter feedback can be found in that rule release.[120]

---

[118] See, for example, letters from EEI, FEI CCR, FEI SPCTF, ICAEW, N. Stofberg, and SVLG.

[119] See, for example, letters from FEE and ICAEW.

[120] Release No. 34-55928.

Strong Indicators of a Material Weakness

Commenters noted there were differences in the list of strong indicators included

in the proposal and the list of strong indicators included in the Proposed Auditing

Standard, raising concern that the failure of the two proposals to provide similar guidance

would cause unnecessary confusion between management and auditors.[121] Commenters

also provided suggested changes, additions or deletions to circumstances that were

included on the list of strong indicators. For example, commenters raised questions about

the "identification of fraud of any magnitude on the part of senior management,"

questioning the appropriateness of the term "of any magnitude" or which individuals

were encompassed in the term "senior management."[122] Commenters also felt the

Commission's proposed list of indicators should be expanded to include the indicator

relating to an ineffective internal audit function or risk assessment function that was

included in the Proposed Auditing Standard.[123] One commenter felt that the list of strong

indicators needed to be made more specific, and should include more illustrative

examples.[124] Another commenter stated that the indicator of "significant deficiencies

that have been identified and remain unaddressed after some reasonable period of time"

should be clarified to mean unremediated deficiencies.[125] Other commenters suggested

that the list of strong indicators be eliminated completely, stating that designating these

items as strong indicators creates a presumption that such items are, in fact, material

---

[121] See, for example, letters from BDO, BR, Center, Cleary, CSC, Deloitte, KPMG, M&P, and Schneider Downs & Co., Inc. (Schneider).

[122] See, for example, letters from 100 Group, Eli Lilly, FEI CCR, and P&G.

[123] See, for example, letters from BR, Crowe Chizek & Company LLC (Crowe), Deloitte, and M&P.

[124] See, for example, letter from Chamber.

[125] See, for example, letter from EEI.

weaknesses, and may impede the use of judgment to properly evaluate the identified control deficiency in light of the individual facts and circumstances.[126]  Commenters also felt the Commission should clearly indicate that a company may determine that no deficiency exists despite the fact that one of the identified strong indicators was present.[127]

After consideration of the comments, we have decided to modify the proposed guidance.  We believe judgment is imperative in determining whether a deficiency is a material weakness and that the guidance should encourage management to use that judgment.  As a result, we have modified the guidance to emphasize that the evaluation of control deficiencies requires the consideration of all of the relevant facts and circumstances.  We agreed with the concerns that an overly detailed list may create a list of de facto material weaknesses or inappropriately suggest that identified control deficiencies not included in the list are of lesser importance.  At the same time, however, we continue to believe that highlighting certain circumstances that are indicative of a material weakness provides practical information for management.  As a result, rather than referring to "strong indicators," the final guidance refers simply to "indicators." This change should further emphasize that the presence of one of the indicators does not mandate a conclusion that a material weakness exists.  Rather management should apply professional judgment in this area.  These examples include indicators related to the results of the financial statement audit, such as material audit adjustments and restatements, and indicators related to the overall evaluation of the company's oversight of financial reporting, such as the effectiveness of the audit committee and incidences of

---

[126] See, for example, letters from Cleary, Institute of Internal Auditors (IIA), and NYC Bar.

[127] See, for example, letters from Chamber, Cleary, CSC, PPL, and Schneider.

fraud among senior management. These examples are by no means an exhaustive list. For example, under COSO, risk assessment and monitoring are two of the five components of an effective system of internal control. If management concludes that an internal control component is not effective, or if required entity-level or pervasive elements of ICFR are not effective, it is likely that internal control is not effective.

Lastly, we agreed with commenters that it is appropriate for the Commission's guidance in this area to mirror the PCAOB's auditing standard. As a result, we have worked with the PCAOB in reaching conclusions regarding the guidance in this area, and we anticipate the PCAOB's auditing standard will align with our final management guidance.

## G. Management Reporting and Disclosure

Comment letters expressed various viewpoints regarding the information management provides as part of its report on the effectiveness of ICFR. For example, commenters raised concerns regarding the "point in time" assessment and suggested various alternative approaches.[128] Commenters also made suggestions regarding the disclosures management provides when a material weakness has occurred. Certain commenters felt the suggested disclosures indicated in the proposing release should be mandatory,[129] while other commenters wanted the Commission to specify where in the Form 10-K management must provide its disclosures.[130] Commenters also requested that

---

[128] See, for example, letters from BHP Billiton Limited, Eli Lilly, and IIA.

[129] See, for example, letters from HFS, IDW, and Tatum.

[130] See, for example, letters from Crowe and KPMG.

the Commission include in its release additional possible disclosures for consideration by management to include in its report.[131]

In addition, commenters expressed concerns regarding the language in the Proposing Release with respect to management's ability to determine that ICFR is ineffective due solely to, and only to the extent of, the identified material weakness(es). Some commenters felt that this language was essentially the same as a qualified opinion, which is prohibited by the guidance,[132] while two others stated that the Commission needed to provide additional guidance around the circumstances under which this approach would be appropriate.[133]

Based on the feedback we received, we have eliminated this from the final interpretive guidance and revised the proposed guidance to simply state that management may not state that the company's ICFR is effective. However, management may state that controls are ineffective for specific reasons.

Additionally, certain of the requests received seemed inconsistent with the statutory obligation. For example, Section 404(a)(2) of Sarbanes-Oxley requires that management perform the assessment as of the end of its most recent fiscal year. As a result, we do not believe any further changes to the proposed guidance around management's expression of its assessment of the effectiveness of ICFR are necessary.

---

[131] See, for example, letters from PCG Worldwide Limited and PepsiCo, Inc. (Pepsi).

[132] See, for example, letters from BDO and CFA.

[133] See, for example, letters from Crowe and Deloitte.

## H. Previous Staff Guidance and Staff Frequently Asked Questions

Commenters raised questions regarding the status of guidance previously issued

by the Commission and its staff, on May 16, 2005,[134] as well as the Frequently Asked

Questions ("FAQs").[135] Some commenters requested the FAQs be retained in their

entirety,[136] while others requested that some particular FAQs be retained.[137] As we

indicated in the proposed guidance, the May 2005 guidance remains relevant.

Additionally, we have instructed the staff to review the FAQs and, as a result of the final

issuance of this guidance, update them as appropriate.

## I. Foreign Private Issuers

The Commission received comments directed towards the information included in

the proposed guidance related to foreign private issuers. While three commenters noted

that no additional guidance for foreign private issuers was necessary,[138] other

commenters suggested changes. Commenters raised concerns regarding potential

duplicative efforts and costs foreign registrants are subject to, as a result of similar

regulations in their local jurisdictions.[139] These commenters requested that the

Commission attempt to minimize or remove any duplicative requirements, with some

---

[134] Commission Statement on Implementation of Internal Control Reporting Requirements, Press Release No. 2005-74 (May 16, 2005); Division of Corporation Finance and Office of the Chief Accountant: Staff Statement on Management's Report on Internal Control Financial Reporting (May 16, 2005), available at http://www.sec.gov/spotlight/soxcom/.htm.

[135] Office of the Chief Accountant and Division of Corporation Finance: Management's Report on Internal Control Over Financial Reporting and Certification of Disclosure in Exchange Act Periodic Reports Frequently Asked Questions (revised Oct. 6, 2004), available at http://www.sec.gov/info/accountants/controlfaq1004.htm.

[136] See, for example, letters from BP p.l.c. (BP), GT, IIA, ISACA, MSFT, and Tatum.

[137] See, for example, letters from BDO, EY, KPMG, and Stantec Inc.

[138] See, for example, letters from BP, Manulife, and Pepsi.

[139] See, for example, letters from 100 Group, Banco Itaú Holding Financeira SA, CCMR, Eric Fandrich, and FEI CCR.

requesting the Commission exempt foreign registrants entirely from the ICFR reporting

requirements if the registrant was subject to similar regulations in their home country.

Other commenters raised concerns relating to the unique challenges that foreign

registrants face in evaluating their ICFR, including language and cultural differences and

international legal differences.[140]

Commenters also made suggestions regarding how the reconciliation to U.S.

GAAP should be handled in the evaluation of ICFR. Certain commenters expressed

support for the Commission's position that foreign private issuers should scope their

evaluation effort based on the financial statements prepared in accordance with home

country GAAP, rather than based on the reconciliation to U.S. GAAP.[141]  However, other

commenters requested that the Commission exempt the reconciliation to U.S. GAAP

from the scope of the evaluation altogether,[142] while others sought further clarification as

to whether and how the reconciliation was included in the evaluation of ICFR,[143] with

one commenter suggesting the Commission staff publish additional Frequently Asked

Questions to address any implementation issues.[144]  One commenter requested the

Commission exclude from the evaluation process those financial statement disclosures

that are required by home country GAAP but not under U.S. GAAP to minimize the

differences in the ICFR evaluation efforts between U.S. registrants and foreign filers as

much as possible.[145]

---

[140] See, for example, letters from IIA and GT.

[141] See, for example, letters from 100 Group, BDO, and ICAEW.

[142] See, for example, letters from CCMR, Cleary, EALIC, and NYC Bar.

[143] See, for example, letters from Deloitte, EY, KPMG, and N. Stofberg.

[144] See, for example, letter from Ohio.

[145] See, for example, letter from ING.

After considering the comments received, the Commission has determined not to exempt foreign registrants from the ICFR reporting requirements, regardless of whether they are subject to similar home country requirements. The Commission's requirement for all issuers to complete an evaluation of ICFR is not derived from the Commission's Interpretive Guidance for Management; this requirement has been established by Congress. Further, the Commission does not believe it is appropriate to exclude the U.S. GAAP reconciliation from the scope of the evaluation as long as it is a required element of the financial statements. Currently, however, the Commission is evaluating, as part of another project, the acceptance of International Financial Reporting Standards ("IFRS") as published by the International Accounting Standards Board ("IASB") without reconciliation to U.S. GAAP.[146]

In light of the comment letters, the Commission realizes that there are certain implementation concerns and issues that are unique to foreign private issuers. As a result, the Commission has instructed the staff to consider whether these items should be addressed in a Frequently Asked Questions document.

---

[146] In a press release on April 24, 2007, the Commission announced its next steps pertaining to acceptance of IFRS without reconciliation to U.S. GAAP. In that press release, the Commission stated that it anticipates issuing a Proposing Release in summer 2007 that will request comments on proposed changes to the Commission's rules which would allow the use of IFRS, as published by the IASB, without reconciliation to U.S. GAAP in financial reports filed by foreign private issuers that are registered with the Commission. The press release is available at http://www.sec.gov/news/press/2007/2007-72.htm.

**List of Subjects**

17 CFR Part 241

Securities.

## TEXT OF AMENDMENTS

For the reasons set out in the preamble, the Commission is amending Title 17, chapter II, of the Code of Federal Regulations as follows:

## PART 241 – INTERPRETATIVE RELEASES RELATING TO THE SECURITIES EXCHANGE ACT OF 1934 AND GENERAL RULES AND REGULATIONS THEREUNDER

Part 241 is amended by adding Release No. 34-55929 and the release date of June 20, 2007 to the list of interpretative releases.

By the Commission.

Nancy M. Morris
Secretary

Dated: June 20, 2007

# About the CD-ROM

## INTRODUCTION

This appendix provides you with information on the contents of the CD that accompanies this book. For the latest and greatest information, please refer to the ReadMe file located at the root of the CD.

## SYSTEM REQUIREMENTS

- A computer with a processor running at 120 Mhz or faster
- At least 32 MB of total RAM installed on your computer; for best performance, we recommend at least 64 MB
- A CD-ROM drive

  **Note:** Many popular word processing programs are capable of reading Microsoft Word files. However, users should be aware that a slight amount of formatting might be lost when using a program other than Microsoft Word.

## USING THE CD WITH WINDOWS

To install the items from the CD to your hard drive, follow these steps:

1. Insert the CD into your computer's CD-ROM drive.

2. The CD-ROM interface will appear. The interface provides a simple point-and-click way to explore the contents of the CD.

If the opening screen of the CD-ROM does not appear automatically, follow these steps to access the CD:

1. Click the Start button on the left end of the taskbar and then choose Run from the menu that pops up.

2. In the dialog box that appears, type **d:\setup.exe.** (If your CD-ROM drive is not drive d, fill in the appropriate letter in place of d.) This brings up the CD Interface described in the preceding set of steps.

## WHAT'S ON THE CD

The following sections provide a summary of the software and other materials you'll find on the CD.

## Content

The CD ROM contains all of the practice aids in this book. They cover all the main phases in the internal control assessment: planning, documentation, testing and reporting. Each form and checklist from this book is included to aid in your information gathering and assessment and to help you document conclusions. You will find this material on the CD-ROM in the folder named "Content."

## Applications

The following applications are on the CD:

### OPENOFFICE.ORG

OpenOffice.org is a free multi-platform office productivity suite. It is similar to Microsoft Office or Lotus SmartSuite, but OpenOffice.org is absolutely free. It includes word processing, spreadsheet, presentation, and drawing applications that enable you to create professional documents, newsletters, reports, and presentations. It supports most file formats of other office software. You should be able to edit and view any files created with other office solutions.

*Shareware programs* are fully functional, trial versions of copyrighted programs. If you like particular programs, register with their authors for a nominal fee and receive licenses, enhanced versions, and technical support.

*Freeware programs* are copyrighted games, applications, and utilities that are free for personal use. Unlike shareware, these programs do not require a fee or provide technical support.

*GNU software* is governed by its own license, which is included inside the folder of the GNU product. See the GNU license for more details.

*Trial, demo, or evaluation versions* are usually limited either by time or functionality (such as being unable to save projects). Some trial versions are very sensitive to system date changes. If you alter your computer's date, the programs will "time out" and no longer be functional.

# TROUBLESHOOTING

Wiley has attempted to provide programs that work on most computers with the minimum system requirements. Alas, your computer may differ, and some programs may not work properly for some reason.

The two likeliest problems are that you don't have enough memory (RAM) for the programs you want to use, or you have other programs running that are affecting installation or running of a program. If you get an error message such as "Not enough memory" or "Setup cannot continue," try one or more of the following suggestions and then try using the software again:

Turn off any antivirus software running on your computer. Installation programs sometimes mimic virus activity and may make your computer incorrectly believe that it's being infected by a virus.

Close all running programs. The more programs you have running, the less memory is available to other programs. Installation programs typically update files and programs; so if you keep other programs running, installation may not work properly. Have your local computer store add more RAM to your computer. This is, admittedly, a drastic and somewhat expensive step. However, adding more memory can really help the speed of your computer and allow more programs to run at the same time.

## CUSTOMER CARE

If you have trouble with the CD-ROM, please call the Wiley Product Technical Support phone number at (800) 762-2974. Outside the United States, call (317) 572-3994. You can also contact Wiley Product Technical Support at **http://www.wiley.com/techsupport.** John Wiley & Sons will provide technical support only for installation and other general quality control items. For technical support on the applications themselves, consult the program's vendor or author.

To place additional orders or to request information about other Wiley products, please call (877) 762-2974.

# Index